'In the wind's eye'

BYRON'S LETTERS AND JOURNALS
VOLUME 9
1821–1822

In the wind's eye I have sailed, and sail; but for
   The stars, I own my telescope is dim;
But at the least I have shunned the common shore,
   And leaving land far out of sight, would skim
The Ocean of Eternity; the roar
   Of breakers has not daunted my slight, trim,
But *still* sea-worthy skiff; and she may float
Where ships have foundered, as doth many a boat.

DON JUAN, 10, 4

BYRON.   From a portrait by W. E. West

Reproduced by courtesy of The Governors of Harrow School

'In the wind's eye'

BYRON'S LETTERS AND JOURNALS

Edited by
LESLIE A. MARCHAND

*The complete and unexpurgated text of
all the letters available in manuscript and
the full printed version of all others*

VOLUME 9
1821–1822

JOHN MURRAY

© Editorial, Leslie A. Marchand 1979
© Byron copyright material, John Murray 1979

First published 1979 by
John Murray (Publishers) Ltd
50 Albemarle Street, London, W1X 4BD

British Library Cataloguing in Publication Data

Byron, George Gordon, *Baron Byron*
Byron's letters and journals
Vol. 9, 1821–1822: 'In the wind's eye'
1. Byron, George Gordon, *Baron Byron*
I. Marchand, Leslie Alexis   II. 'In the wind's eye'
821'.7   PR4381.A3

ISBN 0-7195-3630-8

Printed in Great Britain by
William Clowes & Sons Limited
Beccles and London

CONTENTS

As soon as Byron arrived in Pisa, in November, 1821, he was closely associated with Shelley and his circle, including Edward Williams, Thomas Medwin, John Taaffe, and later Trelawny. Since Teresa Guiccioli and her family, who had been exiled from Ravenna for political activities, lived near by they saw each other daily and fewer letters passed between them. His unique journal, called "Detached Thoughts", begun in Ravenna, was finished in Pisa soon after his arrival. His principal correspondents were still Murray, Kinnaird, Hobhouse, and Moore. After the death of his mother-in-law Lady Noel he was engrossed with money matters connected with the division of the property, and he signed himself henceforth Noel Byron. His correspondence with Murray shows his increasing displeasure with his publisher's delays and indecision and timidity which led to an eventual break, brought to a climax by Byron's association with the Hunts. His letters to Mary Shelley, the Hunts, and Trelawny after the death of Shelley add to the interest of this volume.

EDITORIAL NOTE

As in earlier volumes the repetition of editorial principles following this note is intended to make the volume as self-contained as possible. The appendices are likewise designed to make useful information available to the reader without reference to other sources, and the index of proper names will serve until the general index appears in the last volume.

ACKNOWLEDGMENTS. (Volume 9). Once more my publisher, John Murray, deserves my gratitude for his unflagging interest in and deep concern for every aspect of the publication of this edition. And I am indebted to the personnel of the Harvard University Press for their efficient production of the American edition. The continuing support of the National Endowment for the Humanities has facilitated my work in many ways. For this I am grateful to the Division of Research Grants. Donald H. Reiman, editor of *Shelley and his Circle* for the Carl H. Pforzheimer Library, has been a constant source of help and guidance. I want to thank Doris Langley Moore for her interest and encouragement. John Gibbins of the Murray editorial staff has given valuable help on copy and proof. And I want to thank Ricki B. Herzfeld for translating a few Italian letters in this volume, Stewart Perowne for reading the proofs and making corrections and suggestions for notes, and Sir Rupert Hart-Davis for his help in locating some of Byron's obscure references.

For permission to get photocopies of letters in their possession and to use them in this volume I wish to thank the following libraries and individuals: Henry E. and Albert A. Berg Collection, New York Public Library; Biblioteca Classense, Ravenna; Biblioteca Labronica, Leghorn; British Library (Department of Manuscripts); Fales Collection, New York University; Goethe Collection, Yale University Library; Harrow School Library; Houghton Library, Harvard University; Henry E. Huntington Library; The Milton S. Eisenhower Library, The Johns Hopkins University; Keats-Shelley Memorial, Rome; Lord Kinnaird; University of Leeds Library; The Earl of Lytton; John S. Mayfield Library, Syracuse University; Pierpont Morgan Library; John Murray; National Library of Scotland; Österreichische Nationalbibliothek, Vienna; Carl H. Pforzheimer

Library; Roe-Byron Collection, Newstead Abbey; Rosenbach Foundation, Philadelphia; Stark Library, University of Texas; Robert H. Taylor Collection, Princeton University Library; Ludwig Walter Trinast.

For assistance of various kinds I wish to thank the following: Joseph Byrnes; James L. Clifford; John Clubbe; Sir Moore Crosthwaite; Mario Curreli; Doucet D. Fischer; Paul Fussell; Leon M. Guilhamet; Mihai Handrea; Mrs. Rachel McClellan; Jerome J. McGann; Paul Magnuson; Jo Modert; Gordon N. Ray; Philip Sheridan; William St. Clair; Charles E. Robinson; Elizabeth M. Trinast; Carl Woodring; Dr. C. J. Wright.

* * * * * *

EDITORIAL PRINCIPLES. With minor exceptions, herein noted, I have tried to reproduce Byron's letters as they were written. The letters are arranged consecutively in chronological order. The name of the addressee is given at the top left in brackets. The source of the text is indicated in the list of letters in the Appendix. If it is a printed text, it is taken from the first printed form of the letter known or presumed to be copied from the original manuscript, or from a more reliable editor, such as Prothero, when he also had access to the manuscript. In this case, as with handwritten or typed copies, or quotations in sale catalogues, the text of this source is given precisely.

When the text is taken from the autograph letter or a photo copy or facsimile of it, the present whereabouts or ownership is given, whether it is in a library or a private collection. When the manuscript is the source, no attempt is made to indicate previous publication, if any. Here I have been faithful to the manuscript with the following exceptions:

1. The place and date of writing is invariably placed at the top right in one line if possible to save space, and to follow Byron's general practice. Fortunately Byron dated most of his letters in this way, but occasionally he put the date at the end. Byron's usual custom of putting no punctuation after the year is followed throughout.

2. Superior letters such as S^r or 30th have been lowered to Sr. and 30th. The & has been retained, but $\&^c$ has been printed &c.

3. Byron's spelling has been followed (and generally his spelling is good, though not always consistent), and *sic* has been avoided except in a few instances when an inadvertent misspelling might change the meaning or be ambiguous, as for instance when he spells *there* t-h-e-i-r.

2

4. Although, like many of his contemporaries, Byron was inconsistent and eccentric in his capitalization, I have felt it was better to let him have his way, to preserve the flavour of his personality and his times. With him the capital letter sometimes indicates the importance he gives to a word in a particular context; but in the very next line it might not be capitalized. If clarity has seemed to demand a modification, I have used square brackets to indicate any departure from the manuscript.

5. Obvious slips of the pen crossed out by the writer have been silently omitted. But crossed out words of any significance to the meaning or emphasis are enclosed in angled brackets ⟨ ⟩.

6. Letters undated, or dated with the day of the week only, have been dated, when possible, in square brackets. If the date is conjectural, it is given with a question mark in brackets. The same practice is followed for letters from printed sources. The post mark date is given, to indicate an approximate date, only when the letter itself is undated.

7. The salutation is put on the same line as the text, separated from it by a dash. The complimentary closing, often on several lines in the manuscript, is given in one line if possible. The P.S., wherever it may be written in the manuscript, follows the signature.

8. Byron's punctuation follows no rules of his own or others' making. He used dashes and commas freely, but for no apparent reason, other than possibly for natural pause between phrases, or sometimes for emphasis. He is guilty of the "comma splice", and one can seldom be sure where he intended to end a sentence, or whether he recognized the sentence as a unit of expression. He did at certain intervals place a period and a dash, beginning again with a capital letter. These larger divisions sometimes, though not always, represented what in other writers, particularly in writers of today, correspond to paragraphs. He sometimes used semicolons, but often where we would use commas. Byron himself recognized his lack of knowledge of the logic or the rules of punctuation. He wrote to his publisher John Murray on August 26, 1813: "Do you know anybody who can *stop*—I mean point—commas and so forth, for I am I fear a sad hand at your punctuation". It is not without reason then that most editors, including R. E. Prothero, have imposed sentences and paragraphs on him in line with their interpretation of his intended meaning. It is my feeling, however, that this detracts from the impression of Byronic spontaneity and the onrush of ideas in his letters, without a compensating gain in clarity. In fact, it may often arbitrarily impose a

meaning or an emphasis not intended by the writer. I feel that there is less danger of distortion if the reader may see exactly how he punctuated and then determine whether a phrase between commas or dashes belongs to one sentence or another. Byron's punctuation seldom if ever makes the reading difficult or the meaning unclear. In rare instances I have inserted a period, a comma, or a semicolon, but have enclosed it in square brackets to indicate it was mine and not his.

9. Words missing but obvious from the context, such as those lacunae caused by holes in the manuscript, are supplied within square brackets. If they are wholly conjectural, they are followed by a question mark. The same is true of doubtful readings in the manuscript.

Undated letters have been placed within the chronological sequence when from internal or external evidence there are reasonable grounds for a conjectural date. This has seemed more useful than putting them together at the end of the volumes. Where a more precise date cannot be established from the context, these letters are placed at the beginning of the month or year in which they seem most likely to have been written.

ANNOTATION. I have tried to make the footnotes as brief and informative as possible, eschewing, sometimes with reluctance, the leisurely expansiveness of R. E. Prothero, who in his admirable edition of the *Letters and Journals* often gave pages of supplementary biographical information and whole letters *to* Byron, which was possible at a time when book publishing was less expensive, and when the extant and available Byron letters numbered scarcely more than a third of those in the present edition. Needless to say, I have found Prothero's notes of inestimable assistance in the identification of persons and quotations in the letters which he edited, though where possible I have double checked them. And I must say that while I have found some errors, they are rare. With this general acknowledgment I have left the reader to assume that where a source of information in the notes is not given, it comes from Prothero's edition, where additional details may be found.

The footnotes are numbered for each letter. Where the numbers are repeated on a page, the sequence of the letters will make the reference clear.

In an appendix in each volume I have given brief biographical sketches of Byron's principal correspondents first appearing in that volume. These are necessarily very short, and the stress is always on

Byron's relations with the subject of the sketch. Identification of less frequent correspondents and other persons mentioned in the letters is given in footnotes as they appear, and the location of these, as well as the biographical sketches in the appendix, will be indicated by italic numbers in the index. Similarly italic indications will refer the reader to the principal biographical notes on persons mentioned in the text of the letters.

With respect to the annotation of literary allusions and quotations in the letters, I have tried to identify all quotations in the text, but have not always been successful in locating Byron's sources in obscure dramas whose phrases, serious or ridiculous, haunted his memory. When I have failed to identify either a quotation or a name, I have frankly noted it as "Unidentified". When, however, Byron has quoted or adapted some common saying from Shakespeare or elsewhere, I have assumed it is easily recognizable and have passed it by. I have likewise passed by single words or short phrases (quoted or not quoted) which may have had a source in Byron's reading or in conversation with his correspondents, but which it is impossible to trace. And when he repeats a quotation, as he frequently does, I have not repeated the earlier notation, except occasionally when it is far removed from its first occurrence in the letters, hoping that the reader will find it in the general index or the subject index in the last volume. No doubt readers with special knowledge in various fields may be able to enlighten me concerning quotations that have baffled me. If so, I shall try to make amends in later volumes.

Since this work will be read on both sides of the Atlantic, I have explained some things that would be perfectly clear to a British reader but not to an American. I trust that English readers will make allowance for this. As Johnson said in the Preface to his edition of Shakespeare: "It is impossible for an expositor not to write too little for some, and too much for others . . . how long soever he may deliberate, [he] will at last explain many lines which the learned will think impossible to be mistaken, and omit many for which the ignorant will want his help. These are censures merely relative, and must be quietly endured."

I have occasionally given cross references, but in the main have left it to the reader to consult the index for names which have been identified in earlier notes.

SPECIAL NOTES. The letters to Thomas Moore, first published in Moore's *Letters and Journals of Lord Byron* (1830), were printed with many omissions and the manuscripts have since disappeared. Moore generally indicated omissions by asterisks, here reproduced as in his text.

Beginning with Volume 7 I have divided some of the longer letters into paragraphs, where a pause or a change of subject is indicated. This helps with proof correcting and makes easier reading of the text, without distracting significantly from the impression of Byron's free-flowing and on-rushing style of composition.

BYRON CHRONOLOGY

1821 Nov. 1—Arrived at the Casa Lanfranchi, Pisa.
Nov. 5—Shelley introduced Edward Williams to Byron.
Nov.—Met Thomas Medwin and John Taaffe.
Dec. 12—Incensed by report of proposed "auto da fé".
Dec. 19—*Sardanapalus, The Two Foscari, Cain* published together.

1822 Jan. 3—Began sittings for bust by Bartolini.
Jan. 15—Met Trelawny.
Jan.—Commissioned Captain Roberts through Trelawny to build a boat for him in Genoa.
Jan. 28—Lady Noel, Byron's mother-in-law, died. Byron took name of Noel Byron and shared the estate.
Feb. 5—Wrote reply to Southey's attack in *The Courier*.
Feb. 7—Wrote note to challenge Southey to a duel.
Feb.—Sent £250 to Hunt for his voyage to Italy.
March 9—Medwin left for Rome.
March 24—"Affray" with Sergeant-Major Masi.
March 28—Tita arrested.
April 20—Samuel Rogers arrived in Pisa.
April 20—His daughter Allegra died.
April 26—Shelley and Williams left Pisa for Casa Magni near Lerici.
May 21—Visited American squadron in Leghorn harbour.
May 22?—Moved to Villa Dupuy, Montenero.
June 18—Trelawny brought the *Bolivar* to Leghorn.
July 1?—Leigh Hunt and family arrived in Leghorn.
July 3—Hunt established in Casa Lanfranchi, where Byron and Teresa returned—Gambas went to Lucca.
July 8—Shelley and Williams drowned in Bay of Spezia.
July—Resumed work on *Don Juan*.
Aug. 16—Witnessed cremation of Shelley's remains at Viareggio.
Sept. 15—Hobhouse arrived in Pisa for a short visit.
Sept. 27—Left for Genoa.
Sept. 29—Ill for four days at Lerici.

BYRON'S LETTERS AND JOURNALS

DETACHED THOUGHTS
October 15, 1821–May 18, 1822

I have been thinking over the other day on the various comparisons good or evil which I have seen published of myself in different journals English and foreign.—This was suggested to me by my accidentally turning over a foreign one lately—for I have made it a rule latterly never to search for anything of the kind—but not to avoid the perusal if presented by Chance.———To begin then—I have seen myself compared personally or poetically—in English French *German* (*as* interpreted to me) Italian and Portuguese within these nine years—to Rousseau—Goethe—Young—Aretine—Timon of Athens—"An Alabaster Vase lighted up within", Satan—Shakespeare—Buonaparte—Tiberius—Æschylus—Sophocles—Euripides—Harlequin—The Clown—Sternhold and Hopkins—to the Phantasmagoria—to Henry the 8th, to Chenier—to Mirabeau—to young R. Dallas (the Schoolboy) to Michael Angelo—to Raphael—to a petit maitre—to Diogenes, to Childe Harold—to Lara—to the Count in Beppo—to Milton—to Pope—to Dryden—to Burns—to Savage—to Chatterton—to "oft have I heard of thee my Lord Biron" in Shakespeare,[2] to Churchill the poet—to Kean the Actor—to Alfieri &c. &c. &c. —the likeness to Alfieri was asserted very seriously by an Italian who had known him in his younger days—it of course related merely to our apparent personal dispositions——he did not assert it to *me* (for we were not then good friends) but in society.[3] ——

The object of so many contradictory comparisons must probably be like something different from them all, —but what *that* is, is more than *I* know, or any body else.———My Mother before I was twenty—would have it that I was like Rousseau—and Madame de Stael used to say so too in 1813—and the Edin[burgh] Review has something of ye sort in it's critique on the 4th Canto of Ch[ild]e Ha[rold]e.——I can't see any point of resemblance—he wrote prose—I verse—he was of the people—I of the Aristocracy—he was a philosopher—I am none—he published his first work at forty—I mine at eighteen,—his first essay

---

[1] Continued in the same notebook in which the Journal dated May 15, 1821, was begun.
[2] *Love's Labour's Lost*, Act V, scene 2.
[3] Probably Count Guiccioli. See Vol. 6, p. 276.

brought him universal applause—mine the contrary—he married his housekeeper—I could not keep house with my wife—he thought all the world in a plot against *him*; my little world seems to think *me* in a plot against it—if I may judge by their abuse in print and coterié—he liked Botany—I like flowers and herbs and trees but know nothing of their pedigrees—he wrote Music—I limit my knowledge of it to what I catch by *Ear*—I never could learn any thing by *study*—not even a language—it was all by rote and ear and memory.—He had a bad memory—I *had* at least an excellent one (ask Hodgson the poet—a good judge for he has an astonishing one) he wrote with hesitation and care—I with rapidity—& rarely with pains——he could never ride nor swim "nor was cunning of fence"[4]——I was an excellent swimmer —a decent though not at all a dashing rider—(having staved in a rib at eighteen in the course of scampering) & was sufficient of fence—particularly of the Highland broadsword—not a bad boxer—when I could keep my temper—which was difficult—but which I strove to do ever since I knocked down Mr. Purling and put his knee-pan out (with the gloves on) in Angelo's and Jackson's rooms in 1806 during the sparring, and I was besides a very fair Cricketer—one of the Harrow Eleven when we play[ed] against Eton in 1805.——

Besides Rousseau's way of life—his country—his manners—his whole character—were so very different—that I am at a loss to conceive how such a comparison could have arisen—as it has done three several times and all in rather a remarkable manner. I forgot to say—that *he* was also short-sighted—and that hitherto my eyes have been the contrary to such a degree that in the largest theatre of Bologna—I distinguished and read some busts and inscriptions printed near the stage—from a box so distant—& so *darkly* lighted—that none of the company (composed of young and very bright-eyed people some of them in the same box) could make out a letter—and thought it was a trick though I had never been in that theatre before.—Altogether, I think myself justified in thinking the comparison not well founded. I don't say this out of pique—for Rousseau was a great man—and the thing if true were flattering enough—but I have no idea of being pleased with a chimera.——

1

When I met old Courtenay[1] the Orator at Rogers the poet's in 1811-1812—I was much taken with the portly remains of his fine figure—and

4 *Twelfth Night* Act III, scene 4.
1 John Courtenay (1741–1816) M.P. for Tamworth and later for Appleby, had been private secretary to Viscount Townshend when the latter was Lord Lieutenant of Ireland (1767–1772).

the still acute quickness of his conversation. It was *he* who silenced Flood[2] in the English House by a crushing reply to a hasty debût of the rival of Grattan in Ireland.—I asked Courtenay (for I like to trace motives) if he had not some personal provocation—for the acrimony of his answer seemed to me (as I had read it) to involve it.—Courtenay said "he had—that when in Ireland—(being an Irishman) at the *bar* of the Irish house of Commons that Flood had made a personal and unfair attack upon *himself*—who not being a member of that house—could not defend himself—& that some years afterwards the opportunity of retort offering in the English Parliament—he could not resist it.—" He certainly repaid F[lood] with interest—for Flood never made any figure—and only a speech or two afterwards in the H[ouse] of Commons.—I must except however his speech on Reform in 1790, which "Fox called the best he ever heard upon that Subject".

2

When Fox was asked what he thought the best speech he had ever heard—he replied "Sheridan's on the Impeachment of Hastings in the house of Commons".—(*not* that in Westminster Hall)—When asked what he thought of his *own* speech on the breaking out of the War? he replied "that was a damned good speech too".—*From Ld. Holland*

3

When Sheridan made his famous speech already alluded to—Fox advised him to speak it over again—in Westminster Hall on the trial—as nothing better *could* be made of the subject—but Sheridan made his new speech as different as possible—and according to the best Judges—very inferior to the former—notwithstanding the laboured panegyric of Burke upon his *Colleague.—Ld. H[olland]*

4

Burke spoilt his own speaking afterwards by an imitation of Sheridan's in Westminster Hall—this Speech he called always "the grand desideratum—which was neither poetry nor eloquence—but something *better* than both."

5

I have never heard any one who fulfilled my Ideal of an Orator.— Grattan would have been near it but for his Harlequin delivery.——

2 Henry Flood (1732–1791), Irish statesman and orator, had entered the Irish Parliament in 1759. He was a rival of Grattan. In 1782 he became an M.P. for Winchester and in the English House of Commons brought in a reform bill based on household suffrage in counties. Courtenay's attack was made December 3, 1783, in the debate on Fox's East India Bill.

Pitt I never heard.—Fox but once—and then he struck me as a debater —which to me seems as different from an Orator as an Improvisatore or a versifier from a poet.——Grey is great—but it is not oratory.— Canning is sometimes very like one.—Windham I did not admire though all the world did—it seemed sad sophistry.——Whitbread was the Demosthenes of bad taste and vulgar vehemence—but strong and English.——Holland is impressive from sense and sincerity—Ld. Lansdowne good—but still a debater only—Grenville I like vastly—if he would prune his speeches down to an hour's delivery——Burdett is sweet and silvery as Belial himself—and *I* think the greatest favourite in Pandemonium—at least I always heard the Country Gentleman & the ministerial devilry praise his speeches *up*stairs—and run down from Bellamy's[1] when he was upon his legs.——I heard Bob Milnes make his second speech—it made an impression.——I like Ward,—studied —but keen and sometimes eloquent.—Peel—my School and form-fellow—(we sate within two of each other) strange to say I have never heard—though I often wished to do so—but from what I remember of him at Harrow—he *is* or *should* be—among the best of them. Now I do *not* admire Mr. Wilberforce's speaking—it is nothing but a flow of *words*—"words—words alone".[2]——

I doubt greatly if the English *have* any eloquence—properly so called—and am inclined to think that the Irish *had* a great deal, and that the French *will* have—and have had in Mirabeau.—Lord Chatham & Burke are the nearest approach to Oratory in England.——I don't know what Erskine may have been at the *bar*, but in the house I wish him at the Bar once more. Lauderdale is shrill—& Scotch, and acute. ——Of Brougham—I shall say nothing as I have a personal feeling of dislike to the man.—But amongst all these good—bad—and indifferent —I never heard the speech which was not too long for the auditors—& not very intelligible except here and there.——The whole thing is a grand deception—and as tedious and tiresome as may be to those who must be often present. I heard Sheridan only once—and that briefly— but I liked his voice—his manner—and his wit—he is the only one of them I ever wished to hear at greater length.——In society I have met him frequently—he was superb!—he had a sort of liking for me—and never attacked me—at least to my face, and he did every body else— high names & wits and orators some of them poets also——I have seen [him] cut up Whitbread—quiz Me. de Stael—annihilate Colman—and do little less by some others—(whose names as friends I set not down)

---

1 A famous pastry cook.
2 *Troilus and Cressida*, Act V, scene 3.

of good fame and abilities.—Poor fellow! he got drunk very thoroughly and very soon.—It occasionally fell to my lot to convey him home—no sinecure—for he was so tipsy that I was obliged to put on his cock'd hat for him—to be sure it tumbled off again and I was not myself so sober as to be able to pick it up again.— —

6

There was something odd about Sheridan. One day at a dinner he was slightly praising that pert pretender and impostor Lyttelton[1]— (The Parliament puppy, still alive, I believe)— —I took the liberty of differing from him—he turned round upon me—and said "is that your real opinion?" I confirmed it.—Then said he—"fortified by this concurrence I beg leave to say that it in fact is also *my* opinion—and that he is a person—whom I do absolutely and utterly—despise,—abhor—and detest"—he then launched out into a description of his despicable qualities—at some length—& with his usual wit—and evidently in earnest (for he hated Lyttelton) his former compliment had been drawn out by some preceding one—just as it's reverse was by my hinting that it was unmerited.—

7

One day I saw him take up his own "Monody ⟨to⟩ on Garrick".—He lighted upon the dedication to the Dowager Lady Spencer—on seeing it he flew into a rage—exclaimed "that it must be a forgery—that he had never dedicated anything of his to such a d— —d canting b— —h &c. &c. &c." and so went on for half an hour abusing his own dedication, or at least—the object of it—if all writers were equally sincere—it would be ludicrous.— —

8

He told me that on the night of the grand success of his S[chool] for S[candal]—he was knocked down and put into the watch house for making a row in the Street & being found intoxicated by the watchmen.— —

9

Latterly when found drunk one night in the kennel and asked his *Name* by the Watchman he answered—"Wilberforce"— —The last time I met him was I think at Sir Gilbert Elliot's[1] where he was as quick as ever—no—it—it was not the last time—the last time was at

[1] William Henry Lyttelton, third Baron Lyttelton of the second creation (1782–1837), was M.P. for Worcestershire, 1807–1820. He was a Whig and had the reputation of an eloquent orator.

[1] Sir Gilbert Elliot, first Earl of Minto (1751–1814), was Governor-General of India from 1807 to 1813.

Douglas K[innaird]'s——I have met him in all places and parties—at Whitehall with the Melbournes—at the Marquis of Tavistock's—at Robins[2] the Auctioneer's—at Sir Humphrey Davy's—at Sam Rogers's —in short in most kinds of company—and always found him very convivial & delightful.—

10

Sheridan's liking for me (whether he was not mystifying me I do not know—but Lady C[arolin]e L[amb] & others told me he said the same both before and after he knew me) was founded upon "English Bards & S[cotch] Reviewers"—he told me that he did not care about poetry (or about mine—at least any but *that* poem of mine) but that he was sure from *that* and other symptoms—I should make an Orator if I would but take to speaking and grow a parliament man—he never ceased harping upon this to me—to the last—and I remember my old tutor Dr. Drury had the same notion when I was a *boy*—but it never was my turn of inclination to try—I spoke once or twice as all young *peers* do—as a kind of introduction into public life—but dissipation—shyness —haughty and reserved opinions—together with the short time I lived in England—after my majority (only about five years in all) prevented me from resuming the experiment—as far as it went it was not discouraging—particularly my *first* speech (I spoke three or four times in all) but just after it my poem of C[hild]e H[arol]d was published— & nobody ever thought about my *prose* afterwards, nor indeed did I—it became to me a secondary and neglected object, though I sometimes wonder to myself *if* I should have succeeded?—

11

The Impression of Parliament upon me—was that it's members are not formidable as *Speakers*—but very much so as an *audience*—because in so numerous a body there may be little Eloquence (after all there were but *two* thorough Orators in all Antiquity—and I suspect still *fewer* in modern times) but must be a leaven of thought and good sense sufficient to make them *know* what is right—though they can't express it nobly.——

12

Horne Tooke and Roscoe both are said to have declared that they left Parliament with a higher opinion of it's aggregate integrity and abilities than that with which they had entered it.—The general

2 George Henry Robins (1778–1847) was a famous auctioneer who was a shareholder of Drury Lane Theatre while Byron was on the sub-committee of management in 1815. The dinner at which Byron met Sheridan, Colman, Kinnaird, Kemble, and others was in 1813.

amount of both in most parliaments is probably about the same—as also the number of *Speakers* and their *talent*—I except *Orators* of course because *they* are things of Ages and not of Septennial or triennial reunions.—Neither house ever struck me with more awe or respect than the same number of Turks in a Divan—or of Methodists in a barn would have done.—Whatever diffidence or nervousness I felt—(& I felt both in a great degree) arose from the number rather than the quality of the assemblage, and the thought rather of the *public without* than the persons within—knowing (as all know) that Cicero himself—and probably the Messiah could never have alter'd the vote of a single Lord of the Bedchamber or Bishop.——I thought *our* house dull—but the other animating enough upon great days.——

12 [so repeated by Byron]

Sheridan dying was requested to undergo "an operation" he replied that he had already submitted to *two* which were enough for one man's life time.—Being asked what they were he answered "having his hair cut—and sitting for his picture".—

13

Whenever an American requests to see me—(which is *not* unfrequently) I comply—1stly. because I respect a people who acquired their freedom by firmness without excess—and 2dly. because these transatlantic visits "few and far between"[1] make me feel as if talking with Posterity from the other side of the Styx;—in a century or two the new English & Spanish Atlantides will be masters of the old Countries in all probability—as Greece and Europe overcame their Mother Asia in the older or earlier ages as they are called.

14

Sheridan was one day offered a bet by M. G. Lewis——"I will bet you, Mr. Sheridan, a very large sum—I will bet you what you *owe me* as Manager for my 'Castle Spectre'"——"I never make *large bets*—said Sheridan—but I will lay you a *very small* one—I will bet you *what it is worth*!['"]

15

Lewis, though a kind man—hated Sheridan—and we had some words upon that score when in Switzerland in 1816.—Lewis afterwards sent me the following epigram upon Sheridan from Saint Maurice.—

"For worst abuse of finest parts
Was Misophil begotten;

[1] Campbell, *The Pleasures of Hope*, Part II, line 378.

17

There might indeed be *blacker* hearts
But none could be more *rotten.*"

16

Lewis at Oatlands[1] was observed one morning to have his eyes red—
& his air sentimental—being asked why?—replied—"that when people
said any thing *kind* to him—it affected him deeply—and just now the
Duchess has said something *so* kind to me that"———here "tears began
to flow" again———"Never mind, Lewis—said Col. Armstrong to him
—never mind—don't cry— *She could not mean it.*"

17

Lewis was a good man—a clever man—but a bore—a damned
bore—one may say.—My only revenge or consolation used to be
setting him by the ears with some vivacious person who hated Bores
especially—Me. de Stael or Hobhouse for example.—But I liked
Lewis—he was a Jewel of a Man had he been better set—I don't mean
personally, but less *tiresome*—for he was tedious—as well as contradictory to every thing and every body.———Being short-sighted—when
we used to ride out together near the Brenta in the twilight in Summer
he made me go *before* to pilot him—I am absent at times—especially
towards evening—and the consequence of this pilotage was some
narrow escapes to the Monk[1] on horseback.———Once I led him *into* a
ditch—over which I had passed as usual forgetting to warn my Convoy
—once I led him nearly into the river instead of *on* the *moveable* bridge
which *in*commodes passengers—and twice did we both run against the
diligence which being heavy and slow did communicate less damage
than it received in its leaders who were *terrassé'd* by the charge.—
Thrice did I lose him in the gray of the Gloaming and was obliged to
bring to to his distant signals of distance and distress.—All the time he
went on talking without interruption for he was a man of many words.
—Poor fellow—he died a martyr to his new riches—of a second visit
to Jamaica—

> "I'd give the lands of Deloraine—
> Dark Musgrave were alive again!"[2]

------

that is

I would give many a Sugar Cane
Monk Lewis were alive again!

[1] The estate near Weybridge, Surrey, bought by the Duke of York in 1794.
[1] See Vol. 3, p. 205, 2nd note 2.
[2] Scott's *Lay of the Last Minstrel*, Canto 5.

Lewis said to me—"why do you talk *Venetian* (such as I could talk
not very fine to be sure) to the Venetians? & not the usual Italian?" I
answered—partly from habit—& partly to be understood—if possible,
—"It may be so [''']—said Lewis—"but it sounds to me like talking
with a *brogue* to an *Irishman*."———

19

Baillie (commonly called Long Baillie—a very clever man—but
odd) complained in riding to our friend Scrope B. Davies—"that he had
a *stitch* in his side"—"I don't wonder at it (said Scrope) for you ride
like a *tailor*."———Whoever had seen B[aillie] on horseback with his
very tall figure on a small nag—would not deny the justice of the
repartée.

20

In 1808—Scrope and myself being at supper at Steevens's (I think
Hobhouse was there too) after the Opera—young Goulburne[1] (of the
Blues and of the Blueviad) came in full of the praise of his horse Grimaldi
—who had just won a race at Newmarket.—"Did he win easy?" said
Scrope—"Sir['']—replied Goulburne—['']he did not even condescend
to *puff* at coming in"———["]No—(said Scrope) and so *you puff for*
him.['']—

21

Captain Wallace a notorious character of that day—and *then* intimate
with most of the more dissipated young men of the day—asked me one
night at the Gaming table where I thought *his Soul* would be found
after death? I answered him—"in *SilverHell*" (a cant name for a second
rate Gambling house)———

22

When the Hon[oura]ble J. W. Ward quitted the Whigs;—he
facetiously demanded at Sir James Macintosh's table in the presence of
Mad.e de Stael, Malthus,—and a large and goodly company of all
parties & countries "what it would take—to *re-Whig him*—as he
thought of turning again['']—"Before you can be *re-whigged* (said I)
I am afraid you must be *re-Warded*.['']———This pun has been attributed
to others—they are welcome to it—but it was mine notwithstanding—
as a numerous company—& Ward Himself doth know. I believe
Luttrel versified it afterwards to put into the M[orning] Chronicle—at

[1] Edward Goulburn (1787–1868), barrister, previously served in the Horse
Guards. He published two satirical poems and a novel. He was later M.P. for
Leicester.

least the late Lady Melbourne told me so. Ward took it good-humouredly at the time.—

23

When Sheridan was on his death-bed Rogers aided him with purse and person—this was particularly kind in Rogers—who always spoke ill of Sheridan—(to me at least) but indeed he does that of every-body to any body.—Rogers is the reverse of the line—

> "The *best good man* with the *worst natured* Muse"[1]

being—

> "The *worst* good man with the *best* natured Muse"

His Muse being all Sentiment and Sago & Sugar—while he himself is a venomous talker. I say "*worst good* man" because he is (perhaps) a *good* man—at least he does good now & then—as well he may—to purchase himself a shilling's worth of Salvation for his Slanders.— They are so *little* too—small talk—and old Womanny—and he is malignant too—& envious—and—he be damned!——

24

Curran!—Curran's the Man who struck me most—such Imagination! —there never was any thing like it—that ever I saw or heard of—his *published* life—his published speeches—give you *no* idea of the Man— none at all——he was a *Machine* of Imagination—as some one said that Piron[1] was an "Epigrammatic Machine.["]——I did not see a great deal of Curran—only in 1813—but I met him at home (for he used to call on me) and in society—at MacIntosh's—Holland House— &c. &c. &c. And he was wonderful even to me—who had seen many remarkable men of the time.——

25

A young American named Coolidge called on me not many months ago—he was intelligent—very handsome and not more than twenty years old according to appearances.—A little romantic but that sits well upon youth—and mighty fond of poesy as may be suspected from his approaching me in my cavern.——He brought me a message from an old Servant of my family (Joe Murray) and told me that *he* (Mr. Coolidge) had obtained a copy of my bust from Thorwal[d]sen at Rome to send to America—I confess I was more flattered by this young en-

---

[1] John Wilmot, Earl of Rochester, "To Lord Brockhurst".

[1] Alexis Piron, French poet (1689–1773), was famous for his epigrams. His election to the Academy in 1753 was not confirmed by Louis XV. Voltaire, whom he had offended, wrote: "Pauvre Piron, qui ne fut rien, Pas même Academicien."

thusiasm of a solitary trans-atlantic traveller than if they had decreed me a Statue in the Paris Pantheon—(I have seen Emperors and demagogues cast down from their pedestals even in my own time—& Grattan's name razed from the Street called after him in Dublin) I say that I was more flattered by it—because it was *single—un-political* & was without motive or ostentation—the pure and warm feeling of a boy for the poet he admired.———It must have been expensive though———*I* would not pay the price of a Thorwaldsen bust for any human head & shoulders—except Napoleon's—or my children's—or some *"absurd Womankind's"* as Monkbarns[1] calls them—or my Sister's.—If asked —*why* then I sate for my own—answer—that it was at the request particular of J. C. Hobhouse Esqre.—and for no one else.—A *picture* is a different matter—every body sits for their picture—but a bust looks like putting up pretensions to permanency—and smacks something of a hankering for *public* fame rather than private remembrance.——

26

One of the cleverest men I ever knew in Conversation was Scrope Beardmore [sic] Davies—Hobhouse is also very good in that line, though it is of less consequence to a man who has other ways of showing his talents than in company—Scrope was always ready—and often witty—H[obhouse] as witty—but not always so ready—being more diffident.—

27

A drunken man ran against Hobhouse in the Street.—A companion of the Drunkard not much less so cried out to Hobhouse—*"An't* you ashamed to run against a drunken man? couldn't you see that he was *drunk?"* "Damn him—(answered Hobhouse) "isn't *he* ashamed to run against *me?* couldn't he see that *I* was *sober*.["]——

28

When Brummell was obliged (by that affair of poor Meyler[1]—who thence acquired the name of "Dick the Dandy-killer"—it was about money and debt & all that) to retire to France—he knew no French & having obtained a Grammar for the purpose of Study—our friend Scrope Davies was asked what progress Brummell had made in French

---

[1] Jonathan Oldbuck, the Laird of Monckbarns, in Scott's *The Antiquary*.

[1] Richard Meyler, a wealthy sugar-baker, a frequenter of Harriette Wilson's drawing room (and bedroom), entered into a deal with others to raise £30,000 for Brummell. Meyler's contribution was £7,000. When he learned that there was not the remotest prospect of ever getting any of his money back he was furious, and he exposed Brummell at White's Club. By this he earned the nickname of "Dick the Dandy-killer". (See *Harriette Wilson's Memoirs*, 1929, pp. 602–604.)

—to which he responded—"that B[rummell] had been stopped like Buonaparte in Russia by the *Elements*"—I have put this pun into "Beppo"[2] which is "a fair exchange and no robbery"—for Scrope made his fortune at several dinners (as he owned himself) by repeating occasionally as his own some of the buffooneries with which I had encountered him in the Morning.—

29

I liked the Dandies—they were always very civil to *me*—though in general they disliked literary people—and persecuted and mystified Me. de Stael,—Lewis,—Horace Twiss—and the like—damnably.— They persuaded Me. de Stael that Alvanley[1] had a hundred thousand a year &c. &c. till she praised him to his *face* for his *beauty*!—and made a set at him for Albertine—(*Libertine* as Brummell baptized her—though the poor Girl was—& is as correct as maid or wife can be—& very amiable withal—) and a hundred fooleries besides—The truth is— that though I gave up the business early—I had a tinge of Dandyism in my minority—& probably retained enough of it—to conciliate the great ones—at four & twenty.——I had gamed—& drank—& taken my degrees in most dissipations—and having no pedantry & not being overbearing—we ran quietly together.——I knew them all more or less—and they made me a Member of Watier's (a superb Club at that time) being I take it—the only literary man (except *two others* both men of the world M.—& S.[2]) in it.—Our Masquerade was a grand one —as was the Dandy Ball—too at the Argyle—but *that* (the latter) was given by the four Chiefs—B. M. A. and P.[3]—if I err not.—

30

I was a member of the Alfred too—being elected—while in Greece. ——It was pleasant—a little too sober & literary—& bored with Sotheby and Sir Francis D'Ivernois[1]—but one met Peel—and Ward— and Valentia—and many other pleasant or known people—and was upon the whole a decent resource on a rainy day—in a dearth of parties —or parliament—or an empty season.—

[2] Stanza 61.

[1] Lord Alvanley, one of the Dandies, was a close friend of Beau Brummell.

[2] Moore and William Robert Spencer (1769–1843), poet and wit, writer of society verse.

[3] Brummel, Mildmay, Alvanley, and Pierrepoint?

[1] Sir François d'Ivernois (1757–1842) was a Swiss economist and politician who took refuge in England because of his political beliefs and resided there from 1792 to 1814; when he returned to Switzerland he became a Counsellor of State and held various diplomatic posts. He represented Switzerland at the Congress of Vienna.

I belonged or belong to the following Clubs or Societies—to the Alfred, to the Cocoa tree—to Watier's—to the Union—to Racket's (at Brighton) to the Pugilistic—to the Owls or "Fly by Night"—to the *Cambridge* Whig Club—to the Harrow Club—Cambridge—and to one or two private Clubs—to the Hampden political Club—and to the Italian Carbonari &c. &c. &c. "though last *not least*"[1]—I got into all these—and never stood for any other—at least—to my own knowledge. ——I declined being proposed to several others though pressed to stand Candidate.——

If the papers lie not (which they generally do) Demetrius Zograffo of Athens is at the head of the Athenian part of the present Greek Insurrection.—He was my Servant in 1809—1810—1811—1812—at different intervals in those years—(for I left him in Greece when I went to Constantinople) and accompanied me to England in 1811—he returned to Greece—Spring 1812.—He was a clever but not *apparently* an enterprizing man—but Circumstances make men.—His two sons (*then* infants) were named Miltiades—and Alcibiades—May the Omen be happy!——

I have a notion that Gamblers are as happy as most people—being always *excited*;—women—wine—fame—the table—even Ambition—*sate* now & then—but every turn of the card—& cast of the dice—keeps the Gambler alive—besides one can Game ten times longer than one can do any thing else.—I was very fond of it when young—that is to say of "Hazard" for I hate all *Card* Games even Faro—When Macco (or whatever they spell it) was introduced I gave up the whole thing—for I loved and missed the *rattle* and *dash* of the box & dice—and the glorious uncertainty not only of good luck or bad luck—but of *any luck at all*—as one had sometimes to throw *often* to decide at all.——I have thrown as many as fourteen mains running—and carried off all the cash upon the table occasionally—but I had no coolness or judgement or calculation.—It was the *delight* of the thing that pleased me.—Upon the whole I left off in time without being much a winner or loser.— Since One and twenty years of age—I played but little & then never above a hundred or two—or three.——

[1] *Julius Caesar*, Act III, scene 1.

As far as Fame goes (that is to say *living* Fame) I have had my share
—perhaps—indeed—*certainly* more than my deserts.——Some odd
instances have occurred to my own experience of the wild & strange
places to which a name may penetrate, and where it may impress.—
Two years ago (almost three—being in August or July 1819) I received at Ravenna a letter in *English* verse from *Drontheim* in Norway
—written by a Norwegian—and full of the usual compliments &c. &c.
—It is still somewhere amongst my papers.——In the same month I
received an invitation into *Holstein* from a Mr. Jacobsen (I think) of
Hamburgh—also (by the same medium) a translation of Medora's song
in the "Corsair" by a Westphalian Baroness (*not* "Thunderton-
tronck")[1] with some original verses of hers (very pretty and Klopstock-
ish) and a prose translation annexed to them—on the subject of my
wife;—as they concerned *her* more than me—I sent them to her together with Mr. J's letter.—It was odd enough to receive an invitation
to pass the *summer* in *Holstein*—while in *Italy*—from people I never
knew.—The letter was addressed to Venice.—Mr. J[acobsen] talked
to me of the "wild roses growing in the Holstein summer" why then
did the Cimbri & Teutones emigrate?

What a strange thing is life and man? were I to present myself at the
door of the house where my daughter now is—the door would be shut
in my face—unless (as is not impossible—) I knocked down the porter
—and if I had gone in that year—(& perhaps now) to Drontheim (the
furthest town in Norway) or into Holstein—I should have been received with open arms into the mansions of Strangers & foreigners—
attached to me by no tie by [but?] that of mind and rumour. As far as
Fame goes—I have had my share—it has indeed been leavened by other
human contingencies—and this in a greater degree than has occurred
to most literary men—of a *decent* rank in life—but on the whole I take
it that such equipoise is the condition of humanity.———I doubt sometimes whether after all a quiet & unagitated life would have suited me—
yet I sometimes long for it——my earliest dreams—(as most boys'
dreams are) were martial—but a little later they were all for *love* &
retirement—till the hopeless attachment to M[ary] C[haworth] began
—and continued (though sedulously concealed) *very* early in my teens
—& so upwards—for a time.——*This* threw me out again "alone on
a wide—wide sea".[2]—In the year 1804—I recollect meeting my

[1] The mother of Cunegonde, the "heroine" of Voltaire's *Candide*, was the
Westphalian Baroness Thunder-ten-tronckh.
[2] *Ancient Mariner*, Part IV, line 203.

Sister at General Harcourt's[3] in Portland Place.—I was then *one thing* and *as* she had always till then found me.——When we met again in 1805—(she tells me since) that my temper and disposition were so completely altered that I was hardly to be recognized.—I was not then sensible of the change—but I can believe it—and account for it.—

35

A private play being got up at Cambridge a Mr. Tulk greatly to the inconvenience of Actors and audience declined his part on a sudden—so that it was necessary to make an apology to the Company.—In doing this—Hobhouse (indignant like all the rest at this inopportune caprice of the Seceder) stated to the audience "that in consequence of *a* Mr. Tulk having unexpectedly thrown up his part—they must request their indulgence &c. &c.["]—Next day the furious Tulk demanded of Hobhouse "did you, Sir, or did you not use *that* expression"—"Sir (said Hobhouse) I *did* or *did not* use that expression"——"perhaps—(said Scrope Davies—who was present)—you object to the *indefinite article*, and prefer being entitled *the Mr. Tulk*?["] *the* Tulk eyed Scrope indignantly but aware probably that the said Scrope besides being a profane Jester had the misfortune to be a very good shot & had already fought two or three duels—he retired without further objections to either article—except a conditional menace—*if* he should ascertain that an intention &c. &c.

36

I have been called in as Mediator or Second at least twenty times in violent quarrels—and have always contrived to settle the business without compromising the honour of the parties or leading them to mortal consequences, & often too sometimes in very difficult and delicate circumstances—and having to deal with very hot and haughty Spirits—Irishmen—Gamesters—Guardsmen—Captains & Cornets of horse—and the like.—This was of course in my youth—when I lived in hot-headed company.—I have had to carry challenges—from Gentlemen to Noblemen—from Captains to Captains—from lawyers to Counsellors—and once from a Clergyman to an officer in the Lifeguards—it may seem strange—but I have found the latter by far the most difficult

"... to compose
The bloody duel without blows."[1]

---

[3] General the Hon. William Harcourt (1742–1830) distinguished himself in the War against the Americans. He succeeded his brother as the last Earl Harcourt in 1809. His wife was a friend of Augusta.

[1] Samuel Butler, *Hudibras*, First Part, Canto I, lines 721–726.

The business being about a woman.—I must add that I never saw a *woman* behave so ill—like a cold-blooded heartless whore as she was—but very handsome for all that.—A certain Susan C. was she called—I never saw her but once—and that was to induce her but to say two words (which in no degree compromised herself) & which would have had the effect of saving a priest or a Lieutenant of Cavalry.—She would *not* say them—and neither N. or myself (the son of Sir E. N. and a friend of one of the parties)—could prevail upon her to say them—though both of us used to deal in some sort with Womankind.—At last I managed to quiet the combatants without her talisman—and I believe to her great disappointment.—She was the d——st bitch—that I ever saw—& I have seen a great many.——Though my Clergyman was sure to lose either his life or his living—he was as war-like as the Bishop of Beauvais—& would hardly be pacified—but then he was in love—and that is a martial passion.[2]——

37
[12 lines heavily crossed out]

38
Somebody asked Schlegel (the Dousterswivel of Madame de Stael) "whether he did not think *Canova* a great Sculptor?["]—["]Ah!["] replied the modest Prussian—"did you ever see *my bust* by *Tiecke?*"

39
At Venice in the year 1817—an order came from Vienna for the Archbishop to go in State to Saint Mark's in his Carriage and four horses—which is much the same as commanding the Lord Mayor of London to proceed through Temple Bar in his Barge.——

40
When I met Hudson Lowe the Jailor at Lord Holland's before he sailed for Saint Helena, the discourse turned on the battle of Waterloo. —I asked him whether the dispositions of Napoleon were those of a great General?—he answered disparageingly—"that they were very *simple*"——I had always thought that a degree of Simplicity was an ingredient of Greatness.—

41
I was much struck with the simplicity of Grattan's manners in private life—they were odd—but they were natural—Curran used to take him

---

[2] See Nov. 16, 1811, to Hobhouse (Vol. 2, pp. 129–130.)

off bowing to the very ground—and "thanking God that he had no peculiarities of gesture or appearance" in a way irresistibly ludicrous—and Rogers used to call him "a Sentimental Harlequin" but Rogers back-bites every body—and Curran who used to quiz his great friend Godwin to his very face—would hardly respect a fair mark of mimicry in another—to be sure Curran *was* admirable! to hear his description of the examination of an Irish witness—was next to hearing his own speeches—the latter I never heard—but I have the former.——

42

I have heard that when Grattan made his first speech in the English Commons—it was for some minutes doubtful whether to laugh or cheer him.—The debût of his predecessor Flood had been a complete failure, under nearly similar circumstances.—But when the ministerial part of our Senators had watched Pitt (their thermometer) for their cue and saw him nod repeatedly his stately nod of approbation—they took the hint from their huntsman and broke out into the most rapturous cheers.——Grattan's speech indeed deserved them it was a Chef d'oeuvre.——I did not hear *that* speech of his (being then at Harrow) but heard most of his others on the same question—also that on the war of 1815—I differed from his opinions on the latter question—but co-incided in the general admiration of his eloquence.

43

At the Opposition Meeting of the peers in 1812 at Lord Grenville's —when Ld. Grey & he read to us the correspondence upon Moira's negociation—I sate next to the present Duke of Grafton—when it was over—I turned to him—& said "What is to be done next?"— "Wake the Duke of Norfolk["] (who was snoring away near us) replied he—"I don't think the Negociators have left anything else for us to do this turn."

44

In the debate or rather discussion afterwards in the House of Lords upon that very question—I sate immediately behind Lord Moira—who was extremely annoyed at G[rafton?]'s speech upon the subject—& while G. was speaking turned round to me repeatedly—and asked me whether I agreed with him? It was an awkward question to me who had not heard both sides.—Moira kept repeating to me "it was *not so*—it was so and so &c."—I did not know very well what to think—but I sympathized with the acuteness of his feelings upon the subject.——

27

Lord Eldon affects an Imitation of two very different Chancellors—
Thurlow and Loughborough—& can indulge in an oath now & then—
on one of the debates on the Catholic question—when we were either
equal or within one (I forget which) I had been sent for in great haste
to a Ball which I quitted I confess somewhat reluctantly to emancipate
five Millions of people——I came in late—and did not go immediately
into the body of the house—but stood just behind the Woolsack.—
Eldon turned round & catching my eye—immediately said to a peer
(who had come to him for a few minutes on the Woolsack as is the
custom of his friends) "Damn them! they'll have it now by G. .d!—the
vote that is just come in will give it them."—

46

When I came of age—some delays on account of some birth & marriage certificates from Cornwall occasioned me not to take my seat for
several weeks.—When these were over, and I had taken the Oath.—
the Chancellor apologized to me for the delay—observing "that these
forms were a part of his *duty*"—I begged him to make no apology—
and added (as he certainly had shown no violent hurry) "your Lordship
was exactly like 'Tom Thumb' (which was then being acted) "You did
your *duty*—and you did *no more*."

47

In a certain Capital abroad—the Minister's Secretary (the Minister
being then absent) was piqued that I did not call upon him.—When I
was going away Mr. W. an acquaintance of mine applied to him for my
passport which was sent—but at the same time accompanied by a formal
note from the Secretary stating "that at *Mr. W's request* he had granted
&c." & in such a manner as appeared to *hint* that it was only to oblige
Mr. W. that he had given me that which in fact he had no right to refuse
to Any-body.——I wrote him the following answer—"Ld. B. presents
his Compliments to L—— and is extremely obliged to *Mr. W.* for
the passport.["]

48

There was a Madman of the name of Battersby that frequented
Steevens's & the Prince of Wales Coffee-houses about the time when I
was leading a loose life about town—before I was of age.—One night
he came up to some hapless Stranger whose coat was not to his liking
and said "Pray Sir did the tailor cut your coat in that fashion—or did
the rats gnaw it?["]

The following is—(I believe) better known.—A beau (*dandies* were not then christened) came into the P[rince] of W[ales] and exclaimed—"Waiter bring me a glass of Madeira Negus with a Jelly—and rub my plate with a Chalotte" This in a very soft tone of voice.——A Lieutenant of the Navy who sate in the next box immediately roared out the following rough parody——"Waiter—bring me a glass of d——d stiff Grog—and rub my a—e with a brick-bat.["]

50

Sotheby is a good man—rhymes well (if not wisely) but is a bore.— He seizes you by the button—one night of a route at Mrs. Hope's he had fastened upon me—(something about Agamemnon or Orestes—or some of his plays—) notwithstanding my symptoms of manifest distress—(for I was in love & had just nicked a minute when neither mothers nor husbands—not rivals—nor gossips—were near my then idol who was beautiful as the Statues in the Gallery where we stood at the time) Sotheby I say had seized upon me by the button and the heart-strings—and spared neither.—W. Spencer who likes fun—and don't dislike mischief—saw my case—and coming up to us both—took me by the hand—and pathetically bade me farewell—for said he "I see it is all over with you"—Sotheby then went away; "Sic me Servavit, Apollo".[1]

51

It is singular how soon we lose the impression of what ceases to be *constantly* before us.—A year impairs, a lustre obliterates.—There is little distinct left without an *effort* of memory,—*then* indeed the lights are rekindled for a moment—but who can be sure that the Imagination is not the torch-bearer?—Let any man try at the end of *ten* years to bring before him the features—or the mind—or the sayings—or the habits of his best friend—or his *greatest* man—(I mean his favourite—his Buonaparte—his this—that, or tother)[.] And he will be surprized at the extreme confusion of his ideas.——I speak confidently on this point having always past for one who had a good eye—an excellent memory.—I except indeed—our recollections of Womankind—— there is no forgetting *them*—(and be d——d to them) any more than any other remarkable Era—such as "the revolution" or "the plague"—or "the Invasion" or "the Comet"—or "the War" of such— and such an Epoch—being the favourite dates of Mankind who have so many *blessings* in their lot that they never make their Calendars from

[1] "Thus did Apollo rescue me." The concluding words of the 9th *Satire* of Horace.

them—being too common.—For instance you see "the great drought" —"the Thames frozen over"—"the Seven years war broke out"—the E[nglish] or F[rench] or S[panish] "Revolution commenced"—"The Lisbon Earthquake"—"the Lima Earthquake"—"the Earthquake of Calabria"—"the Plague of London"—"Ditto of Constantinople"— "the Sweating Sickness"—"The Yellow fever of Philadelphia" &c. &c. &c.—but you don't see "the abundant harvest"—"the fine Summer"— "the long peace"—"the wealthy speculation"—"the wreckless voyage" recorded so emphatically?—By the way there has been a *thirty years war* and a *Seventy years war*—was there ever a *Seventy or a thirty years peace?*—or was there even a day's *Universal* peace—except perhaps in China—where they have found out the miserable happiness of a stationary & unwarlike mediocrity?—And is all this—because Nature is niggard or savage? or Mankind ungrateful?—let philosophers decide.——I am none.—

52

In the year 1814—as Moore and I were going to dine with Lord Grey in P[ortman] Square—I pulled out a "Java Gazette" (which Murray had sent to me) in which there was a controversy on our respective merits as poets.——It was amusing enough that we should be proceeding peaceably to the same table—while they were squabbling about us in the Indian Seas (to be sure the paper was dated six months before) and filling columns with Batavian Criticism.—But this is fame I presume.—

53

In general I do not draw well with Literary men—not that I dislike them but—I never know what to say to them after I have praised their last publication.—There are several exceptions to be sure—but they have either been men of the world—such as Scott—& Moore &c. or visionaries out of it—such as Shelley &c. but your literary every day man—and I never went well in company——especially your foreigner —whom I never could abide—except Giordani[1] & and—and (I really can't name any other)—I do not remember a man amongst them— —whom I ever wished to see twice—except perhaps Mezzophanti[2]— who is a Monster of Languages—the Briareus[3] of parts of Speech—a

[1] Byron met Pietro Giordani in Venice.
[2] Giuseppe Mezzofanti was the librarian of the Bologna Library. He later became a Cardinal.
[3] In Greek mythology one of three hundred-handed monsters, children of Heaven and Earth.

walking Polyglott and more—who ought to have existed at the time
of the tower of Babel as universal Interpreter.—He is indeed a Marvel
—unassuming also—I tried him in all the tongues of which I knew a
single oath (or adjuration to the Gods against Postboys—Lawyers—
Tartars — boatmen, — Sailors, pilots, — Gondoliers — Muleteers —
Camel-drivers—Vetturini—Postmasters—post-horses—post-houses
—post-everything) and Egad! he astonished me even to my English.—

54

Three Swedes came to Bologna knowing no tongue but Swedish— —
the inhabitants in despair presented them to Mezzophanti.—Mezzophanti (though a great Linguist) knew no more Swedish than the
Inhabitants.—But in two days by dint of dictionary he talked with them
fluently and freely, so that they were astonished—and every body else,
at his acquisition of another tongue in forty eight hours—I had this
anecdote first from Me. Albrizzi—& afterwards confirmed by *himself*
—& he is not a boaster.—

55

I sometimes wish that—I had studied languages with more attention
—those which I know, even the classical (Greek and Latin in the usual
proportion of a sixth form boy) and a smattering of modern Greek—
the Armenian & Arabic Alphabets—a few Turkish & Albanian phrases,
oaths, or requests—Italian tolerably—Spanish less than tolerably—
French to read with ease—but speak with difficulty—or rather not at
all— —all have been acquired by ear or eye—& never by anything like
Study:—like "Edie Ochiltree"— —"I never dowed to bide a hard turn
o'wark in my life"[1]— —To be sure—I set in zealously for the Armenian
and Arabic—but I fell in love with some absurd womankind both times
before I had overcome the Characters and at Malta & Venice left the
profitable Orientalists for—for—(no matter what—) notwithstanding
that my master the Padre Pasquale Aucher (for whom by the way I
compiled the major part of two Armenian & English Grammars) assured me "that the terrestrial Paradise had been certainly in *Armenia*"
—I went seeking it—God knows where—did I find it?—Umph!—Now
& then—for a minute or two.

56

Of Actors—Cooke was the most natural—Kemble the most supernatural—Kean a medium between the two—but Mrs. Siddons worth
them all put together—of those whom I remember to have seen in
England.— —

[1] In Scott's *The Antiquary.*

I have seen Sheridan weep two or three times—it may be that he was maudlin—but this only renders it more impressive for who would see?

"From Marlborough's eyes the tears of dotage flow
And Swift expire a driveller and a show?["]¹

Once I saw him cry at Robin's the Auctioneer's after a splendid dinner full of great names and high Spirits.—I had the honour of sitting next to Sheridan.—The occasion of his tears was some observation or other upon the subject of the sturdiness of the Whigs in resisting Office—& keeping to their principles—Sheridan turned round——"Sir—it is easy for my Lord G.—or Earl G.—or Marquis B.—or Lord H. with thousands upon thousands a year some of it either *presently* derived or *inherited* in Sinecures or acquisitions from the public money—to boast of their patriotism—& keep aloof from temptation—but they do not know from what temptations those have kept aloof who had equal pride—at least equal talent, & not unequal passions—& nonetheless—knew not in the course of their lives—what it was to have a shilling of their own. ["]——And in saying this he wept.——

I have more than once heard Sheridan say that he never "had a shilling of his own"—to be sure he contrived to extract a good many of other people's.——In 1815—I had occasion to visit my Lawyer—in Chancery Lane—he was with Sheridan.—After mutual greetings &c. Sheridan retired first.—Before recurring to my own business—I could not help enquiring *that* of S.——"Oh (replied the Attorneo) the usual thing—to stave off an action from his Wine-Merchant—my Client. —["] "Well (said I) & what do you mean to do?" "Nothing at all for the present—said he—would you have us proceed against old Sherry? —what would be the use of it?["]—And here he began laughing & going over Sheridan's good gifts of Conversation.——Now from personal experience I can vouch that my Attorneo is by no means the tenderest of men, or particularly accessible to any kind of impression out of the Statute or record.—And yet Sheridan in half an hour had found a way to soften and seduce him in such a manner that I almost think he would have thrown his Client (an honest man with all the laws and some justice on his side) out of the window had he come in at the moment.—Such was Sheridan!—he could soften an Attorney!—there has been nothing like it since the days of Orpheus.——

¹ Quoted, not quite accurately, from Johnson's "The Vanity of Human Wishes," lines 317–318.

When the Bailiff (for I have seen most kinds of life) came upon me in 1815—to seize my chattels (being a peer of parliament my person was beyond him) being curious (as is my habit)—I first asked him "what Extents elsewhere he had for Government"? upon which he showed me one upon *one house only*—for *seventy thousand pounds!*—Next I asked him if he had nothing for Sheridan?—"Oh—Sheridan—said he—Aye I have this (pulling out a pocket-book &c.) but—my L[ord] I have been in Mr. Sheridan's house a twelve-month at a time, a civil gentleman—knows how to deal with *us* &c. &c.["] Our own business was then discussed—which was none of the easiest for me at that time.—But the Man was civil—& (what I valued more) communicative——I had met many of the brethren years before in affairs of my friends—(Commoners that is) but this was the first (or second) on my own account;—a civil Man, feed accordingly;—probably he anticipated as much.—

No man would live his life over again—is an old & true saying which all can resolve for themselves.—At the same time there are probably *moments* in most men's lives—which they would live over the rest of life to *regain*?—Else why do we live at all? because Hope recurs to Memory—both false—but—but—but—but—and—this *but* drags on till—What? I do not know—& who does?—"He that died o' Wednesday"[1]—by the way—there is a poor devil to be shot tomorrow here—(Ravenna) for murder;—he hath eaten half a Turkey for his dinner—besides fruit & pudding—and he refuses to confess?—shall I go to see him exhale?—No.—And why?—because it is to take place at *Nine*;—Now—could I *save* him—or a fly even from the same catastrophe—I would out-watch years—but as I cannot—I will not get up earlier to see another man shot—than I would to run the same risk in person.—Besides—I have seen more than one die that death (and other deaths) before to-day.—It is not cruelty which actuates mankind—but excitement—on such occasions—at least I suppose so;—it is detestable to *take* life in that way—unless it be to preserve two lives.——

Old Edgeworth—the fourth—or fifth Mrs. Edgeworth—and *the* Miss Edgeworth were in London—1813.—Miss Edgeworth liked—Mrs. Edgeworth not disliked—old Edgeworth a bore—the worst of bores—a boisterous Bore.—I met them in society—once at a breakfast

---

[1] *Henry IV*, Part I, Act. V, scene 1.

of Sir H[umphry] D[avy]'s—Old Edgeworth came in late boasting that he had given "Dr. Parr a dressing the night before"———(no such easy matter by the way)———I thought *her* pleasant.—They all abused Anna Seward's memory.—

62

When on the road—they heard of *her* brother's—and *his* Son's death —what was to be done? their *London* Apparel was all ordered & made! —so they sunk his death for the six weeks of their Sojourn—and went into mourning on their way back to Ireland—*Fact*!

63

While the Colony were in London—there was a book with a Subscription for the "recall of Mrs. Siddons to the Stage" going about for signatures.—Moore moved for a similar subscription for the "recall of *Mr. Edgeworth to Ireland*"![1]———

64

Sir Humphrey Davy told me that the Scene of the French Valet and Irish postboy in "Ennui"[1]—was taken from *his* verbal description to the Edgeworths in Edgeworthtown—of a similar fact on the road occurring to himself—So *much* the better—being *life*.———

65

When I was fifteen years of age—it happened that in a Cavern in Derbyshire—I had to cross in a boat—(in which two people only could lie down—) a stream which flows under a rock—with the rock so close upon the water—as to admit the boat only to be pushed on by a ferryman (a sort of Charon) who wades at the stern stooping all the time.— —The Companion of my transit was M[ary] A. C[haworth] with whom I had been long in love and never told it—though *she* had discovered it without.—I recollect my sensations—but cannot describe them—and it is as well.———We were a party—a Mr. W.—two Miss W's—Mr. & Mrs. Cl[ar]ke—Miss R. and *my* M. A. C.—Alas! why do I say *My*? —our Union would have healed feuds in which blood had been shed by our fathers—it would have joined lands—broad and rich—it would have joined at least *one* heart and two persons not ill-matched in years (she is two years my elder) and—and—and—what has been the result?—*She* has married a man older than herself—been wretched— and separated.—I have married—& am separated.—and yet *we* are *not* united.———

1 See Diary, Jan. 19, 1821 (Vol. 8, pp. 29–30).
1 *Ennui* was one of the first set of Maria Edgeworth's *Tales of Fashionable Life.* It was published in 1809.

One of my notions different from those of my contemporaries, is, that the present is not a high age of English Poetry——there are *more* poets (soi-disant) than ever there were and proportionally *less* poetry.—— This *thesis*—I have maintained for some years—but strange to say—it meeteth not with favour with my brethren of the Shell[1]—even Moore shakes his head—& firmly believe[s] that it is the grand Era of British Poesy.——

When I belonged to the D[rury] L[ane] Committee and was one of the S[ub] C[ommittee] of Management—the number of *plays* upon the shelves were about *five* hundred;—conceiving that amongst these there must be *some* of merit—in person & by proxy I caused an investigation. —I do not think that of those which I saw—there was one which could be conscientiously tolerated.——There never were such things as most of them.—Mathurin was very kindly recommended to me by Walter Scott—to whom I had recourse—firstly—in the hope that he would do something for us himself—& secondly—in my despair—that he would point out to us any young (or old) writer of promise.—Mathurin sent his Bertram—and a letter *without* his address—so that at first—I could give him no answer.—When I at last hit upon his residence I sent him a favourable answer and something more substantial.—His play succeeded—but I was at that time absent from England.——I tried Coleridge too—but he had nothing feasible in hand at the time.—Mr. Sotheby obligingly offered *all* his tragedies—and I pledged myself— and notwithstanding many squabbles with my Committe[e]d Brethren —did get "Ivan" accepted—read—& the parts distributed.—But lo! in the very heart of the matter—upon some *tepid*-ness on the part of Kean—or warmth upon that of the Authour—Sotheby withdrew his play.——Sir J. B. Burgess[1] did also present four tragedies and a farce —and I moved Green-room & S[ub] Committee—but they would not. —Then the Scenes I had to go through!—the authours—and the authoresses——the Milliners—the wild Irishmen—the people from Brighton—from Blackwell—from Chatham—from Cheltenham— from Dublin—from Dundee—who came in upon me!—to all of whom it was proper to give a civil answer—and a hearing—and a reading—— Mrs. Glover's father an Irish dancing Master of Sixty years—called upon me to request to play "*Archer*"—drest in silk stockings on a frosty morning to show his legs—(which were certainly good & Irish for his

[1] The name of a form at Harrow School.
[1] Sir James Bland Burges, an uncle by marriage of Lady Byron.

age—& had been still better)—Miss Emma Somebody with a play entitled the "Bandit of Bohemia"—or some such title or production— Mr. O' Higgins—then resident at Richmond—with an Irish tragedy in which the unities could not fail to be observed for the protagonist was chained by the leg to a pillar during the chief part of the performance.— He was a wild man of a salvage appearance—and the difficulty of *not* laughing at him was only to be got over—by reflecting upon the probable consequences of such cachinnation.——As I am really a civil & polite person—and *do* hate giving pain—when it can be avoided—I sent them up to Douglas Kinnaird—who is a man of business—and sufficiently ready with a negative—and left them to settle with him— and as at the beginning of next year—I went abroad—I have since been little aware of the progress of the theatres.

68

Players are said to be an impracticable people.—They are so.—But I managed to steer clear of any disputes with them—and excepting one debate with the Elder Byrne about Miss Smith's Pas de (Something— I forget the technicals) I do not remember any litigation of my own.— I used to protect Miss Smith—because she was like Lady Jane Harley in the face—and likenesses go a great way with me.—Indeed in general I left such things to my more bustling colleagues—who used to reprove me seriously—for not being able to take such things in hand without buffooning with the Histrions—& throwing things into confusion by treating light matters with levity.

69

Then the Committee!—then the Sub-Committee! we were but few— & never agreed!—There was Peter Moore who contradicted Kinnaird —& Kinnaird who contradicted everybody——then our two managers Rae and Dibdin—and our Secretary Ward! and yet we were all very zealous—& in earnest to do good & so forth;——Hobhouse furnished us with prologues to our revived Old English plays—but was not pleased with me for complimenting him as "the *Upton*"[1] of our theatre (Mr. Upton is or was the poet who writes the songs for Astley's) and almost gave up prologuizing in consequence.——

70

In the Pantomime of 1815–16—there was a Representation of the Masquerade of 1814—given by "us Youth" of Watier's Club to Wellington & Co.—Douglas Kinnaird—& one or two others with my-

[1] See April 11, 1818, to Murray, note 2. (Vol. 6, p. 27.)

self—put on Masques—and went *on* the Stage amongst the οἱ πολλοί —to see the effect of a theatre from the Stage.—It is very grand.—— Douglas danced amongst the figuranti too—& they were puzzled to find out who we were—as being more than their number.—It was odd enough that D. K. & I should have been both at the *real* Masquerade— & afterwards in the Mimic one of the same—on the stage of D. L. Theatre.

71

When I was a youth—I was reckoned a good actor.—Besides "Harrow speeches"—(in which I shone) I enacted "Penruddock" in the "Wheel of Fortune"[1] and "Tristram Fickle" in Allingham's farce of "the Weathercock"—for three nights (the duration of our compact) in some private theatricals at Southwell in 1806—with great applause. —The occasional prologue for our volunteer play—was also of my composition.— —The other performers were young ladies and gentlemen of the neighbourhood—& the whole went off with great effect upon our good-natured audience.—

72

When I first went up to College—it was a new and a heavy hearted scene for me.—Firstly—I so much disliked leaving Harrow that though it was time—(I being seventeen) it broke my very rest for the last quarter—with counting the days that remained.—I always *hated* Harrow till the last year and a half—but then I liked it.—2dly. I wished to go to Oxford and not to Cambridge.—3dly. I was so completely alone in this new world that it half broke my Spirits.—My companions were not unsocial but the contrary—lively—hospitable—of rank—& fortune—& gay far beyond my gaiety—I mingled with—and dined— & supped &c. with them—but I know not how—it was one of the deadliest and heaviest feelings of my life to feel that I was no longer a boy.—From that moment I began to grow old in my own esteem—and in my esteem age is not estimable.—I took my gradations in the vices —with great promptitude—but they were not to my taste—for my early passions though violent in the extreme—were concentrated—and hated division or spreading abroad.—I could have left or lost the world with or for that which I loved—but though my temperament was naturally burning—I could not share in the common place libertinism of the place and time—without disgust.— —And yet this very disgust and my heart thrown back upon itself—threw me into excesses perhaps more fatal than those from which I shrunk—as fixing upon one (at a

[1] See Vol. 1, p. 101.

time) the passions which spread amongst many would have hurt only myself.—

73

People have wondered at the Melancholy which runs through my writings.—Others have wondered at my personal gaiety——but I recollect once after an hour in which I had been sincerely and particularly gay—and rather brilliant in company—my wife replying to me when I said (upon her remarking my high spirits) "and yet Bell—I have been called and mis-called Melancholy—you must have seen how falsely frequently." "No—B—(she answered) it is not so—at *heart* you are the most melancholy of mankind, and often when apparently gayest. [")]——

74

If I could explain at length the *real* causes which have contributed to increase this perhaps *natural* temperament of mine—this Melancholy which hath made me a bye-word—nobody would wonder——but this is impossible without doing much mischief.———I do not know what other men's lives have been—but I cannot conceive anything more strange than some of the earlier parts of mine———I have written my memoirs—but omitted *all* the really *consequential* & *important* parts—from deference to the dead—to the living—and to those who must be both.—

75

I sometimes think that I should have written the *whole*—as a *lesson*——but it might have proved a lesson to be *learnt*—rather than *avoided*—for passion is a whirlpool, which is not to be viewed nearly without attraction from it's Vortex.——

76

I must not go on with these reflections—or I shall be letting out some secret or other—to paralyze posterity.—

77

One night Scrope Davies at a Gaming house—(before I was of age) being tipsy as he mostly was at the Midnight hour—& having lost monies—was in vain intreated by his friends one degree less intoxicated than himself to come or go home.—In despair—he was left to himself and to the demons of the dice-box.——Next day—being visited about two of the Clock by some friends just risen with a severe headache and empty pockets—(who had left him losing at four or five in the morning) he was found in a sound sleep—without a nightcap—& not particularly encumbered with bed-cloathes———a Chamber-pot stood by the bedside—*brim-full* of—*Bank Notes!*—all won—God knows how—and crammed—Scrope knew not where—but *there* they were—all good legitimate notes—and to the amount of some thousand pounds.—

78

At Brighthelmstone—(I love orthography at length) in the year 1808 Hobhouse, Scrope Davies, Major Cooper—and myself—having dined together with Lord Delvin—Count (I forget the french Emigrant nomenclature) and others—did about the middle of the night—(we *four*) proceed to a house of Gambling—being then *amongst us* possest of about *twenty guineas* of ready cash—with which we had to maintain about as many of your whoreson horses & servants—besides household and whorehold expenditure. We had I say—twenty guineas or so—& we lost them—returning home in bad humour.—Cooper went home. ——Scrope and Hobhouse and I (it being high Summer) did first-ly strip and plunge into the Sea—whence after half an hour's swimming of those of us (Scrope & I) who could swim—we emerged in our dressing-gowns to discuss a bottle or two of Champaigne and Hock (according to choice) at our quarters.—In the course of the discussion —words arose——Scrope seized H[obhouse] by the throat—H. seized a knife in self-defence and stabbed Scrope in the shoulder to avoid being throttled.——Scrope fell bathed in blood & wine—for the *bottle* fell with him.—Being infinitely intoxicated—with Gaming—Sea-bathing at two in the morning—and supplementary Champaigne—The skirmish had past before I had time or thought to interfere.—Of course I lectured against quarrelling—

"Pugnare Thracum est"[1]—

and then examined Scrope's wound which proved to be a gash long and broad—but not deep nor dangerous.——Scrope was furious—first he wanted to fight—then to go away in a post-chaise & then to *shoot himself*—which last intention I offered to forward—provided that he did not use my *pistols*—which in case of suicide would become a deo-dand to the king. At length with many oaths & some difficulty he was gotten to bed—in the morning Cool reflection & a Surgeon came—and by dint of loss of blood—& Sticking plaister—the quarrel (which Scrope had begun) was healed as well as the wound—& we were all friends as for years before and after.

[1] Horace, *Odes*, I, 27. Literally the meaning is "To fight is Thracian" or "To fight is what Thracians do". In the Loeb Classics edition of Horace's *Odes*, the translator, C. E. Bennett, gives the sense of the whole passage thus: "To fight with goblets meant for pleasure's service is fit for none but Thracians. Banish such barbarous ways! Protect from bloody brawls our Bacchus, who loves what's seemly."

My first dash into poetry, was as early as 1800.——It was the ebul-
lition of a passion for my first Cousin Margaret Parker (daughter and
grand-daughter of the two Admirals Parker)[1] one of the most beautiful
of Evanescent beings.—I have long forgotten the verses—but it would
be difficult for me to forget her——Her dark eyes!—her long eye-
lashes! her completely Greek cast of face and figure!—I was then about
twelve—She rather older—perhaps a year.——She died about a year
or two afterwards—in consequence of a fall which injured her spine and
induced consumption.—Her Sister Augusta—(by some thought still
more beautiful) died of the same malady—and it was indeed in attending
her that Margaret met with the accident which occasioned her own
death.—My Sister told me that when she went to see her shortly before
her death—upon accidentally mentioning my name—Margaret coloured
through the paleness of mortality to the eyes—to the great astonishment of my Sister—who (residing with her Grand-mother Lady
Holderness—saw at that time but little of me for family reasons) knew
nothing of our attachment—nor could conceive why my name should
affect her at such a time.——I knew nothing of her illness—(being at
Harrow and in the country) till she was gone.——Some years after I
made an attempt at an Elegy.—A very dull one.—I do not recollect
scarcely anything equal to the *transparent* beauty of my cousin—or to
the sweetness of her temper—during the short period of our intimacy—
—she looked as if she had been made out of a rainbow—all beauty and
peace.—My passion had it's effects upon me—I could not sleep—I
could not eat—I could not rest—and although I had reason to know that
she loved me—it was the torture of my life—to think of the time which
must elapse before we could meet again—being usually about *twelve
hours*—of separation!——But I was a fool then—and am not much
wiser now.

My passions were developed very early—so early—that few would
believe me—if I were to state the period—and the facts which accompanied it.—Perhaps this was one of the reasons which caused the
anticipated melancholy of my thoughts—having anticipated life.—My
earlier poems are the thoughts of one at least ten years older than the age
at which they were written,—I don't mean for their solidity—but their
Experience—the two first Cantos of C[hild]e H[arold]e were completed
at twenty two—and they were written as if by a man—older than I
shall probably ever be.—

1 See Nov. 8, 1798, to Mrs. Parker, note 1. (Vol. 1, p. 39.)

81 [omitted by Byron]

82

Upon Parnassus going to the fountain of Delphi (Castri) in 1809—
I saw a flight of twelve Eagles—(Hobhouse says they are Vultures—
at least in conversation) and I seized the Omen.—On the day before, I
composed the lines to Parnassus—(in Childe Harold) and on beholding
the birds—had a hope—that Apollo had accepted my homage.——I
have at least had the name and fame of a Poet—during the poetical
period of life (from twenty to thirty) whether it will last is another
matter—but I *have been*—a votary of the Deity—and the place—and am
grateful for what he has done in my behalf—leaving the future in his
hands as I left the past.—

83

Like Sylla—I have always believed that all things depend upon
Fortune & nothing upon ourselves.—I am not aware of any one thought
or action worthy of being called good to myself or others—which is not
to be attributed to the Good Goddess—*Fortune*!—

84

Two or three years ago, I thought of going to one of the Americas—
English or Spanish.—But the accounts sent from England in consequence
of my enquiries—discouraged me.—After all—I believe most countries
properly balanced are equal to *a Stranger* (by no means to the *native*
though)——I remembered General Ludlow's domal inscription—

"Omne solum forti patria"[1]—

And sate down free in a country of Slavery for many centuries.——But
there is *no* freedom—even for *Masters*—in the midst of slaves——it
makes my blood boil to see the thing.—I sometimes wish that I was the
Owner of Africa—to do at once—what Wilberforce will do in time—
viz—sweep Slavery from her desarts—and look on upon the first dance
of their Freedom. ——As to *political* slavery—so general—it is men's
own fault—if they *will* be slaves let them!——yet it is but "a word and
a blow"[2]—see how England formerly—France—Spain—Portugal—
America—Switzerland—freed themselves!——there is no one instance
of a *long* contest in which *men* did not triumph over Systems.—If
Tyranny misses her *first* spring she is cowardly as the tiger and retires
to be hunted.——

[1] See Alpine Journal, Sept. 18, 1816. (Vol. 5, p. 97.)
[2] *Romeo and Juliet*, Act III, scene 1.

An Italian—(the younger Count Ruota) writing from Ravenna to his friend at Rome in 1820—says of me by way of compliment—"that in society no one would take me for an Englishman—though he believes that I *am* English at bottom—my manners were so different"——this he meant as a grand eulogy—and I accept it as such.——The letter was shown to me this year by the Correspondent Count P[ietro] G[amba] or by his Sister.——

I have been a reviewer.—In "the Monthly Review" I wrote some articles which were inserted.——This was in the latter part of 1811.[1] In 1807—in a Magazine called "Monthly Literary Recreations" I reviewed Wordsworth's trash of that time.[2]—Excepting these—I cannot accuse myself of anonymous Criticism (that I recollect) though I have been *offered* more than one review in ⟨both "Edinburgh" and "Quarterly"⟩ our principal Journals.——

Till I was eighteen years old (odd as it may seem) I had never read a review.—But while at Harrow my general information was so great on modern topics as to induce a suspicion that I could only collect so much information from *reviewers*—because I was never *seen* reading—but always idle and in mischief—or at play.—The truth is that I read eating —read in bed—read when no one else read—and had read all sorts of reading since I was five years old—and yet never *met* with a review which is the only reason that I know of—why I should not have read them.——But it is true—for I remember when Hunter & Curzon in 1804—told me this opinion at Harrow—I made them laugh by my ludicrous astonishment in asking them *"what is* a review?"—to be sure they were then less common——In three years more I was better acquainted with that same—but the first I ever read was in 1806–7.

At School—I was (as I have said) remarked for the extent and readiness of my *general* information—but in all other respects idle—capable of great sudden exertions—(such as thirty or forty Greek Hexameters —of course with such prosody as it pleased God) but of few continuous drudgeries.—My qualities were much more oratorical and martial—

[1] Byron reviewed *Poems*, by William Robert Spencer (Vol. 67, 1812, pp. 54–60); and *Neglected Genius*, by W. H. Ireland (Vol. 70, 1813, pp. 203–205).

[2] Wordsworth's *Poems* (2 vols., 1807) in the *Monthly Literary Recreations* for July, 1807.

than poetical—and Dr. D[rury] my grand patron—(our head-master) had a great notion that I should turn out an Orator—from my fluency—my turbulence—my voice—my copiousness of declamation—and my action.—I remember that my first declamation[1]—astonished him into some unwonted (for he was economical of such) and sudden compliments—before the declaimers at our first rehearsal.—My first Harrow verses (that is English as exercises) a translation of a Chorus from "the Prometheus" of Æschylus—were received by him but coolly———no one—had the least notion that I should subside into poesy.—

89

Peel the Orator and Statesman—("that was—or is—or is to be")[1] was my form-fellow—& we were both at the top of our remove—(A public School phrase) we were on good terms—but his brother was my intimate friend.—There were always great hopes of Peel—amongst us all, Masters & Scholars—and he has not disappointed them.—As a Scholar—he was greatly my Superior,—as a declaimer & actor—I was reckoned at least his equal——as a school-boy *out* of School—I was always *in* scrapes—and *he never*—and *in School*—he always knew his lesson—and I rarely—but *when* I knew it—I knew it nearly as well.——In general information—history—&c. &c.—I think I was *his* superior—as also of most boys of my standing.——

89 [repeated]

The prodigy of our School days—was George Sinclair (Son of Sir John) he made exercises for half the School (*literally*) verses at will—and themes without it.—When in the Shell[1]—he made exercises for his Uncle Dudley Macdonald (a dunce who could only play upon the flute) in the sixth. He was a friend of mine and in the same remove—and used at times to beg me to let him to do [sic] my exercise—a request always most readily accorded,—upon a pinch—or when I wanted to do something else—which was usually once an hour.——On the other hand—he was pacific—and I savage—so I fought for him—or thrashed others for him—or thrashed himself to make him thrash others when it was necessary as a point of honour—and stature—that he should so chastise, —or—we talked politics for he was a great politician—and were very

[1] From here to the end of the paragraph, this portion of the diary is missing from the Murray MS. The leaf was sent to Robert Peel on May 30, 1829. The text here is from the original MS. now in the Manuscript Division of the New York Public Library. Paragraph 89 to "*when* I knew it" is also in that library.

[1] Perhaps an adaptation of *Revelations* I: 4.

[1] See No. 66, note 1.

good friends—I have some of his letters—written to me from School
—still.

90

Clayton was another School Monster of learning and talent—and
hope—but what has become of him—I do not know—he was certainly
a Genius.

91

My School friendships were with *me passions* (for I was always violent) but I do not know that there is one which has endured (to be sure
some have been cut short by death) till now—that with Lord Clare
began one of the earliest and lasted longest—being only interrupted by
distance—that I know of.—I never hear the word *"Clare"* without a
beating of the heart—even *now*, & I write it—with the feelings of
1803–4–5—ad infinitum.—

92

In 1812, at Middleton (Lord Jersey's) amongst a goodly company—
of Lords—Ladies—& wits—&c.—there was poor old Vice Leach the
lawyer[1]—attempting to play off the fine gentleman.—His first exhi-
bition—an attempt on horseback I think to escort the women—God
knows where—in the month of November—ended in a fit of the Lum-
bago—as Lord Ogleby says—"a grievous enemy to Gallantry and
address"[2]—and if he could have but heard Lady Jersey quizzing him
(as I did) the next day for the *cause* of his malady——I don't think
that he would have turned a "Squire of dames" in a hurry again.—He
seemed to me the greatest fool (in that line) I ever saw.——This was
the last I saw of old Vice Leach—except in town where he was creeping
into assemblies —and trying to look young—& gentlemanly.—

93

Erskine too![1]—Erskine—was there—good—but intolerable—he
jested—he talked—he did every thing admirably but then he *would* be
applauded for the same thing twice over—he would read his own verses
—his own paragraph—and tell his own story—again and again—and
then "the trial by Jury!!!"—I almost wished it abolished, for I sate next
him at dinner——As I had read his published speeches—there was no
occasion to repeat them to me.—Chester (the fox hunter) surnamed
"Cheeks Chester"—and I sweated the Claret—being the only two who

---

[1] Leach defended James Johnston, when a movement for an injunction was
brought against him in 1816 for publishing in Byron's name some poems of his
own. See Dec. 9, 1816, to Murray, note 1. (Vol. 5, p. 138.)

[2] Colman and Garrick, *The Clandestine Marriage*, Act II, scene 1.

[1] See Diary, March 6, 1814, note 1. (Vol. 3, p. 247.)

did so.—Cheeks who loves his bottle—and had no notion of meeting with a "bon vivant" in a scribbler—in making my eulogy to somebody one evening summed it up in—"by G—d he *drinks like a Man!*"

94

Nobody drank however but Cheeks and I—to be sure there was little occasion—for we swept off what was on the table (a most splendid board—as may be supposed at Jersey's) very sufficiently.—However we carried our liquor discreetly—like "the Baron of Bradwardine".[1]

95

If I had to live over again—I do not know what I would change in my life—unless it were *for*—*not to have lived at all*[.] All history and experience—and the rest—teaches us that the good and evil are pretty equally balanced in this existence—and that what is most to be desired is an easy passage out of it.——What can it give us but *years*? & those have little of good but their ending.—

96

Of the Immortality of the Soul—it appears to me that there can be little doubt—if we attend for a moment to the action of Mind.—It is in perpetual activity;—I used to doubt of it—but reflection has taught me better.—It acts also so very independent of body—in dreams for instance incoherently and madly—I grant you;—but still it is *Mind* & much more *Mind*—than when we are awake.——Now—that *this* should not act *separately*—as well as jointly—who can pronounce?— The Stoics Epictetus & Marcus Aurelius call the present state "a Soul which drags a Carcase"———a heavy chain to be sure, but all chains being material may be shaken off.—How far our future life will be *individual*—or rather—how far it will at all resemble our *present* existence—is another question—but that the *Mind* is *eternal*—seems as possible as that the body is not so.—Of course—I have venture[d] upon the question without recurring to Revelation—which however is at least as rational a solution of it—as any other.—A *material* resurrection seems strange and even absurd except for purposes of punishment—and all punishment which is to *revenge* rather than *correct*—must be *morally wrong*—and *when* the *World is at an end*—what moral or warning purpose *can* eternal tortures answer?—human passions have probably disfigured the divine doctrines here—but the whole thing is inscrutable. —It is useless to tell one *not* to *reason* but to *believe*——you might as well tell a man not to wake but *sleep*—and then to *bully* with torments!

[1] In Scott's *Waverley.*

—and all that!—I cannot help thinking that the *menace* of Hell makes as many devils as the severe penal codes of inhuman humanity make villains.———Man is born *passionate* of body—but with an innate though secret tendency to the love of Good in his Main-spring of Mind.——— But God help us all!—It is at present a sad jar of atoms.———

97

Matter is eternal—always changing—but reproduced and as far as we can comprehend Eternity—Eternal—and why not Mind?—Why should not the Mind act with and upon the Universe?—as portions of it act upon and with the congregated dust—called Mankind?—See—how one man acts upon himself and others—or upon multitudes?—The same Agency in a higher and purer degree may act upon the Stars &c. ad infinitum.

98

I have often been inclined to Materialism in philosophy—but could never bear it's introduction into *Christianity*—which appears to me essentially founded upon the *Soul*.—For this reason, Priestley's Christian Materialism—always struck me as deadly.—Believe the resurrection of the *body*—if you will—but *not without* a *Soul*—the devil's in it—if after having had a Soul—(as surely the *Mind* or what- ever you call it—*is*)—in this world we must part with it in the next— even for an Immortal Materiality;—I own my partiality for *Spirit*.—

99

I am always most religious upon a sunshiny day—as if there was some association between an internal approach to greater light and purity—and the kindler of this dark lanthorn of our external exist- ence.——

100

The Night is also a religious concern—and even more so—when I viewed the Moon and Stars through Herschell's telescope—and saw that they were worlds.—

101

If according to some speculations—you could prove the World many thousand years older than the Mosaic Chronology—or if you could knock up Adam & Eve and the Apple and Serpent—still what is to be put up in their stead?—or how is the difficulty removed? things must have had a beginning—and what matters it *when*—or *how*?——I some- times think that *Man* may be the relic of some higher material being wrecked in a former world—and degenerated in the hardships and

46

struggle through Chaos into Conformity—or something like it—as we see Laplanders—Esquimaux—&c. inferior in the present state—as the Elements become more inexorable——but even then this higher pre-Adamite Supposititious Creation must have had an Origin and a *Creator* —for a *Creator* is a more natural imagination than a fortuitous concourse of atoms—all things remount to a fountain—though they may flow to an Ocean.—

102

What a strange thing is the propagation of life!—A bubble of Seed which may be spilt in a whore's lap—or in the Orgasm of a voluptuous dream—might (for aught we know) have formed a Caesar or a Buonaparte—there is nothing remarkable recorded of their Sires— that I know of.——

103

Lord Kames has said—(if I misquote not) "that a power to call up agreeable ideas at will would be something greater for mortals than all the boons of a fairy tale."——I have found increasing upon me (without sufficient cause at times) the depression of Spirits (with few intervals) which I have some reason to believe constitutional or inherited.

104

Plutarch says in his life of Lysander—that Aristotle observes "that in general great Geniuses are of a melancholy turn and instances Socrates—Plato and Hercules (or Heracleitus) as examples—and Lysander—though not—*while* young—yet—as inclined to it when approaching towards age."—Whether I am a Genius or not—I have been called such by my friends as well as enemies—and in more countries and languages—than one—and also within a no very long period of existence.—Of my Genius—I can say nothing—but of my melancholy that it is "increasing—& ought to be diminished"[1] but how?—

105

I take it that most men are so at bottom—but that it is only remarked in the remarkable.——The Duchesse de Broglie—in reply to a remark of mine on the errors of clever people said "that they were not *worse* than others—only being more in view—more noted; especially in all that could reduce them to the rest—or raise the rest to them.["] In 1816, this was.—

[1] Perhaps a reference to Lord Ashburton's motion in the Commons in 1780, "That the power of the Crown has increased, is increasing, and ought to be diminished".

In fact (I suppose—that) if the follies of fools were all set down like those of the wise—the wise (who seem at present only a better sort of fools) would appear almost intelligent.——

I have met George Colman occasionally and thought him extremely pleasant and convivial—Sheridan's humour or rather wit—was always saturnine—and sometimes savage—but he never laughed (at least that *I* saw—and I watched him) but Colman did—I have got very drunk with them both—but if I had to *choose*—and could not have both at a time—I should say—"let me begin the evening with Sheridan and finish it with Colman."—Sheridan for dinner—Colman for Supper— Sheridan for Claret or port—but Colman for every thing—from the Madeira & Champaigne—at dinner—the Claret with a *layer* of *port* between the Glasses—up to the Punch of the Night—and down to the Grog—or Gin and water of day-break—all these I have threaded with both the same——Sheridan was a Grenadier Company of Life-Guards —but Colman a whole regiment of *light Infantry* to be sure—but still a regiment.

Alcibiades is said to have been "successful in all his battles"—but *what* battles? name them—if you mention Caesar—or Annibal—or Napoleon—you at once rush upon Pharsalia—Munda—Alesia; — Cannæ—Thrasimene—Trebia; Lodi—Marengo—Jena—Austerlitz— Friedland—Wagram—Mowska[sic]—but it is less easy to pitch upon the victories of Alcibiades—though they may be named too—though not so readily as the Leuctra and Mantinea of Epaminondas—the Marathon of Miltiades—the Salamis of Themistocles—and the Thermopylae of Leonidas.—Yet upon the whole it may be doubted whether there be a name in Antiquity which comes down with such a general charm as that of *Alcibiades*——*Why*?—I cannot answer—who can?

The vanity of Victories is considerable—of all who fell at Waterloo or Trafalgar—ask any man in company to *name you ten off hand*——they will stick at Nelson;—the other will survive himself—*Nelson was* a hero —the other is a mere Corporal—dividing with Prussians and Spaniards —the luck—which he never deserved—he even—but I hate the fool— and will be silent.——

The Miscreant Wellington is the Cub of Fortune—but she will never lick him into shape—if he lives he will be beaten—that's certain.— Victory was never before wasted upon such an unprofitable soil—as this dunghill of Tyranny—whence nothing springs but Viper's eggs.—

111

I remember seeing Blucher in the London Assemblies—and never saw anything of his age less venerable.—With the voice and manners of a recruiting Sergeant—he pretended to the honours of a hero—just as if a stone could be worshipped because a Man had stumbled over it.——

112

There is nothing left for Mankind but a Republic—and I think that there are hopes of Such—the two Americas (South and North) have it —Spain and Portugal approach it—all thirst for it—Oh Washington!—

113

Pisa Novr. 5th. 1821

"There is a strange coincidence sometimes in the little things of this world—Sancho" says Sterne in a letter[1] (if I mistake not) and so I have often found it.——Page 128 article 91 of this collection of scattered things—I had alluded to my friend Lord Clare in terms such as my feelings suggested.—About a week or two afterwards I met him on the road between Imola and Bologna—after not having met for seven or eight years.—He was abroad in 1814—and came home just as I set out in 1816.——This meeting annihilated for a moment all the years between the present time and the days of *Harrow*—It was a new and inexplicable feeling like rising from the grave to me.—Clare too was much agitated—more—in *appearance*—than even myself—for I could feel his heart beat to the fingers' ends—unless indeed—it was the pulse of my own which made me think so.—He told me that I should find a note from him left at Bologna—I did.—We were obliged to part for our different journeys—he for Rome—I for Pisa—but with the promise to meet again in Spring.—We were but five minutes together—and in the public road—but I hardly recollect an hour of my existence which could be weighed against them.———He had heard that I was coming on—& had left his letter for me at B[ologna] because the people with whom he was travelling could not wait longer.——Of all I have ever known—he has always been the least altered in every thing from the excellent qualities and kind affections which attracted me to him so strongly at

[1] Letter to Ignatius Sancho, Sterne's black friend. (*Letters of Laurence Sterne*, ed. Lewis Perry Curtis, 1935, p. 285.)

School.—I should hardly have thought it possible for Society—(or the World as it is called) to leave a being with so little of the leaven of bad passions.——I do not speak from personal experience only—but from all I have ever heard of him from others during absence and distance.—

114

I met with Rogers at Bologna—staid a day there—crossed the Appennines with him.—He remained at Florence——I went to Pisa— 8bre. 29—30th. &c. 1821.

115

I revisited the Florence Gallery &c. my former impressions were confirmed—but there were too many visitors there to allow me to *feel* anything properly. When we were (about thirty or forty) all stuffed into the Cabinet of Gems & knick-nackeries in a corner of one of the Galleries—I told R[ogers] that I "felt like being in the Watch-house." I left him to make his obeisances to some of his acquaintances—& strolled on alone—the only few minutes I could snatch of any feeling for the works around me.—I do not mean to apply this to a tete a tete scrutiny with Rogers—who has an excellent taste & deep feeling for the Arts (indeed much more of both than I possess for of the *former* I have not much) but to the crowd of jostling starers & travelling talkers around me.——I heard one bold Briton declare to the woman on his arm looking at the Venus of Titian—"well now—this is very fine indeed . ." —an observation which like that of the landlord in Joseph Andrews— "on the certainty of death"—was (as the landlord's wife observed) "extremely true"[1]——In the Pitti palace—I did not omit Goldsmith's prescription for a Connoisseur—viz: "that the pictures would have been better if the painter had taken more pains—and to praise the works of Pietro Perugino[".][2]——

116

I have lately been reading Fielding over again.[1]—They talk of Radicalism—Jacobinism &c. in England (I am told) but they should turn over the pages of "Jonathan Wild the Great".—The inequality of conditions and the littleness of the great—were never set forth in stronger terms—and his contempt for Conquerors and the like is such that had he lived *now* he would have been denounced in the "Courier" as the grand Mouth-piece and Factionary of the revolutionists.—And

[1] Fielding, *Joseph Andrews*, Book I, Chapter 2.
[2] *Vicar of Wakefield*, Chapter 20.
[1] Paragraphs 116 and 117 are written over and between the lines of 114 and 115 in the manuscript, which makes it extremely difficult to read all of them.

yet I never recollect to have heard this turn of Fielding's mind noticed though it is obvious in every page.————

117

The following dialogue passed between me and a very pretty peasant Girl (Rosa Benini married to Domenico Ovioli or Oviuoli the Vetturino) at Ravenna.—

Rosa. "*What* is the Pope?"

I. "Don't *you* know?"

Rosa. "No, I don't know, what or who is he—is he a Saint?"

I. "He is an old man."

Rosa. "What nonsense to make such a fuss about an old man.—have *you ever* seen him?"

I. "Yes—at Rome."—

Rosa. "You English don't believe in the Pope?"

I. "No—we don't—but you do—"

Rosa. "I don't know what I believe—but the priests talk about him——I am sure I did not know what he was."

This dialogue I have translated nearly verbatim—& I don't think that I have either added to or taken away from it.——The speaker was under eighteen & an old acquaintance of mine.——It struck me as odd that I should have to instruct her *who* the Pope was—I think they might have found it out without me—by this time.——The fact is indisputable & occurred but a few weeks ago, before I left Ravenna.—

Pisa Novr. 6th. 1821

118

1

Oh! talk not to me of a name great in story
The days of our Youth, [sic] are the days of our Glory,
And the myrtle and ivy of sweet two and twenty
Are worth all your laurels though ever so plenty.

2

What are garlands and crowns to the brow that is wrinkled,
Tis but as a dead flower with May-dew besprinkled,
Then away with all such from the head that is hoary,
What care I for the wreaths that can *only* give Glory?

3

Oh! Fame!—if I eer took delight in thy praises—
'Twas less for the sake of thy high-sounding phrases,
Than to see the bright eyes of the dear One discover
She thought that I was not unworthy to love her.

4

There chiefly I sought thee, *there* only I found thee,
Her Glance was the best of the rays that surround thee,
When it sparkled oer aught that was bright in my story,
I knew it was love, and I felt it was Glory.—

I composed these stanzas (except the fourth added now) a few days ago
—on the road from Florence to Pisa.—

Pisa Novr. 6th. 1821

119

My daughter Ada on her recent birthday the other day (the 10th. of
December 1821) completed her sixth year.—Since she was a Month
old—or rather better—I have not seen her.—But I hear that she is a
fine child with a violent temper.—I have been thinking of an odd circumstance.—My *daughter*—my *wife*—my *half sister*—my *mother*—
my sister's *mother*—my natural daughter—and *myself* are or were all
only children.—My sister's Mother (Lady Conyers) had only my half
sister by that second marriage—(herself too an only child) and my
father had only me (an only child) by his second marriage with my
Mother (an only child too) [.] Such a complication of *only* children all
tending to *one family* is singular enough, & looks like fatality almost.—
But the fiercest Animals have the rarest number in their litters—as
Lions—tigers—and even Elephants which are mild in comparison.

120

May 18th. 1822

I have not taken up this sort of Journal for many months—shall I
continue it? "Chi Cosa"?——I have written little this year—but a good
deal last (1821) *Five* plays in all (two yet unpublished) some Cantos
&c.——I have begun one or two things since—but under some discouragement—or rather indignation at the brutality of the attacks
which I hear (for I have seen few of them) have been multiplied in
every direction against me & my recent writings—but the English
dishonour themselves more than me by such conduct.—It is strange—
but the Germans say—that I am more popular in Germany by far than
in England—and I have heard the Americans say as much of America
—the French too have printed a considerable number of translations in
prose! with good success—but *their* predilection (if it exists) depends
I suspect—upon their belief that I have no great passion for England or
the English.—It would be singular if I had, however I wish them no
harm.—

121   [Here the Ms. ends]

P.S.—I crossed the Appennines with Rogers as far as Florence.
—— On the road from Imola to Bologna I met Lord Clare—whom I
had not seen for seven years—he was one of my earliest & dearest
friends and our meeting was almost pathetic[1]——It sent me back to
Harrow again.——I met Rogers at Bologna—in a florid state—he
is a most agreeable companion in a post-chaise and we slashed away
to right and left—cutting up all our acquaintances,—and indeed—
every body else.——It would have done your heart good to hear
us.—*You* were not spared by any means—but as nobody else was—you
were in very good company—I don't think that I heard & uttered so
much slander for these last seven years.—But *He is* a clever fellow—
that's certain—& said some wonderful things.——

[TO JOHN MURRAY]   *Pisa Novr. 3d. 1821*

Dear Moray/—The two passages cannot be altered without making
Lucifer talk like the Bishop of Lincoln—which would not be in the
character of the former.——The notion is from Cuvier[1] (that of the
old Worlds) as I have explained in an additional note to the preface.—
The other passage is also in Character—if *nonsense*—so much the
better—because then it can do no harm—& the sillier Satan is made
the safer for every body.——As to "alarms" &c. do you really
think such things ever led anybody astray? are these people more
impious than Milton's Satan?—or the Prometheus of Æschylus?—or
even than the Sadducees of your envious parson the "Fall of Jerusalem"
fabricator?[2]—Are not Adam—Eve—Adah—and Abel as pious as
the Catechism?—Gifford is too wise a man to think that such things
can have any *serious* effect—*who* was ever altered by a poem? I beg
leave to observe that there is no creed nor personal hypothesis of
mine in all this—but I was obliged to make Cain and Lucifer talk
consistently—and surely this has always been permitted to poesy.——
Cain is a proud man—if Lucifer promised him kingdoms &c.—it
would *elate* him—the object of the demon is to *depress* him still further
in his own estimation than he was before—by showing him infinite
things—& his own abasement—till he falls into the frame of mind—
that leads to the Catastrophe—from mere *internal* irritation—*not*

---

[1] See "Detached Thoughts", No. 91, and No. 113.
[1] See Sept. 19, 1821, to Moore, note 5. (Vol. 8, p. 216.)
[2] The Rev. H. H. Milman.

premeditation or envy—of *Abel*—(which would have made him contemptible) but from rage and fury against the inadequacy of his state to his Conceptions—& which discharges itself rather against Life—and the author of Life—than the mere living.——His subsequent remorse is the natural effect of looking on his sudden deed—had the *deed* been premeditated—his repentence would have been tardier.—

The three last M.S. lines of Eve's curse are replaced from *memory* on the proofs—but incorrectly (for I keep no copies)—Either keep *these three*—or *replace* them with the *other three*—whichever are thought least bad by Mr. Gifford——There is no occasion for a *revise*—it is only losing time.—Either dedicate it to Walter Scott[3]—or if you think—he would like the dedication to "the Foscaris" better—put the dedication to "the Foscaris"—Ask him which.——Your first note was queer enough—but your two other letters with Moore's & Gifford's opinions set all right again—I told you before that I can never *recast* anything.—I am like the Tiger—if I miss the first spring—I go growling back to my Jungle again—but if I *do hit*—it is crushing. ——Now for Mr. Mawman.——I received him civilly as *your* friend—and he spoke of you in a friendly manner.—As one of the Squadron of Scribblers—I could not but pay due reverence to a commissioned officer.—I gave him that book with the inscription to show to *you*—that you might correct the errors.—With the rest I can have nothing to do—but he served you very *right.*—You have played the Stepmother to D[on] J[uan]—throughout.—Either ashamed—or afraid—or negligent—to your own loss and nobody's credit. ——Who ever heard before of a *publisher's not* putting *his* name?—The reasons for *my anonyme*—I stated—they were family ones entirely.——Some travelling Englishmen whom I met the other day at Bologna told me—that you affect to wish to be considered as *not* having anything to with that work—which by the way—is sad half and half dealing—for you will be a long time before you publish a better poem.——

You seem hurt at the words *"the publisher" what*! *you*—who won't put your name on the title page—would have had me stick J. M. Esqre. on the blank leaf—no—Murray—you are an excellent fellow—a little variable—& somewhat of the opinion of every body you talk with—(particularly the last person you see) but a good fellow for all that—yet nevertheless—I can't tell you that I think you have acted very gallantly by that persecuted book—which has made it's way entirely by *itself*—without the light of your countenance—or any kind

[3] *Cain* was dedicated to Scott. See Scott's letter to Murray of Dec. 4, 1821, accepting the dedication. (*LJ*, VI, 3n.)

of encouragement—critical—or bibliopolar.—You disparaged the last three cantos to me—& kept them back above a year—but I have heard from England—that (notwithstanding the errors of the press) they are well thought of—for instance—by American Irving—which last is a feather in my (fool's) Cap.——You have received my letter (open) through Mr. Kinnaird—& so pray—send me no more reviews of any kind.——I will read no more of evil or good in that line.—— Walter Scott has not read a review of *himself* for *thirteen years.*—The bust is not *my* property—but *Hobhouse's*—I addressed it to you as an Admiralty man great at the custom house—pray—deduct the expences of the same—& all others.—

yrs. ever & [most?]
BYRON

[TO DOUGLAS KINNAIRD]   *Pisa. Novr. 4th. 1821*

My dear Douglas/—Your epistle has pacified my wrath—& explained every thing—All the accounts I hear from every body agree in saying that the new *Dons* are liked—but that M[urray] has neither given them nor their predecessors fair play,—from timidity I presume.—Rogers with whom I crossed the Appennines—says— that *M[urray]* affects *not* to wish to be considered as having any thing to do with that work.—Upon this score I have written him a trimmer.—I rejoice that you accept the dedication[1]—especially as you liked the play.—The most opposite people—Irving—Moore— Hoppner—and yourself for instance—like the Juans & many others— so I suppose that they will do.—The *misprinting* was shameful—such nonsense!—in some of the clearest passages too.———Now you see how people can never pretend to anticipate accurately—Murray and others kept back the Cantos a whole year & more—because they were *dull*—& wanted alterations &c. &c.—I would alter nothing—well— the work appears—with a lukewarm publisher and all these previous impressions against it—& still it succeeds.—I thought it would *not* because it's real qualities are not on the *surface*—but still if people will dive a little—I think it will reward them for their trouble.— Nearly *five hundred* pounds from Sir Jacob!—how is this?—it is more than I thought.—As to *M[ealey?]*—you may pay him *ten pounds*— which is double his merit—he is the greatest rascal that ever emptied a brandy bottle.—Pay *him*! quotha! what do you take me for? that I

---

[1] To *Marino Faliero.* The dedication was not published with the play until 1832.

should pay any body?——And Claughton's money too!—I presume that you have got *sure* account of it from Hanson.——Sir Jacob's money must be reserved for *Self*—except deduction of such monies as you have paid away for me already. I hate to bore you—but what can I do?—I have no other active friend—and you always go to the point—with the scoundrels of all kinds.——I look for a decent sum at Christmas I assure you——but I long to hear that we are out of the funds—I would sacrifice the interest cheerfully—for a year—to be sure of a safe mortgage at the end of it.—I am in cash sufficiently— as you will perceive—but this changing residences—& removing establishments—has taken a sum out of my pocket—as I removed all my furniture &c. &c. We were all obliged to retire on account of our politics——my relations (the Gambas—exiles &c.) are here too lodged about a quarter of a mile from me——the place—and air—&c. are very agreeable hitherto.——I left Sam Rogers at Florence—& met my old friend Lord Clare between Ravenna—& Bologna—he seemed delighted to meet me—& our meeting was almost pathetic.— Rogers and I abused every body in our journey to Florence—as you may suppose.——I am glad that you approved of my epistle to Murray —it was become necessary.——But he does not mention it in his late answers.——They are very civil about *"Cain"*—but alarmed at it's *tendency*—as they call it—for my part—I maintain that it is as orthodox as the thirty nine articles. There is or ought to be—*another* poem now at Murray's.——Remember me to Hobhouse &c. and believe me ever & most truly

[Scrawl]

P.S.—I ought to mention to you that Rogers said—that the bruit was that Murray was *ruined* by buying eight & twenty thousand pounds of copyrights last year—in Northern & Loo Choo voyages travels &c. &c. if true it is some comfort that he made no purchases of *me then* but the single drama.—You will be in the way of knowing this—but if true it would form a clue to his costiveness.—I will acquiesce in whatever bargain you make with him.—

[TO AUGUSTA LEIGH]   *Pisa. Novr. 4th. 1821*]

My dearest Augusta/—You will see by the date that I have arrived here safely.—I am writing in a room inconvenient from the extreme heat of the *Sun*—it is like Summer—so fine is the climate.—If the Girls are delicate in health—as you say—you had better bring them out here for a year or two.—The Climate is you know a *medical* one for [?] people.—I have an immense house and could lodge you *all* without the least inconvenience—it would save you expences & you would see your brother.———I recommend this to your thoughts seriously.—Let me know.—I send you some hair *darker* than the other though from the same head—but it is only in parts that it is *so* grey.———Have you sent any to Ada—as requested?

yrs [Scrawl]

P.S.—I am *alone* in my house—which is immense—you could bring your drone of a husband with you—it would do him good—and probably save the lives of some of the children, if they are delicate.—As to expences—I will *frank* you *all here*—if you like to take the journey—and I have carriages &c. for you—things don't cost here—what they do amongst you in England.——

[TO JOHN MURRAY] *Pisa. Nov. 9th. 1821*

I *never read* the Memoirs at all, not even since they were written; and I never will: the pain of writing was enough; you may spare me that of a perusal. Mr. Moore has (or may have) a discretionary power to omit any repetition, or expressions which do not seem *good* to *him*, who is a better judge than you or I.

[TO LORENZO BARTOLINI] *Pisa 10 9bre. 1821*

[In the handwriting of Teresa Guiccioli—signed by Byron]

Signore—Le vostre gentili espressioni mi onorano—e mi obbligano moltissimo—ed avrei assai piacere di potervi corrispondere—col farvi cosa grata.—Quando verrete in Pisa avrò caro di vedervi—perchè è probabile che io abbia bisogno di un Opera vostra.—Intanto col rinnovarvi le proteste della mia gratitudine—e sincera stima ho il piacere di dirmi———

Di voi Pregiatissimo Sig.re   U[milimissi]mo Ser[vitor]e
                                 BYRON   Pair d'Angleterre

[TRANSLATION] *Pisa 10 9bre. 1821*

Sir—I am honoured by your kind expressions—and very much obliged—and I would have a great deal of pleasure in being able in return to do something pleasing for you.———When you come to Pisa I will want very much to see you—because it is probable that

I may have a need for one of your Works.[1] In the meantime with renewed declarations of my gratitude to you—and my sincere esteem I have the pleasure of declaring myself, most esteemed Signore,

> your most humble Servant
> BYRON   Peer of England[2]

Dear Sir/—I have marked on the back of the enclosed proof of the letter to Mr. Wilson[1]—the names of the writings mostly unpublished which if collected together—would form a volume or two which might be entitled Miscellanies.—You must recollect however that the letter on the British review signed *Clutterbuck*[2] must have a note stating that the name of *Clutterbuck* was adopted long before (a year I think) the publication of the Monastery & Abbot.—If you don't do this—I shall be accused (with the usual justice) of plagiarism from Walter Scott.———The whole of these tracts might be published simply and unostentatiously—with the letter on B[owles]'s Pope at the head of them.———Be careful about their dates—Let me know your intention—

> yr. hum[b]le Sert.
> BN

Opened by *me*—this day Novr. 14th. 1821 and sent to Mr. Kinnaird.—

> B

Dear Sir/—Enclosed is a lyrical drama (entitled a Mystery from it's subject)[1] which perhaps may arrive in time for the volume.—If it should not (for I must have *the proofs first* as it is not very legibly written) you can add it to the volume with the Pulci and Dante.— Perhaps—you might publish it in a separate appendix form of the

---

[1] Early in the following year Byron commissioned the famous Italian sculptor then at Florence to make a bust of him and one of the Countess Guiccioli.

[2] Translated by Ricki B. Herzfeld of the Carl H. Pforzheimer Library.

[1] Byron's reply to an article in *Blackwood's Edinburgh Magazine* of August, 1819, which was not by Wilson ("Christopher North"). The reply did not appear until after Byron's death.

[2] Wortley Clutterbuck was the pseudonym Byron used in his "Letter to the Editor of 'My Grandmother's Review'".

[1] *Heaven and Earth*, which was published in the second number of *The Liberal*, Jan. 1, 1823.

same type &c. for the purchasers of "Cain" so that they might bind it up with the new volume and then put it together with the others in a second edition—supposing a second edition possible.———You will find *it pious* enough I trust—at least some of the Chorus might have been written by Sternhold and Hopkins[2] themselves for that—and perhaps for melody.—As it is longer and more lyrical & Greek than I intended at first—I have not divided it into *acts* but called what I have sent—*Part first*[3]—as there is a suspension of the action which may either close there without impropriety—or be continued in a way that I have in view.—I wish the first part to be published before the second—because if it don't succeed—it is better to stop there—than to go on in a fruitless experiment.———I desire you to acknowledge the arrival of the packet by return of post—if you can conveniently—with a proof.——

yr. obedt. Sert.

B

P.S.—My wish is to have it published at the same time—and if possible—in the same volume with the others; because whatever the merits or demerits of these pieces may be—it will perhaps be allowed that each is of a different kind and in a different style—so that including the prose and the D[on] J[uan]'s &c.—I have at least sent you *variety* during the last year or two.—The present packet consists of 12 sheets—which will make more than *fifty* printed pages additional to the Volume. I suppose that there is not enough in the four plays (or poems) to make *two* volumes—but they will form *one* large one. Two words to say that you have received the packet will be enough.

[TO JOHN MURRAY]   [*November 15–16? 1821*]

Sir/—The enclosed which I only received by this day's post you addressed by mistake to Ravenna. I presume that the *three plays* are to be published together—because if not—I will not permit their *separate* publication.—I repeat this because a passage in your letter makes it doubtful.———I sent you a fourth by last post (a lyrical drama on a scriptural subject—"the Deluge") which I could wish to be published at the same time and (if possible & in time) in the same volume.—I return you the notes—(not of "the Doge" as you say by mistake) but of the new poems.———Most of the packets have I believe arrived in safety.———I wrote to Mr. K[innair]d to accept

---

[2] See Vol. 4, p. 173, note 2.
[3] The second part was never written.

your proposal for the *three* plays & three cantos of D[on] J[uan] distinctly giving to understand that the *other poems* did *not* enter into that agreement.——

I am yr. obedt. &c.

[Scrawl]

P.S.—What is the reason that I see "Cain"—& the "Foscaris" announced and not "Sardanapalus"?

[TO DOUGLAS KINNAIRD (*a*)]   *Pisa. Novr. 15th. 1821*

My dear Douglas/—Murray has *not* made any proposal to me for the additional play of "Cain"—neither will *I* treat with him—that is to say unless you decline acting for me—I think it is fairer for all parties—that you who are on the spot and can judge at once should pronounce upon all matters of business—and it is even more delicate. ——I repeat to you that I shall never *cavil* at nor annul your *decision*—though I may state to you such & such reasons &c. for such & such an &c.—*before hand*.——Murray has received from me two or three tolerably *sharp* letters lately—upon the whole of his late conduct and language—which I am not disposed to tolerate much further.—The former is ambiguous & the latter pert.—What you say of his talk to Matthews[1] is of a piece with the rest.—To me he talks of the *power*—of "Cain" and that Gifford & Moore &c.—all place it among the best &c. as a composition—but he *cants* about it's tendency also.—There never was *such cant*—Abel & Adah &c. are as pious as possible—but would they have me make Lucifer and Cain talk like two prebendaries—looking out for a step higher in the Church?——Milton's Satan is twice as daring and impious—as mine—and what do they say to such lines as these in the "Samson Agonistes?"

"In fine

Just and unjust alike seem miserable
Since both alike oft come to evil end.[2] ["]

Pray *quote* this to him & his *Canters*—& hear what they can say for themselves. I do *not* know why he is shy of *you*—but so it seems—the truth I take to be that he thinks—distance from England must make me take what he says for granted—and that wont pass with you. Besides all the people about him except Gifford—(who I do believe

---

[1] Probably Henry Matthews, brother of Charles Skinner Matthews, Byron's Cambridge friend who was drowned in 1811.

[2] *Samson Agonistes*, lines 703–704.

likes me in his heart) hate me—and well they may—for they can only rise by crushing their opponents—at least this is their opinion.—I am very much obliged to Matthews—for the view he has taken of the question—and am persuaded—that if the thing had fair play—people would never suppose that there was any such tendency—which is quite of the Albemarle Street making.——I came here not very long ago—the situation on the Arno is very fine—and the air &c.—delightful hitherto.——There are some English—but I never see them in public nor in private—except two or three old acquaintances—& one or two not quite of so antient a date.——I ride out &c. as usual—and though Ravenna is quieter—other things are perhaps about equal here—as I have most of my Italian relations near me.—

yrs. ever & truly
[Scrawl]

[TO DOUGLAS KINNAIRD (*b*)]   *Novr. 15th. 1821*

Dear Douglas/—Upon second thoughts I send the revise of a thing meant to be published *anonymously*—and also—of a *prose* pamphlet—which I am not sure of publishing,—that you may give me your opinion.———Recollect—*I do not* apply to my friends—my address to Murray—all I wish is *not* to be bored with *Shop* & *parlour gossip*—nor to read reviews *good*—or bad—flattering—or abusive— nor to hear of them again—unless something requires *actual notice*— and then *you* can tell me.——What do you think of *Quevedo*?[1] and of another publisher—for assuredly Murray will be displaced if he publishes it?——

[Scrawl]

[TO DOUGLAS KINNAIRD]   *Pisa. Novr. 16th. 1821*

My dear Douglas/—Yestreen (as a canny Scotchman you can translate that) I sent you by the post a large packet containing two proofs—and a preface—&c. with a letter.—Today yrs. of the 2d. has arrived.—You like "Cain" then—so do Moore, Matthews and even Mr. Gifford—but you say it is "a puzzler"—do you mean a puzzler to *understand*—or to answer?—I can stand your opinion so fire away.— It is only when I dislike people—that I would rather not hear their

---

[1] Quevedo Redivivus was the pseudonym under which Byron published his *Vision of Judgment*. See Vol. 8, p. 229, note 1.

damned nonsense.———Murray's only reply to my declination of his offer—was that he wished I would leave all these bargains to *"his honour"*—those were his very words.——I responded that I would trust no man's honour in affairs of barter, because a bargain was naturally & essentially an *hostile* transaction—in which "Honour" had no more skill—than She "hath in Surgery", as all mankind—even the most honest—naturally try to make the best they can.—I concluded by saying in short—that I would get as much—and he give as little as he could help.———You say—name a sum—I can't do that because I may say too much—or too little—but I will take what *you* fix upon.— Recollect that "Cain" and "the Vision"—are added since our latter negociations.—"Cain" should be published in the same volume with the two other dramata.——For "the Vision" which is a different sort of thing—you may try another publisher.—With regard to Southey please to recollect that in his preface to his "Vision"—he actually called upon the legislature to fall upon Moore [,] me—& others—now such a cowardly cry deserves a dressing.—He is also the vainest & most intolerant of men—and a rogue besides.—Ergo— he only meets with his deserts.—And he is not such a low prey—as you suppose—being powerfully supported by Government and the Quarterly &c.——As to "serious and ludicrous"—read "Fielding's journey from this world to the next"—or the Spanish Quevedo's Visions—and judge whether I have at all infringed upon the permitted facetiousness upon such topics as means of Satire.—Recollect that I carefully avoid *all profane* allusion to *the Deity*—and as for Saints— Angels—and demons—they have been a sprightly people since the Wife of Bath['s] times—and Lucian's even till now.—The receiving the interest only once a year—does not seem to me any reason against the investment—as it is broad as it is long.———I should like to have the affair settled now—so invest at your pleasure.—By the way—are we as likely to lose a part of the principal by exchequering as funding?— But if we are it don't matter—I would rather be out of those funds in every case.——Do not *wait* for further advice from me—but *act*——I will *never turn* upon you—& say *why* & *wherefore?*—My confidence in your skill is as great as in your integrity—and though I hope that *I* am an honest man too—I am a mere child in business—& can neither count nor *ac*count.——I wish too you would come to an agreement with Murray—because though I have a very decent sum of monies in hand—yet I love Monies—& like to have more always.———I have no dislike to anything so much as to paying anybody.——By Xmas—I presume that I shall perhaps survey in circulars—the balance of Sir

Jacob's recent payment—half year's fee (if not sold out before hand—but p[ray] don't delay selling out on that account—[it] is so much more important to conserve the *principal* in its integrity) and Mr. Murray's disbursement—which ought to be fair—as he hath had a quantum of the article.——I am collecting gradually a lot of *modern* Gold coins—Napoleons &c. (with the *real* Emperor on them) which are scarce—now what will they fetch in England if sent there by and by?—

yrs. ever & truly
[Scrawl]

P.S.—As to my question of *"right"* I have written to Murray repeatedly—referring him entirely to *you* on all matters of business—as my *trustee*—and declining discussion with *him* through any other Channel upon subjects of disbursement.—The bill I allude to will be for books & tooth powder &c. since the publication of "Beppo"—which settled the former account.——Has Hobhouse got the bust yet—Murray has lately asked me for it—for *himself*!! tell Hobhouse to claim his property—for it is his own.—It is valuable as being a work of Thorwaldsen's.——

[TO THOMAS MOORE]   *Pisa. November 16th. 1821*

There is here Mr. * * [Taaffe][1], an Irish genius, with whom we are acquainted. He hath written a really *excellent* Commentary on Dante, full of new and true information, and much ingenuity. But his verse is such as it hath pleased God to endue him withal. Nevertheless, he is so firmly persuaded of its equal excellence, that he won't divorce the Commentary from the traduction, as I ventured delicately to hint,—not having the fear of Ireland before my eyes, and upon the presumption of having shotten very well in his presence (with common pistols too, not with my Manton's) the day before.

But he is eager to publish all, and must be gratified, though the Reviewers will make him suffer more tortures than there are in his original. Indeed, the *Notes* are well worth publication; but he insists upon the translation for company, so that they will come out together, like Lady C**t chaperoning Miss * *. I read a letter of yours to him yesterday, and he begs me to write to you about his Poeshie. He is really a good fellow, apparently, and I dare say that his verse is very good Irish.

[1] See Appendix IV for a biographical sketch of Taaffe.

Now what shall we do for him? He says he will risk part of the expense with the publisher. He will never rest till he is published and abused—for he has a high opinion of himself—and I see nothing left but to gratify him, so as to have him abused as little as possible; for I think it would kill him. You must write, then, to Jeffrey to beg him *not* to review him, and I will do the same to Gifford, through Murray. Perhaps they might notice the Comment without touching the text. But I doubt the dogs—the text is too tempting.

* * * * * * * * * * * * * * *

I have to thank you again, as I believe I did before, for your opinion of "Cain", &c.

You are right to allow [Lord Lansdowne] to settle the claim; but I do not see why you should repay him out of your *legacy*[2]—at least, not yet. If you *feel* about it (as you are ticklish on such points), pay him the interest now, and the principal when you are strong in cash; or pay him by instalments; or pay him as I do my creditors—that is, *not* till they make me.

I address this to you at Paris, as you desire. Reply soon, and believe me ever &c.

P.S.—What I wrote to you about low spirits is, however, very true. At present, owing to the climate, &c. (I can walk down into my garden, and pluck my own oranges,—and, by the way, have got a diarrhoea in consequence of indulging in this meridian luxury of proprietorship,) my spirits are much better. You seem to think that I could not have written the "Vision," &c., under the influence of low spirits; but I think there you err. A man's poetry is a distinct faculty, or soul, and has no more to do with the every-day individual than the Inspiration with the Pythoness when removed from her tripod.

[TO LADY BYRON][1]   *Pisa. Novr. 17th. 1821*

I have to acknowledge the receipt of "Ada's hair" which is very soft and pretty—and nearly as dark already as mine was at twelve years old—if I may judge from what I recollect of some in Augusta's possession—taken at that age.—But it don't curl—perhaps from it's being let grow.—I also thank you for the inscription of the date and

[2] See Oct. 28, 1821, to Moore, note 8. (Vol. 8, p. 251.)
[1] This letter, like a number of others which Byron wrote to Lady Byron to relieve his feelings, was never sent, but he later sent it to Lady Blessington and it was first published by Moore.

name—and I will tell you why—I believe that they are the only two or three words of yr. handwriting in my possession—for yr. letters I restored—and except the two words or rather one word "*Household*"— written twice in an old accompt book—I have no other—as I burnt yr. last note—for two reasons 1stly. it was written in a style not very agreeable—and 2dly. I wished to take your word without documents—which are the worldly resource of suspicious people.—I suppose that this note will reach you somewhere about Ada's birthday (the 10th Dec.) (I believe)—she will then be six—so that in about twelve more I shall have some chance of meeting her—perhaps sooner—if I am obliged to go to England by business or otherwise.—— Recollect however one thing—either in distance or nearness;—every day which keeps us asunder—should after so long a period of division— rather soften our mutual feelings which must always have one rallying point as long as the child exists—which I presume we both hope will be long after either of her parents.—The time which has elapsed since the separation has been considerably more than the whole brief period of our union—& the not much longer one of our prior acquaintance.——We both made a bitter mistake, but now it is over— & irrevocably so;—at thirty three on my part—and a few years less on yours—though it is no very extended period of life—still it is one when the habits and thoughts are generally so formed as to admit of no modification—and as we could not agree when younger—we should with difficulty do so now.—I say all this—because I own to you that notwithstanding every thing I considered our re-union as not impossible—for more than a year after the separation—but then I gave up the hope entirely—and for ever.—But this very impossibility of re-union—seems to me at least a reason why on all the few points of discussion which can arise between us—we should preserve the courtesies of life—and as much of it's kindness—as people who are never to meet may preserve perhaps more easily than nearer connections.——For my own part—I am violent but not malignant—for only *fresh* provocations can awaken my resentments.——To you who are colder and more concentrated—I would just hint—that you may sometimes mistake the depth of a cold anger—for dignity, and a worse feeling for duty.——I assure you that I bear you *now* (whatever I may have done) no resentment whatever. Remember, that if *you have injured me* in aught—this forgiveness is something—and that if *I have injured you*—it is something more still—if it be true as the Moralists say—that the most offending are the least forgiving.—— Whether the offence has been solely on my side—or reciprocal,—

or on yours chiefly—I have ceased to reflect upon any but two things;—
viz. that you are the Mother of my child—and that we shall never
meet again.———I think that if you also consider the two corresponding
points with reference to myself—it will be better for all three.

yrs. ever

B

[TO LORD KINNAIRD]   *Pisa. Novr. 20th. 1821*

My dear Kinnaird/—I ought to have answered yr. letter long ago—
but I am but just subsiding into my new residence—after all the bore
and bustle of changing.—The traveller can "take his ease at his
Inn"—but those who are settled in a place and must move with bag
and baggage—are (as I suppose you know by experience) more
costive necessarily in their arrangements.—I have got a very good
spacious house upon the Arno—and have nothing to complain of
except that it is less quiet than my house in Ravenna.—And so you
are at Rome—I am glad you have got rid of the Gout, the tumour if
not of podagrous origin—will subside of itself.——At Bologna I
met with *Rogers*—and we crossed the Apennines together—probably
you have got him at Rome by this time.—I took him to visit an old
friend—the Sexton at the Certosa—(where you and I went with
Bianchetti) who looked at him very *hard*—and seemed well disposed
to keep him back in his Skull room.—The said Sexton by the way
brought out his two daughters to renew their acquaintance—one of
them is very pretty—and the other sufficiently so—and he talked
pathetically of the venality of the age—in which young virgins could
not be espoused without a *dower*—so if you are disposed to portion
them in your way to Milan (if you return) you have an opportunity
of exercising your carnal benevolence.——I was obliged to set out
next day with Rogers—remained with him a day at Florence—and
then came on alone to Pisa—where I found all my Romagnole friends
in good plight and spirits.——Rogers looks a little black still about
being called "venerable" but he did not mention it.—It was at his
own request that I met him in the City of Sausages;—he is not a bad
traveller—but bilious.——

As to "Don Juan" it is not impossible that he might have visited
the City which you recommend to his inspection—but "these coster-
monger days" are unfavourable to all liberal extensions of Morality.
——As to his Author—he can hardly come on to Rome again for
the present—but some day or other probably may.—You ask after

Bowles—but he has been so extremely civil—that I could not without app[earing] overbearing and insolent continue the controversy—for I could not answer without saying something sharp or other—and therefore it is better to be silent.———Let me hear from you whenever you think it not a bore to do so and believe me

ever & truly
BYRON

P.S.—You are a pretty fellow to talk of "introductions"—did you not refuse to present me to our "Aunt"?—and I never saw the niece either but once.——If Ld. Clare and Ld. Sligo are at Rome still and of your acquaintance—will you tell them both with my best remembrances—that I will answer their letters soon.——I find my old friends have got a notion (founded I suppose upon an angry note of mine to a poem) that I receive nobody—& renew no old acquaintance. —They are very much mistaken. I only desire no *new* ones.——The silly note (which by the way I desired Murray to suppress before publication—and he printed it notwithstanding) was caused by a really impudent assertion of an anonymous traveller who said that he (or She) "had repeatedly declined an introduction to me"—now I never in my life *proposed*—and rarely would accept an *English* introduction since I came abroad.

[TO JOHN CAM HOBHOUSE]   *Pisa. Novr. 23d. 1821*

My dear Hobhouse/—Murray must have been crazy or tipsy to imagine that the Bust could be for *him*! I distinctly explained (at least I thought so) that it was only addressed to *him* as an *Admiralty* Officer—to get it through the custom house—but at my expence.—I am sure you must see at once that I was not to blame in it.—How could you suppose for a moment the *possibility* of such a transfer?—I thought indeed to save you trouble.—But you have got it and there's an end.——I dare say your opinion about "Cain" is the right one—but as there are opposite opinions upon it—and of sensible men too (for instance our friend's Brother Henry Matthews the "Invalid traveller" and Moore &c.) why—as Fielding said "Damn them let them find that out!"[1]—They (i.e. the public) *will* find it out I dare

---

[1] This episode is no doubt garnered from an essay on Fielding by Arthur Murphy that prefaced an edition of Fielding's *Works*. Murphy wrote: "It was in vain to tell him, that a particular scene was dangerous, on account of its coarseness, or because it retarded the general business with feeble efforts of wit; he doubted the discernment of his auditors, and so thought himself secured by their stupidity."

say fast enough—but I can't burn it—on the contrary it must take it's chance, with the other two, plays or whatever they may be called. ——I have no violent paternal feelings upon the subject—and as a proof of it—I write you this not an hour after getting your letter.—— I know only *one* motive for publishing *any thing* with a sensible man— and I think Johnson has already quoted that.—As to Johnson and Pope—surely *your* admiration cannot surpass *mine* of them—and had they lived now—I would not have published a line of any thing I have ever written.——I thought I had expressed my opinion on such matters already in my letter upon Pope.——But the volume with Murray must take it's chance—because rhymes bring more than *"a sheet of speech"* as the author says in "Andria"[2]—though I recollect now that he says the *reverse*—"the sheet of speech" *then* bringing more than "the rhymes".——

With regard to "the Memoirs" I can only say—that *Moore* acted entirely with *my approbation* in the whole transaction—and that I desire no profit whatever from it.—Do you really mean to say that I have not as good a right to leave such an M.S. after my death—as the thousands before me who have done the same?——Is there no *reason* that I should?—Will not my life (it is egotism but you know this is true of all men who have *had* a name even if they survive it) be given in a false and unfair point of view by others?—I mean *false* as to *praise* as well as *censure*?—If you have any *personal* feelings upon it—I can say as far as I recollect that you are mentioned without anything that could annoy you—and if otherwise it shall be cut out.—— This is all I can do about them—or indeed am disposed to do—whatever blame there is attaches to *me* and not to *Moore*—who merely acted from my suggestion to him—to whom the papers were left as a kind of legacy.—Excuse the haste of this scrawl—and believe me ever & very truly yrs.

[Scrawl]

P.S.—Pray write freely—I think we have both done so for many *years*—and I shall do so by *you* on the first opportunity—I mean of your works.——If you think a little you must allow that there is nothing discreditable to *Moore* in selling "the Memoirs" for he did it at *my* suggestion—and to me there *can* be none—for I neither have nor would accept a sixpence from the purchase.—They are sold

---

When his comedy *The Wedding Day* was in rehearsal, one of the actors begged him to omit a scene which he thought the audience might find offensive. Fielding replied: "No, d—mn 'em, if the scene is not a good one, let them find *that* out."
    [2] Unidentified.

with the express stipulation of not being published during the writer's lifetime.—I gave them to him *three years* ago[3]—and I desired him to sell them *now*—to help him out of his "Bermuda" scrape——now it appears to me that there is nothing but what is honourable in the fact and in *the motive*.—I shall conclude—as you are fond of "Johnson" with a quotation from his life of Edmond Smith.—"Pray, Rag, when were you drunk last?"[4]——

[TO JOHN CAM HOBHOUSE]   *Novr. 24th. 1821*

D[ea]r H.—On recollection I am as sure as Memory can be— that the address I forwarded to Thorwaldsen was to J[ohn] H[obhouse] Esqre. M.P.—to the care of J[ohn] M[urray] &c. &c.——now if Murray did not understand this I do not see how I am to blame.—It appeared to me as simple as the address of a letter—particularly—when *I* was to pay the postage.——If you are anxious to know my opinion of the *style* of yr. letter I refer you [to] Douglas Kinnaird—to whom I have written by this post upon the subject.[1]—You remind me of the new peer quoted by Tom Shuffleton—who "if a single knob is knocked out of his new coronet will make *me* a *much sharper speech* than ever he will produce in *parliament*".[2]—But as I once heard Fletcher observe—"being too often *Chairman spoils* a man's manners."

[Scrawl]

[TO JOHN MURRAY]   *Pisa. Novr. 24th. 1821*

Dear Sir/—By a not very temperate letter from Mr. Hobhouse— in a style which savours somewhat of the London tavern—I perceive that there has been some mistake or misunderstanding about the block of a bust.—This as I do not understand—I cannot explain.—I addressed it to your *care* for Mr. Hobhouse—and indeed with *his* name on the direction—always understood—that *expences* were to be at *my charge*—and that the trouble would not be greater than you have often been willing to take.—I thought that as publisher to the Admiralty &c. you would be able more easily to get it through the Customs house.—Something however has happened it seems to

[3] A lapse of memory. Byron gave the Memoirs to Moore in October, 1819.
[4] Johnson's life of Edmund Smith: "When, Rag, were you drunk last?" "Captain Rag" was the name Smith was given at Oxford because of his negligence of dress.
[1] This letter is not extant.
[2] George Colman the Younger, *John Bull*, Act II, scene 1.

excite Mr. H[obhouse]'s indignation—and I could really wish to be spared such altercations as (were he not one of my oldest friends) must have ended in a total rupture.—For this you must be partly to blame—as surely my directions were extremely clear.———Of his language to *me* I can only say that I can hardly believe him to have been sober when he used it.———Not content with an invective about the marble—he has launched (uncalled for, for I did not solicit his opinion that I recollect at least) into a most violent invective upon the subject of "Cain"—(*not* on *a religious* account at all as he says) and in such terms as make the grossest review in the lowest publication that ever I read upon any scribbler—moderate in comparison.———He then proceeds (still unasked) upon the subject of the M.S.S. sold by Mr. Moore—and I do not know which of the two he bespatters most.— Having thus "bespattered the poetical eminence of the day" as Gifford says to quiz Timothy Adney in the Baviad[1] & Ma[e]viad I should be glad to know whether there *is* anything reproachable in the *means* or the *motive* of that transaction?—*I* can derive no profit from it—and Moore in doing so was merely anticipating a legacy—at *my express desire* often *repeated to him*.—Whatever blame then there may be is *mine*—and ought to be.———Does Mr. Hobhouse dispute my right to leave Memoirs of myself for posthumous publication?—Have not thousands done it?—Are there not—or—*have* there not been circumstances which require it in *my case*—or would he have me leave the tale for him to tell?———But the best is—that I happen to know *he himself* keeps—and has kept for many years a regular diary and disquisition upon all his personal as well as public transactions—and has *he* done this with no view to posthumous publication? I will not believe it.—I shall not quote his expressions—because really some of them, could only be noticed in one way—& that way neither present distance—nor past intimacy—were I *nearer*—would induce me to take—without some overt action accompanied the harshness of his language.—I have even written him as temperate an answer as I believe ever human being did in the like circumstances.—

Is there any thing in the M.S.S. that could be personally obnoxious to *himself*?—I am sure I do not remember—nor intended it.———Mr. Kinnaird & others had read them at Paris and noticed none such.———If there were any—I can only say—that even *that* would not sanction the tone of his letter, which I showed to one or two English & Irish friends of mine here—who were perfectly astonished at the whole of it.—I do not allude to the *opinions*—(which may or may not be

---

[1] *Baviad*, line 187.

founded) but to the language—which seems studiously insulting.——
You see—Murray—what a scene you have superinduced—because
the *original sin* seems to have been about this foolish bust,—or I am
convinced that he would have expressed his opinions less in the Election
style.——However I am more hurt than angry—for I cannot afford
to lose an old friend for a fit of ill humour.—

yrs. ever

P.S.—Have you publicated the three plays in *one* volume—*that*
will be the best way?—And I wish to know what you think about
doing with the *Miscellanies* as I have formed no *positive* determination
about *them*—the *prose* ones I mean.—The "poeshie"—you must
publish, as *heretofore* decided—but whether with or without the *prose*
I leave to your pleasure.—As Liston says that "is all *hoptional* you
know".[2] Have you given the "Irish Avatar" to Mr. Moore?—as I
requested you to do?—You are a pretty fellow upon the whole for
making a confusion.——

[Scrawl]

[TO DOUGLAS KINNAIRD]   *Pisa. Novr. 28th. 1821*

My dear Douglas/—Murray's offer in his letter to *me* is for the
three cantos of Don Juan—and the *three* plays (or whatever you call
them) Sardanapalus—Foscari—and Cain.—As you think it right that
I should accept it (he says two thousand five hundred *guineas*—
recollect *not* pounds is the *word*) I accept it accordingly for the *above
named* works—but distinctly understood that it is *not* for "the Vision
of Judgement" nor *any other* M.S. of mine now in his or other hands.—I
sent you "the Vision of Judgement" to ask you to publish it anonymously (i.e. with the [words?] Quevedo redivivus on the title page)
with *another* publisher.——Murray's plea is that the *Juans* are
pirated—but this is none with me—as it is his *own* fault——what
business had *he* to affect not to put his name on the title page?—I
enclose you his letter to prevent mistakes—for it is best to "deal by
the card"[1] in all matters of business.—I sent him *three* copies of Juan
per post to *correct him* for not *correcting* them.——But of these *I* will
pay the postage of *two*—which deduct.—I leave him to pay the other—

---

[2] John Liston, the actor, "in one of his farces, used to make a strong point, when
asked to 'remember the coachman,' by dividing sixpence between guard and
coachman, and explaining that the gift was 'hoptional.' " (*LJ*, V, 485n.)

[1] "Speak by the card." *Hamlet*, Act V, scene 1.

as a warning to be more precise in printing another time. I shall by no means be guided by *him* about *not* publishing except the three plays this winter—on the contrary I desire that the "Pulci" in particular be published—and "the Vision" if not by him—by some other— but *separately.*———Last week I wrote to you on occasion of a letter from Hobhouse—one of the grossest ever written in style and manner. ———Had it been by any but an old friend—I really think I must have at the least made such an answer as would have produced a scene.—As it was I answered temperately.—I quoted to you *parts* of *his*—from which you may judge of the whole.—I write this merely to acknowledge yrs.

> ever & truly
> [Scrawl]

P.S.—What Sir Henry Halford[2] or you may say of Lady Noel is all very fine—but She is immortal—that you may depend upon—an ill-tempered woman turned of Seventy—never dies—though they may be buried sometimes.—Besides my luck does not run in that family.———Recollect—that I accept M[urray]'s offer *only* for the three Cantos of D. J. and for the *three plays.*—

[TO DOUGLAS KINNAIRD]   *Pisa. Novr. 29th. 1821*

My dear Douglas/—We ought to have had *three thousand* G[uinea]s for the three plays and Cantos only. Murray's present offer was nearly the same as for the 4th. Canto of C[hild]e H[arol]d which is inferior in quantity—and I am bold to say—in quality. But I will do as you please—as I said already.—I have not written to Mr. Murray preferring that he should negociate with you.———"The Vision" you can publish anonymously with some other publisher.— [Will] you forward the enclosed deed [words torn out with seal] which I have signed as [more words missing]—I trouble you with it [to?] spare him postage—on which I have sweated him lately.———I shall not draw back—nor grumble at any bargain you may settle with him—Yours in haste I shall write you again shortly

> [Scrawl]

[2] Sir Henry Halford, 1st Baronet (1766–1844), who was then president of the College of Physicians. At various times he attended George IV, William IV, and Queen Victoria.

[TO DOUGLAS KINNAIRD?]   [*December. 1821?*]

[Undated fragment]

There is a bond of Mr. W. Webster's, dated 1813, with a judgment, principal 1000,[1] interest 500, total 1500; will you get it sold, that is, desire Hanson to do so; I will take any discount, but it must be in monies, and not on Mr. Hanson's account. Messrs. Dawson, Capron, and Rowley of Saville Row, attornies, are not unlikely to treat for it, as they are already in W[ebste]r's affairs.

I really cannot afford to lose the whole, and prefer this method to awaking him, which otherwise I must have done.

[TO DOUGLAS KINNAIRD]   *Pisa. Decr. 4th. 1821*

Dear Douglas/—As fee-time is approaching I should like to know what I am to calculate upon—besides M[urray]'s monies?—I ask this—because if you have *sold out*—the *half years* fee is of course sacrificed to the object of getting out of the funds.—You mentioned a slight balance of Sir Jacob's.——If you have not sold out (nor sell) till January—of course I shall expect the fee from the funds as usual—together with all such cash as has been levied upon Albemarle Street.——As to debts—the interest of them may be kept down—but as for principal—I can't disgorge for the present.——For this there are several reasons—1stly. I have not received from M[urray] what I reckoned upon—2dly. Claughton's money in whatever way disposed of—must have either tended to lighten Hanson's bill or some one else's.——As to what Sir Henry Halford said to your friend of Lady Noel's health—it is little to be depended upon—old ailing women are eternal;—he gave her over before—and she got well—and so she may now.—I believe I long ago mentioned to you my *Umpire* (or Arbiter) in case of her demise before me.—It was either Sir Francis Burdett—Earl Grey—(I forget the third)[1] whoever of the three would accept the office.——You will find it all in the letter of business I sent to you by *Hanson* from Venice in *1818*.——As I wrote to you lately and frequently I wont trouble you further now than to say that I am

                                                        ever [scrawl]

---

[1] See Oct. 10, 1813, to Hanson (*b*). (Vol. 3, pp. 138–139.)
[1] Lord Grenville. (See Vol. 6, p. 79.)

Dear Sir/—By extracts in the English papers in your holy Ally—Galignani's messenger—I perceive that the "two greatest examples of human vanity—in the present age"—are firstly "the Ex-Emperor Napoleon"—and secondly—"his Lordship the noble poet &c."—meaning your humble Servant—"poor guiltless I".[1]——Poor Napoleon!—he little dreamed to what "vile comparisons" the turn of the Wheel would reduce him.—I cannot help thinking however that had our learned brother of the Newspaper Office—seen my very moderate answer to the very scurrile epistle of my radical patron John Hobhouse M.P.—he would have thought the thermometer of my "Vanity" reduced to a very decent temperature.—By the way, you do not happen to know whether Mrs Fry[2] had commenced her reform of the prisoners at the time when Mr. Hobhouse was in Newgate?——there are some of his phrases—and much of his style (in that same letter) which lead me to suspect that either she had not—or that he had profited less than the others by her instructions.—Last week—I sent back the deed of Mr. Moore signed—and witnessed.—It was inclosed to Mr. Kinnaird with a request to forward it to you.—I have also transmitted to him my opinions upon your proposition &c. &c. —but addressed them to himself.——

I have got here into a famous old feudal palazzo on the Arno[3]—large enough for a garrison—with dungeons below—and cells in the walls—and so full of *Ghosts* that the learned Fletcher (my Valet) has begged leave to change his room—and then refused to occupy his *new* room—because there were more Ghosts there than in the other.—It is quite true;—that there are most extraordinary noises (as in all old buildings) which have terrified the servants so—as to incommode me extremely. ——There is one place where people were evidently *walled up*—for there is but one possible passage—*broken* through the wall—& then meant to be closed again upon the inmate.—The house belonged to the Lanfranchi family—(the same mentioned by Ugolino in his dream as his persecutor with Sismondi) and [has] had a fierce owner or two in it's t[ime]. The Staircase &c. is said to have been b[uilt] by Michel Agnolo.———It is not yet cold enough for a fire—what a

---

[1] Pope, "Epistle to Dr. Arbuthnot," line 281.

[2] Mrs. Elizabeth Fry, a Quaker minister, interested herself in prison reform and formed an association for the improvement of female prisoners in Newgate. Byron referred particularly to her attempts to induce the prisoners not to use vile language.

[3] The Casa Lanfranchi was not Gothic nor mediaeval but mid-Renaissance in design. Byron accepted the local traditions concerning it. See Marchand, III, p. 943 and Notes, p. 103.

climate!——I am however bothered about the spectres—(as they say the last occupants were too—) of whom I have as yet seen nothing—nor indeed heard (*myself*)—but all the other ears—have been regaled by all kinds of supernatural sounds.——The first night I thought I heard an odd voice—but it has not been repeated.——I have now been here more than a month.—

yrs. & [scrawl]

P.S.—Pray send me two or three dozen of *"Acton's Corn-rubbers"* in a parcel by the post—*packed dry* & well—if you can.—I have received safely the parcel containing the Seal,—the E[dinburgh] Review—and some pamphlets &c. the others are I presume upon their way.——Are there not designs from *Faust?* send me some—and a translation of it—if such there is—also of Goethe's life if such there be—if not—the original German.——

[TO HENRY DUNN?]   *Decr. 8th. 1821*

Sir/—I should have no objection to the pistols (marked "Janar") but for the price.—You know very well that they cost but 20 guineas in England—which is the regular price of Williams [& Co's] pistols. I will give *seventeen*—which is *three* more than any one will ever give, for second hand pistols.——If not the owner may have them again. ——I have an excellent pair of Manton's of my own—& merely wished these others to spare them—as I am fond of the practice.—I beg leave to add that you are also damned dear in all yr. other commodities—which you ought not to be—as I am likely to prove a constant— and at le[ast] a ready money customer.—

yrs.
B

[TO JOHN SHEPPARD]¹   *Pisa. Decr. 8th. 1821*

Sir,—I have received yr. letter.—I need not say that the Extract which it contains has affected me—because it would imply a want of all feeling to have read it with indifference.—Though I am not quite *sure* that it was intended by the writer for *me*—yet the date—the

¹ John Sheppard (1785–1879), a clothier of Frome, wrote books of travel and devotional works. He wrote to Byron to say that his wife before she died had written a prayer for him [Byron]. She had not mentioned him by name but referred to one whose "transcendent talents" should be turned to good, though his "past conduct and writings have been of evil".

place where it was written—with some other circumstances which you mention—render the allusion probable.—But for whomever it was meant—I have read it with all the pleasure which can arise from so melancholy a topic.—I say *pleasure*—because your brief and simple picture of the life and demeanour of the excellent person whom I trust that you will again meet—cannot be contemplated without the admiration due to her virtues and her pure and unpretending piety.——Her last moments were particularly striking, and I do not know that in the course of reading the story of mankind, and still less in my observations upon the existing portion, I ever met with any thing so unostentatiously beautiful.——Indisputably the firm believers in the Gospel have a great advantage over all others—for this simple reason—that if true—they will have their reward hereafter, and if there be no hereafter—they can be but with the infidel in his eternal sleep—having had the assistance of an exalted hope—through life—without subsequent disappointment—since (at the worst for them) "out of nothing nothing can arise"[2]—not even Sorrow.——But a Man's creed does not depend upon *himself*;—*who* can say I *will* believe—this—that—or the other?—and least of all that which he least can comprehend?—I have however observed that those who have begun life with an extreme faith have in the end greatly narrowed it—as Chillingworth[3]—Clarke[4] (who ended as an Arian) Bayle—and Gibbon (once a Catholic) and some others—while on the other hand nothing is more common than for the early Sceptic to end in a firm belief like Maupertuis[5]—and Henry Kirke White.[6]——

But my business is to acknowledge your letter—and not to make a dissertation.—I am obliged to you for your good wishes—and more than obliged by the extract from the papers of the beloved object whose qualities you have so well described in a few words.——I can assure you that all the fame which ever cheated Humanity into higher notions of it's own importance—would never weigh in my mind against the pure and pious interest which a virtuous being may be pleased to take in my welfare.———In this point of view I would not exchange the prayer of the deceased in my behalf—for the united

[2] Persius, *Satires*, 1, 7, 84 'De nihilo nihilum etc.'.

[3] William Chillingworth (1602–1644) embraced Roman Catholicism, but later abjured it.

[4] Samuel Clarke (1675–1729) founded an "intellectual" school which deduced the moral law from a logical necessity. He carried on a philosophical correspondence with Leibnitz. In 1714 he was accused of Arianism.

[5] See Diary, Feb. 18, 1821, note 2. (Vol. 8, p. 46.)

[6] See Aug. 21, 1811, to Dallas, note 3. (Vol. 2, p. 76.)

glory of Homer Caesar and Napoleon—could such be accumulated upon a living head.——Do me at least the justice to suppose that

"Video meliora proboque"—[7]

however the "Deteriora sequor" may have been applied to my conduct.——I have the honour to be

yr. obliged & obed.t Servt.

Byron

P.S.—I do not know that I am addressing a Clergyman—but I presume that you will not be affronted by the mistake—(if it is one) on the address of this letter.—One who has so well explained—and deeply felt the doctrines of religion—will excuse the error which led me to believe him it's minister.

[TO JOHN MURRAY]   *Pisa. Decr. 10th. 1821*

Dear Sir/—This day and this hour (one on the Clock) my daughter is six years old. I wonder when I shall see her again or if ever I shall see her at all.——I have remarked a curious coincidence which almost looks like a fatality.——My *mother*—my *wife*—my *daughter*—my *half sister*—my *sister's mother*—my natural daughter (as far at least as I am concerned) and *myself* are all *only children*.—My father by his first marriage with Lady Conyers (an only child) had only my sister—and by his second marriage with another only child—an only child again.—Lady B[yron] as you know was one also,—and so is my daughter &c.——Is not this rather odd—such a complication of only children? By the way—Send me my daughter Ada's miniature.—I have only the print—which gives little or no idea of her complexion.—I heard the other day from an English voyager—that her temper is said to be extremely violent.—Is it so?—It is not unlikely considering her parentage.—My temper is what it is—as you may perhaps divine—and my Lady's was a nice little sullen nucleus of concentred Savageness to mould my daughter upon,—to say nothing of her two Grandmothers—both of whom to my knowledge were as pretty specimens of female Spirit—as you might wish to see on a Summer's day.——I have answered yr. letters—&c.—either to you in person—or through Mr. D[ouglas] K[innair]d.——The broken Seal—and

---

[7] Ovid, *Metamorphoses*, VII, 20:

"I know the right, and I approve it too;
Condemn the wrong, and yet the wrong pursue."

Edinburgh R[eview] &c. arrived safely.—The others are I presume upon their way.—

yrs. &c.

B

[TO JOHN TAAFFE, JR.]   *Decr. 12th. 1821*

My dear Taaffe—Your reasons may be good and true—but ought not to weigh against the possibility even of saving a human creature— from so atrocious an infliction.[1]—However without compromising *you*—I could wish you (as a personal favour to *me*) I not having any acquaintance with the Sovereign or his ministers to apply to any of the *latter* in *my name* only—and say that I will and would do any thing either by *money* or *guarantee* or otherwise—to have this man's punishment commuted;—(*saved* if possible) at least for some less cruel mode of destruction.———As to the Government I appeal to the whole of my conduct since I came here to prove whether I meddle or make with their politics.———I defy them to misinterpret my motive—and as to leaving their states—I am a Citizen of the World—content where I am now—but able to find a country elsewhere.—I only beg of you to take any steps in *my name* that may even have the possibility of being useful in saving the World from another reproach to it's Annals.—I am willing to make any sacrifice—of money or otherwise— I could never *bribe* in a better cause than that of humanity.—

yrs. ever & truly

BYRON

P.S.—Try the *priests*—a little cash to the Church might perhaps save the Man yet? *You* know *Lucca* well—I wish you would try there—always *without* compromising yourself.—

[TO PERCY BYSSHE SHELLEY]   *Decr. 12th. 1821*

My dear Shelley/—Enclosed is a note for you from Taaffe.———His reasons are all very true—I dare say—and might & may be of personal inconvenience to us—but that does not appear to me to be a reason to allow a being to be burnt without trying to save him.—[To save] him by any means but *remonstrance* is [of course] out of the question—

---

[1] Thomas Medwin had just brought a report that a man at Lucca had been taken up for sacrilege and was sentenced to be burned alive. Byron and Shelley were incensed and determined to save him. It turned out be a false report.

but I do not see [why] only a *temperate* remonstrance should hurt any one.—Lord *Guilford*[1] is the *man*, if he would undertake it.—He knows the Grand Duke personally—& might perhaps prevail upon him to interfere.—But as he goes tomorrow—you must be quick—or it will be useless.—Make any use of *my name* that you please.—

yrs. ever & truly
BYRON

[TO THE EARL OF GUILFORD]   *Decr. 12th. 1821*

My dear Lord/—There is a man to be *burnt* at Lucca for Sacrilege. ——This is an abrupt beginning but as they say you are going away—I have hardly time to apologize for breaking in upon you.—Some of our Countrymen here as well as myself are shocked at this horrible mode of punishment—whatever the crime may have been.—It is said to be Sacrilege.——We wish to have the punishment commuted, if the man *cannot* be saved.———*You* have influence and acquaintance with these Grand Dukes and Sovereigns—and such people as are able to burn other people still it seems.——You have past your whole life in doing Good.—Surely saving (if in your power by remonstrance) the *Age* from such an infamy—as the destruction of a human being by the Stake—would not be the worst action ever of so honourable a life.——A few words from you—so well known—and so much honoured would avail more than all our attempts—who are not well looked upon in high places.—I write to you in haste and late—excuse both and believe me ever & truly

yr. obliged & faithful St.
BYRON[1]

[TO THOMAS MOORE]   *Pisa. December 12th. 1821*

What you say about Galignani's two biographies is very amusing: and, if I were not lazy, I would certainly do what you desire. But I doubt my present stock of facetiousness—that is, of good *serious* humour, so as not to let the cat out of the bag. I wish *you* would undertake it.[1] I will forgive and *indulge* you (like a Pope) beforehand,

[1] Frederick North, 5th Earl of Guilford.

[1] This was a joint letter with Shelley, who added two pages to Byron's epistle, expressing his horror at the proposed barbaric punishment.

[1] "Mr. Galignani having expressed a wish to be furnished with a short Memoir of Lord Byron, for the purpose of prefixing it to the French edition of his works, I had said jestingly in a preceding letter to his lordship, that it would be but a fair satire on the disposition of the world to 'bemonster his features,' if he would write

for any thing ludicrous, that might keep those fools in their own dear belief that a man is a *loup garou.*

I suppose I told you that the Giaour story had actually some foundation on facts; or, if I did not, you will one day find it in a letter of Lord Sligo's, written to me *after* the publication of the poem.[2] I should not like marvels to rest upon any account of my own, and shall say nothing about it. However, the *real* incident is still remote enough from the poetical one, being just such as, happening to a man of any imagination, might suggest such a composition. The worst of any *real* adventures is that they involve living people—else Mrs. ————'s, ————s, etc., are as "German to the matter"[3] as Mr. Maturin could desire for his novels.

* * * * * * * * * * * * * * *

The consummation you mentioned for poor * * [Taaffe] was near taking place yesterday. Riding pretty sharply after Mr. Medwin and myself, in turning the corner of a lane between Pisa and the hills, he was spilt,—and, besides losing some claret on the spot, bruised himself a good deal, but is in no danger. He was bled and keeps his room. As I was ahead of him some hundred yards, I did not see the accident; but my servant who was behind, did, and says the *horse* did not fall—the usual excuse of floored equestrians. As * * [Taaffe] piques himself upon his horsemanship, and his horse is really a pretty horse enough, I long for his personal narrative,—as I never yet met the man who would *fairly claim a tumble* as his own property.

Could not you send me a printed copy of the "Irish Avatar?"—I do not know what has become of Rogers since we parted at Florence.

Don't let the Angles keep you from writing. Sam told me that you were somewhat dissipated in Paris, which I can easily believe. Let me hear from you at your best leisure.

Ever and truly, etc.

P.S. December 13th

I enclose you some lines written not long ago, which you may do what you like with, as they are very harmless.[4] Only, if copied, or

---

for the public, English as well as French, a sort of mock-heroic account of himself, outdoing in horrors and wonders, all that had been yet related or believed of him, and leaving Goethe's story of double murder at Florence far behind." (Moore, II, 565.)

[2] See Aug. 31, 1813, to Lady Melbourne, note 2. (Vol. 3, p. 102.)

[3] *Hamlet*, Act V, scene 2.

[4] The lines beginning: "Oh! talk not to me of a name great in story", "Detached Thoughts", No. 118.

printed, or set, I could wish it more correctly than in the usual way, in which one's "nothings are monstered,"[5] as Coriolanus says.

You must really get * * [Taaffe] published—he never will rest till he is so. He is just gone with his broken head to Lucca, at my desire, to try to save a *man* from being *burnt*. The Spanish * * *, that has her petticoats over Lucca, had actually condemned a poor devil to the stake, for stealing the wafer box out of a church. Shelley and I, of course, were in arms against this piece of piety, and have been disturbing every body to get the sentence changed. * * [Taaffe] is gone to see what can be done.

B

[TO THOMAS MOORE]   [*December 13? 1921*]

Dear M.—I send you the two notes which will tell you the story I allude to of the Auto da Fe.—Shelley's allusion to his "fellow Serpent" is a buffoonery of mine—Goethe's Mephistofeles calls the Serpent who tempted Eve *"my Aunt the renowned Snake"* and I always insist that Shelley is nothing but one of her Nephews—walking about on the tip of his tail— —

B

[TO DOUGLAS KINNAIRD]   *Pisa. Decr. 14th 1821*

My dear Douglas.—I write only to apprize you as a matter of business—that I sent by this post—a little lyrical drama to Murray[1]— presuming that it may arrive in time for the volume which he is about to publish.—You will not like it—for it is *choral* and mystical—and a sort of Oratorio on a sacred subject—but it will do if "Cain" does and if not—it must at least take it's chance.—I have not heard from you lately—that is very lately—but I do not wish you to bore yourself with writing to me—two words stating that Murray has received the poem (which is about "the Deluge") will be sufficient and oblige

yrs. ever & most truly
B

[TO JOHN CAM HOBHOUSE]   *Pisa. Decr. 16th, 1821*

Dear Hobhouse/—I have waited several posts in the hope that you might perhaps stumble upon the papers I mentioned—the first act of a thing begun in 1815.—called "Werner".—If you can't it don't

5 *Coriolanus,* Act II, scene 2.
1 *Heaven and Earth.*

much matter—only let me know it.—You will by this time have received my very temperate answer to your very tipsy letter.—I forgive you as a Christian should do—that is I never will forgive you as long as I live—and shall certainly pay you in kind with interest the very first opportunity—but that need break no squares between us—as it hath been our custom for several years—the example being first set by yourself at Cambridge and Brighton.—"Don't you remember what happened seven years ago?"

yrs. ever [Scrawl]

[TO DOUGLAS KINNAIRD] *Pisa. Decr. 18th. 1821*

My dear Douglas/—I really can't pay Farebrother or any one else more than the *interest* of their debt at present.——I wish at least for an account of *how* Claughton's money was disposed of—surely I have paid debt enough for one year—when this Nine hundred pounds of Clau[ghton]'s and the one hundred & fifty deducted from the Copy of "the Doge" are calculated—why Man it is a thousand guineas!—and all to Creditors!—I wonder at your profligate expectations of my paying more just now—can't they be content with the interest—until the death of Ly. N[oel]—or my own—sets my capital free—or her income at my disposal, or at least a part of it.——I have also been disappointed at Murray's disbursement—he has behaved as shabbily about "the Juans" as possible.——I sent him by last post—*another drama* (but not a long one) for which I expect monies—I promise you.——I expect also—my half year's fee—Sir Jacob's total balance—& the produce of the copy-rights all *integral* and entire—in your seductive circulars.——Change of house naturally has made expences, & I have been laying in some English household comforts from Leghorn—to which for six years I had been a stranger.—You really must not pay any body——I can't afford it.—Remember I deal with *M[urray]* in *guineas*—pounds are not agreeable.—The new drama is lyrical and you will not like it. I have set my heart on having a good round sum total to commence the year withal.——As to Lady Noel's health—it is not to be calculated upon,—and I can't part with my *ready*—because a tough old woman *may* chance to die at last before one self.—So remember—Dougal—the fee—and the whole entire balance of Sir Jac[ob] [word torn off with seal] and all & sundry the Copy monies—are to be forwarded in due season.——

yrs. ever & truly
B

P.S.—Remember me to Alvanly[1] & all friends.—I have been Clareting a little myself lately—having got some "choice wines" from Leghorn.—But don't speak to me of *paying*—it makes me so very unwell.———Don't forget the funds though.——

P.S.—Will you pay my Sister the bill for the *locket* (ordered by me for my daughter) and deduct it from our banking accompt. Do not omit this—for I fear that Augusta has not much cash to spare.—She will tell you the amount.——

[TO THE REV. DR. BRYCE][1]   *Monday [Water mark, 1822]*

Will you send Mr. Harrington[2] a copy of No. II . . . .

[TO BRYAN WALLER PROCTER]   *Pisa. 1822*

Your friend Captain Medwin is at this moment with me. . . . The story in "Blackwood"[1] (which I have only just heard) is utterly false. I have had no geese (not even one on Michaelmas Day), and I should neither be such a fool nor buffoon as to baptize them if I had. I always thought highly of the dramatic specimens, and look upon "Mirandola"[2] as a work of very great promise and deserved success. It is strange that Mr. Murray has not thought it worth his while to mention (that is, if you know him), that I expressly wrote to him my regret that I had not been aware of "Mirandola" at the date of the preface to "The Doge", etc. The latter work was sent to England in the summer of 1820, and "Mirandola" not announced till the winter following. The first time I saw it mentioned was in a newspaper, many months after my own MS. had been sent to Albemarle Street. I never received the copy from the author, but a single copy sent from the bookseller as his own. Had I been aware of your tragedy (although it is a matter of not the least consequence to you), I should certainly

----

[1] Byron referred to Lord Alvanley as one the Dandies. See "Detached Thoughts", No. 29.

[1] Unidentified.

[2] Unidentified.

[1] *Blackwood's Edinburgh Magazine* makes no mention of Byron's geese in 1821 or 1822. The reference is puzzling, for Medwin, mentioned in the letter, left Pisa on March 9, 1822, and did not return until August or September, when Byron did have some geese.

[2] Procter's drama *Mirandola* was produced at Covent Garden, Jan. 9, 1821, with Macready, Charles Kemble, and Mrs. Foote taking the leading roles. It was acted sixteen times and had a fair success.

not have omitted to insert your name with those of other writers who still do honour to the drama.

My own notions on the subject of the English drama altogether are so very different from the popular ideas of the day, that we differ essentially (as indeed I do from our whole English literati) upon that topic; but I do not contend that I am in the right. I merely say that such is my opinion—and as it is a solitary one, it can do no great harm.

But this does not prevent me from doing justice to the *power* of those who adopt a different system.

I wish you every success, both on and off the stage, and am very truly your old schoolfellow and well wisher.

Yours, etc.
BYRON

P.S.—I should feel it as a compliment if I could have a copy of your new volume—sent by the post; it will reach me more quickly, and you need not have any remorse about the postage, as I am in the habit of having books so sent.

I, too, have been writing on the *Deluge*;[3] but it is on *Noah*! I wonder if our thoughts *hit*: most probably.

[TO DOUGLAS KINNAIRD]   [*Jan. 1822?*] [*Postmark, Jan. 19, 1822*]

P.S.—Please to bear in *mind* (as Murray has lately been troubled with a short memory) that his Bill ought only to *date* from the publication of Beppo in 1818, which at his *own desire* was to cancel all former bookselling accounts between us *up* to that period.—Do *not forget* this—as it is possible that he may.—Also, tell me—if "the Deluge" has arrived at Murray['s]—it was sent on the 15th. Decr. 1821—I have several counts ag[ain]st Murray—1stly he behaved shabbily—& uncivilly—in not th[anking] me for my very civil behaviour about *Galignani's* copyrights.—2dly. Rogers says he went about affecting *not* to be the publisher of "Don Juan"—-&c. at the very time that he was pressing me to write more of it.—3rdly. he has not been very magnifique about the letter on Pope—and 4thly.—you know how he has behaved about the rest—the *Juans* &c.——Pray press the publication of "the Vision"—you will soon find a publisher.——Shelley who has just read your letter (and is witness to the deed) agrees with

[3] Byron wrote his poetic drama *Heaven and Earth* in October, 1821. The heroines refuse to join Noah in the Ark and escape with two angels.

you entirely on the subject of the *deed* that is of the manner in which it is *drawn*.[1]—What is to be done? Moore was undoubtedly signing (as I did) a deed of which he did not fully understand the tenor.— But—as I said before—I cannot have *him troubled about it*—as I am sure it would make him uncomfortable.—Do what you can—but do it *delicately* on Moore's account.—*He* is in no fault whatever.—I *pressed* him repeatedly and anxiously to avail himself of the M.S.S. to get out of his difficulties.—He is under no obligation—for he will have work enough to do for his legacy.——

[TO SIR WALTER SCOTT]   *Pisa. Ja[nuar]y 12th. 1822*

My dear Sir Walter/—I need not say how grateful I am for yr. letter—but I must own my ingratitude in not having written to you again long ago.—Since I left England (and it is not far off the usual term of transportation) I have scribbled to five hundred blockheads on business &c. without difficulty though with no great pleasure;—and yet with the notion of addressing you a hundred times in my head—and always in my heart—I have not done—what I ought to have done.—I can only account for it on the same principle of tremulous anxiety with which one sometimes makes love to a beautiful woman of our own degree with whom one is ⟨in love⟩ enamoured in good earnest;— whereas we attack a fresh-coloured housemaid without (I speak of course of earlier times) any sentimental remorse or mitigation of our virtuous purpose.—

I owe to you far more than the usual obligation for the courtesies of literature and common friendship—for you went out of your way in 1817—to do me a service when it required not merely kindness—but courage to do so;—to have been seconded by you in such a manner would have been a proud memorial at any time—but at such a time— when "all the World and his Wife"[1] (or rather *mine*) as the proverb goes—were trying to trample upon me was something still higher to my Self esteem. I allude to the Quarterly rev[iew] of the 3d. Canto of C[hild]e H[arol]d[2] which Murray told me was written by you—and indeed I should have known it without his information—as there

---

[1] The deed for the sale of Byron's Memoirs to Murray, which Byron co-signed with Moore, who was to benefit from the sale.

[1] Swift, *Polite Conversation*, Dialogue 3.

[2] Scott's review appeared in the October, 1816, number of the *Quarterly*, but Byron did not know that Scott was the reviewer until Murray told him in March, 1817.

could not be *two* who *could* and *would* have done this at the time.—Had it been a common criticism—however eloquent or panegyrical—I should have felt pleased undoubtedly and grateful—but not to the extent which the extraordinary Good-heartedness of the whole proceeding—must induce in any mind capable of such sensations.—The very *tardiness* of this acknowledgement will at least show that I have not forgotten the obligation—[and] I can assure you that my Sense of it has been out at compound interest during the delay.—I shall only add one word upon the subject—which is—that I think—that you and Jeffrey—and Leigh Hunt were the only literary men of numbers whom I know (& some of whom I had served) who dared venture even an anonymous word in my favour just then—and that of those three—I had never seen *one* at all—of the second much less than I desired—and that the third was under no kind of obligation to me whatever—while the other *two* had been actually attacked by me on a former occasion[3]—*one* indeed with some provocation—but the other wantonly enough.—So you see you have been heaping "coals of fire &c."[4] in the true Gospel manner——and I can assure you that they have burnt down to my very heart.—

I am glad that you accepted the Inscription.[5]—I meant to have inscribed "the Foscaris" to you instead—but firstly—I heard that "Cain" was thought the least bad of the two as a composition—and 2dly—I have abused Southey like a pickpocket in a note to the "Foscaris" and I recollected that he is a friend of yours (though not of mine) —and that it would not be the handsome thing to dedicate to one friend —anything containing such matters about another.——However—I'll work the Laureate before I have done with him—as soon as I can master Billingsgate therefor.—I like a row—& always did from a boy—in the course of which propensity I must needs say that I have found it the most easy of all to be gratified—personally and poetically. ——You disclaim "Jealousies" but I would ask as Boswell did of Johnson "Of *whom could* you be jealous"—of none of the living certainly—and (taking all and all into consideration)—of which of the dead?—I don't like to bore you about the Scotch novels (as they call them though two of them are wholly English—and the rest half so) but nothing can or could ever persuade me since I was the first ten minutes in your company that you are *not* the Man.——To me those

[3] Byron had attacked both Scott and Jeffrey in *English Bards and Scotch Reviewers*.
[4] Proverbs, 25: 22.
[5] The dedication of *Cain* to Scott was graciously accepted by Scott in a letter to Murray of Dec. 4, 1821. (*LJ*, VI, 3.)

novels have so much of "Auld lang syne" (I was bred a canny Scot till ten years old) that I never move without them—and when I removed from Ravenna to Pisa the other day—and sent on my library before—they were the only books that I kept by me—although I already knew them by heart.

Ja[nuar]y 27th. 1822—

I delayed till now concluding in the hope that I should have got "the Pirate" who is under way for me—but has not yet hove in sight. ——I hear that your daughter is married and I suppose by this time you are half a Grandfather—a young one by the way.——I have heard great things of Mrs. Lockhart's personal and mental charms—and much good of her Lord;—that you may live to see as many novel Scotts as there are Scot's [sic] novels is the very bad pun but sincere wish of

yrs. ever most affectly
BYRON

P.S.—Why don't you take a turn in Italy—you would find yourself as well-known and as welcome as in the Highlands among the natives.— As for the English you would be with them as in London—and I need not add that *I* would be delighted to see you again—which is far more than I shall ever feel or say for England or (with a few exceptions "of kith—kin—and allies")[6] any thing that it contains.——But my "heart warms to the Tartan"[7] or to any thing of Scotland which reminds me of Aberdeen and other parts not so far from the Highlands as that town—(about Invercauld & Braemar where I was sent to drink Goat's *Fey*[8] in 1795–6 [following a?] threatened decline after the scarlett fever)—but I am gossipping a [illegible] Good night—and the Gods be with your dreams! Pray present my respects to Lady Scott—who may perhaps recollect having seen me in town in 1815.

I see that one of your Supporters (for like Sir Hildebrand I am fond of Gwillim)[9] is a *Mermaid*—it is my *Crest* too—and with precisely the same curl of tail.——There's concatenation for you! I am building a little cutter at Genoa to go a cruising in the summer——I know *you* like the sea too.

---

[6] An adaptation of "acquaintance, kindred and allies" in *Henry IV*, Part I, Act 1, scene 1.

[7] Jeanie Deans uses the phrase in *The Heart of Midlothian*, Chap. 35. See Byron's confession in *Don Juan* (X, 17): "But I am half a Scot by birth, and bred/A whole one."

[8] Another phrase (modified) from *The Heart of Midlothian*, Chap. 49. Effie Deans was sent to Roseneath, "being recommended to drink goat's whey by the physicians."

[9] *Rob Roy*, Chap. 10.

Dear Hobhouse/—You are a pretty fellow to talk about "ballads"[1] and "tu quoques".—Did not you begin first? did you not ballad me at Brighton?—in Piccadilly—and at Venice?——However I am so perfectly in the right—that I forgive and restore you to my good graces.—I don't recollect any thing about the "public"—or a paper war—neither do I see what the "public" could have to do with the matter.——My payment with interest was merely to have talked to you of your speeches—or some new work—in the same style—you bestowed upon me in your epistle—and see how you liked it.——But I can't go on with such nonsense—nor squabble about anything of the kind—that is to say in earnest.—As for "Prison" and "Cain" there is great hope (Murray says) of seeing him the said Murray in durance for publishing the same—a consummation which he deserves for his shuffling with me for some time past—though not about the *bust*— which (*he swears*) he never *meant* to appropriate—when once he knew it to be *yours*—which to be sure he ought to have discovered directly.——So—you shall see that he shan't want a ballad either—in proper place.—

As for "purchasing a biographer under pretext of doing a generous action"[2]—I am willing to bear that imputation rather than have Moore or anyone else suppose that He is at all obliged to me.——I suppose however that like most men who have been talked about—I might have had—(if I did not outlive my reputation which however is not unlikely) a biographer without purchase—since most other scribblers have two or three—gratis.—Besides—I thought that I had written my *own*.——But—damn all this nonsense.——What are you about?—Hunting?——I have not been able to hold out till you fished up the first act of "Werner"—but have written *four new* acts (and am in labour with the fifth) of the same drama.—But I should like to see the old first—nevertheless—to compare it with the subsequent sketch.—I do not know anything here that would interest you at all—nothing but the Russian war—or *not* war—is talked about. ——Douglas has not got "the Vision" publicated—will you axe him *why?*—as he seemed to like it—and to wish it "stampata"——

---

[1] Hobhouse was still smarting from Byron's "Ballad" ridiculing his attachment to the "Mobby-O", written while Hobhouse was in Newgate for publishing an inflammatory pamphlet.

[2] Hobhouse, perhaps somewhat jealous that Byron had given his Memoir to Moore to sell to Murray for posthumous publication, felt that Byron demeaned himself in co-signing the agreement.

What is to be done in politics this year? I think the struggle seems approaching—let me know—

yrs. ever & truly [scrawl]

P.S.—Our late Correspondence reminds me of one of yours at College with poor Matthews in which one of his letters commenced with—"Your *atrabilarious disposition* Hobhouse!" &c. and yours ended with reproaching him with "*p*icking out *p*etty *p*eculiarities and *t*reasuring up *t*rifling defects." A pretty instance of alliteration.—But "I'll have a frisk with you, you dog"[3] notwithstanding.—I have got some good claret from Leghorn—which I wish you was here to ingurgitate.

[TO DOUGLAS KINNAIRD]   *Pisa. J[anuar]y 18th. 1822*

My dear Douglas—I return you your "Happy new year" of the first—and wait patiently for the promised "*Solid*". But I wish you would let me know why "the Vision" is not published—or whether it is to be so or no—and by whom.—You could not of course expect L[ongman?] to have any thing to do with a work which attacks his own ragam[uffin Southey.]—If you are alarmed about its politics—[you] need not be so—*much*—for I should think *that* was my concern.— Murray will of course discourage any further publication as much as he can—to avoid *disbursing* in the first place—and in the next, on account of the *entire* works—which he can turn to better account—than *separate* additions—which distract the attention.—He says—he is to be prosecuted about "Cain"—in that Case—let his lawyer merely quote the daring passages from *Milton.*—"Evil be thou my Good" and "better to reign in Hell than serve in Heaven"—with any given speech of the fallen Angels.—But Master Murray (besides being probably in no great peril) ought to recollect that "Cesarem vehit"[1] (which passage you can translate to him) and be proud of his company. ——I have already written *four acts* of a new drama—to be called "Werner or the Inheritance".—It shall be sent to you when completed —as also the proof of the new Mystery—to dispose of to any publisher you may fix on.—

yrs ever [scrawl]

P.S.—The *funds*! What not *yet*?

[3] What Dr. Johnson said on being knocked up at 3 a.m. by Beauclerk and Langton (*Boswell*, ed. Powell, Vol. I, p. 250).
[1] Julius Caesar was caught in a storm in a small vessel and according to tradition reassured the frightened pilot with the words "Caesarem vehis et fortunam ejus." ("You carry Caesar and his fortunes".)

Pisa. J[anuar]y 22d. 1822

The enclosed letter with the annexed packet will explain it's object.—
I can only say that the work appears a desideratum in literature—
(especially in English literature) and with a lift in the Quarterly
would be likely to go off well.—Foscolo can tell you this better than
I—Taaffe[1] is a very good man—with a great desire to see h[imself] in
print—and will be made very ha[ppy] by such a vision.—He was
persuaded to add his translation—which is *not* good—but the Comment
is really valuable.—If *you* will engage in the work—you will serve
him—and oblige me—if not—at least recommend it to some of the
other publishers—as I should feel sorry to disappoint a very good
natured man—who is publishing an useful work.——He stipulates
for no terms—at any rate let us have an answer.

yrs. [scrawl]
B

His politics and religion are all in your own damned way—so that
there will be no dispute about that.

[TO JOHN MURRAY (*b*)] *Pisa. J[anuar]y 22d. 1822*

I write merely to say that I have returned by this post the proofs
to Mr. Kinnaird—so that you may not be surprized at not receiving
them—or suppose that I have not acknowledged their arrival.—In
a post or two I shall send you a version of the extract from "Petrarch"
as you wished—but you must not expect it to be good, I have not
the turn for those things.—I also (as a piece of courtesy) inform you—
t[hat] in a few days (as soon as it can be fairly c[opied] out) I shall
send to Mr. K[innaird] the drama of "Werner or the Inheritance"
in five acts—which were completed on the twentieth.——As you
have lately published more of mine than you seem to think convenient—
it is probable that I shall not trouble you with the publication of these—
but transfer them to some other publisher,—and I merely apprize
you of this—because it may be proper after the length of the connection
—not to terminate it abruptly without such advice of my intention.—

I am yrs. very truly
[Scrawl]

It is probable that the new things will be published anonymously.—

[1] Taaffe had written a Commentary on Dante and a translation of the *Divine
Comedy*.

Pisa. J[anuar]y 22d. 1822

Dear Douglas/—I enclose you the new Mystery—for which you will please to contract with any publisher you please.——If you choose to offer Murray the refusal—do so.—If not—perhaps Mawman or some other may suit you.—At the same time also (I do not mean to publish *it alone*) state that I have another drama in five acts entitled "Werner or the Inheritance" ready, as soon as copied out fairly.— probably [in a] few posts.——It was completed on the twentieth— (the day before yesterday) and Those who have seen it—like it— hitherto.——I am surprized to have no news of "the Vision"—let me know by return of post—that this is ar[rived].—"Werner" is rather long—and with the "Mystery" w[ill] form a fair-sized volume. ——I leave the terms to you and the Bibliopole—and do not m[uch] care who is the publisher—(except Longman—whom I do not wish to have anything to do with) if you prefer it—we can publish anony- mously.—Whether he may give more or less than Murray—I think what we have lately seen of that gentleman—renders any continuance of our connection no more desirable to him than to me—I speak only *quoad* publisher—he is a very good fellow I dare say in other respects, but a man's trade always brings out his worst qualities.

yrs. ever & truly [scrawl]

P.S.—Let me have an answer at your convenience.——

Pisa. J[anuar]y 23rd. 1822

Sir,—I have just received the parcel—all right—and well.—But I am greatly surprized to see that you have omitted the dedication of "Sardanapalus" to Goethe which if any opportunity of replacing it occurs I desire may be done—and a copy forwarded to Goethe from the author.——I sent you a heavy parcel by the post [yes]terday—& request that you will [app]ly to Mr. Kinnaird for payment of the postage of the same—as also for any books that you send me—that we may not incur long accounts.—

I am &c. yrs. truly
[Scrawl]

[On cover] There are some mistakes in the printing which I shall notice by and bye.

My dear Douglas/—I have to acknowledge the first remittance of circulars—i.e. eighteen hundred pounds worth.—I did not expect expences to have been so great—as to swallow up almost the whole of Sir Jacob's balance—but nevertheless I shall not quarrel with your disposition as it is so much debt lessened.——I am glad too that you have paid Mr. Murray's bill—and if in future—you would pay *him* at the *time* and deduct it from my accompt with you—it would save us long bills.—You did right to retain the eighty pounds—for my commissions & so forth.—I am not ill off—for the coming year—as I had still *two* thousand circulars unspent—& unmortgaged—before the arrival of this reinforcement.—Nevertheless I shall be glad to see the other eighteen hundred £.S.D.—With regard to what you say about further publication—I have before said—that I cannot take it ill.—it is the *manner* and not the matter—of such things—which can offend—& yours (in the present instance) is plain—to the purpose —meant well—and I trust not ill taken.—No one has a greater right to say what he pleases to me than you—who have so much bother and trouble on my account.——But acknowledging all this—I shall not the less contrive to publish till I have run my *vein dry.*——If it is not profitable—be it so—I shall do so for nothing (till it becomes actually a loss) and this because it is an occupation of mind—like *play*—or any other stimulus.—

With regard to what I sent you a few days ago (the Mystery) and what I shall send you in a few days (the drama of "Werner") I shall publish them with another publisher.—and *anonymously* if you like.———Indeed—I am much surprized that you say nothing of "the Vision" as you seemed delighted with it and eager to get it published.— Published it *shall be*—though even on my own account.—As I said before the profit is a *secondary* object—*pleasant*—if it comes—but to be borne without—if it does not.——If you cannot settle with any *English publisher*—forward them to Galignani—at Paris——& make any agreement you please—conditional for example——as each to share—or if he chooses to purchase the Copyright—or to divide profit or loss—what you please.——You can get my M.S.S. out of Murray's hand—the Pulci—&c. as I shall most likely collect the whole of what I have in M.S.S. and publish them at once—*My* object is not *immediate* popularity in my present productions which are written on a different system from the rage of the day.—But *mark what I now say*—that the time will come—when *these* will be preferred to any I have before written;—it is not from the cry, or depression of a month or two that such things are to be decided upon.—

In the mean time I mean to be as [word torn off with seal] as Calderon and Lope de Vega.——After all—I rather suspect that Murray has not played fairly with me—I have heard lately two or three instances of his crookedness—that make me almost believe that he wishes to depress me—and is set on by something higher than himself.—But never mind—all I require of you of [sic] is to get these things I send you published—& for the consequences—I can meet them.——As I make no stipulations but leave that to you—you can have less difficulty—as I shall not [murmur?].——Will you desire Mr. Murray to give up the M.S. (Pulci &c.) and to place before "Sardanapalus" the dedication to "Goethe" which he has (like a beast) omitted to prefix.

P.S.—There is one thing I wish you to state to Mr. Murray—it was understood and exprest? (by his particular wish) that the *Copyright* of *Beppo* was to cancel all bills of his *up* to *1818* the date of that publication.—Now your House *date his bill* from March *1816*—If this is not a mistake—all I can say is that it *ought* to *be one*.—But I have little more to say of that Gentleman.—I wrote to Galignani & Mr. Moore by this post to Paris—about the publication. Also to Mr. Murray to place in your hands the "Pulci" & other things in his hands.—If I agree with Galignani—you can send them all—"the Vision" the "Mystery"—&c. to Moore at Paris (17, Rue d'Anjou St. Honoré) where I shall also forward "Werner"——I perceive that Murray had not even the grace to mention the "Letter on Pope" which is of a piece with his incivility when I gave up to him the *French* copyright—for which Galignani offered me my *own terms* a year or two ago.——

J[anuar]y 24th. Pisa

I have just written both to *Moore* and Galignani—will you forward to the *former* the things you have in hand (17 Rue d'Anjou St. Honoré. Paris)

[TO DOUGLAS KINNAIRD]   *Pisa. J[anuar]y 26th. 1822*

My dear Douglas/—Since I wrote to you two days ago—I perceive Murray has omitted the *dedication* to *Goethe*—which I had set my heart upon! is this his insolence or negligence?——Apprize him of this.——I enclose you two of his letters—in which he expressly says that "as far as he is concerned the tragedies are all sold"———In the other he speaks of the "outcry &c."———Now once for all about publication—I [n]*ever courted* the public—and I never will *yield* to it.—As long as I can find a *single* reader I will publish my Mind (while it lasts) and write whilst I feel the impetus.—As to profit, that is another matter—if none is to be attained—it must be dispensed with.—Profit or loss;—they shall never subdue me while I keep my senses.—I have written to Moore and Galignani—and if you can't find a publisher I will try what I can do—though at a distance.—— You talk of "too much"—*number* the *volumes* with Scott! or Southey!— But let this be as it may—I can assure you that I will not swerve from my purpose—though I should share the lot of all who have ever done good or attempted to instruct or better mankind.—I can sustain their persecution—it is not the first time either, and console myself for their neglect—always employing my own mind to the best of my understanding.

yrs [scrawl]

[TO DOUGLAS KINNAIRD]   *Pisa. J[anuar]y 29th. 1822*

My dear Douglas/—By this post I forward to Moore at Paris (17 Rue d'Anjou St. Honoré) the drama of "Werner or the Inheritance"———I write to request you to forward the "Quevedo["] & new Mystery (which I sent to you lately) and the Pulci—& all unpublished poeshie in Mr. Murray's hands—to Moore also.—I have written to Mr. Murray to consign them to you—of course I presume (as you say nothing) that the Quevedo is still unpublished—Murray will [let] you have proofs of the others.———I replied to your last letter—stating my reasons for quitting Murray as a publisher—and also my determination to continue to publish;—as to the profit—that must be as it pleases the Gods—but I shall not give way to discouragement—as long as I do not feel my mind failing.——With regard to the *public* I have expected *that* to *change* this many a good year—but I may perhaps find a reader or two even yet in Germany or America—

yrs. ever & truly
[Scrawl]

[TO ?]   [*Feb., 1822?*]

[Fragment of a letter]

... preaching at it from Oxford to Pisa.[1]—It ... priests who do
more ... all the Infidels that ... Catechism.—

[TO BRYAN WALLER PROCTER]   [*Feb.? 1822*]

[Fragments of a letter]

... ever were formed.—The wit of the one consists in the repetition and play upon a quaint phrase—and of the other in the very
cheap humour of fustian.—Falstaff himself is anything but a *natural*
Character—a moment's reflection will show that such a character
never did—nor ever will have the remotest approach to *real* existence.—
But ... of Pyrrhonism—whatever their opinions may do.—Twice has
he embarked[1]—& twice landed again—between the Nore and the
Lizard—and of course I cannot calculate exactly upon the progress
of such a pilgrim.—But he is hoped for in the Spring—which is already
arrived in Tuscany.—I suppose we shall see him by Xmas next.——

[TO THOMAS MEDWIN][1]   *Pisa. F[ebruar]y 3d. 1822*

Dear M.—Could you favour me if not with the letter[2] with the
principal *personal* outline thereof.—

                                            yrs. ever & truly
                                            [Scrawl]

[TO THE EDITOR OF THE COURIER]   *Pisa. F[ebruar]y 5th. 1822*

Sir/—I have read in your Journal some remarks of Mr. Southey
⟨purporting⟩ which he is pleased to entitle a reply to "a note relating
to himself." appended to the "two Foscari".—Mr. Southey denies

[1] Concerning the outcry of the parsons over *Cain*.
[1] Leigh Hunt, who had been invited by Shelley on behalf of Byron to come to
Italy to be a joint editor of a new literary journal, embarked with his family on Nov.
15, 1821, but was turned back by storms. He spent the winter in Plymouth and
left again in May but did not arrive in Leghorn until the first of July.
[1] See Biographical Sketch, Appendix IV.
[2] Robert Southey had written a letter to the *Courier* replying to Byron's attack
on him in a note to *The Two Foscari*. When he saw Southey's letter Byron boiled with
rage and wanted to challenge him to a duel. When he calmed down he wrote a long
letter of reply, but sent the challenge through Kinnaird also. More happily he
resolved to publish his *Vision of Judgment* whose ridicule effectively silenced
Southey. Medwin first told him about the letter in the *Courier* and he could not rest
until he saw it.

positively "having scattered abroad calumnies knowing them to be such against Ld. Byron & others on his return from Switzerland in 1817."—I can only say that my authority was such as I had no reason to doubt—and that authority—as well as any other sort of Satisfaction shall be at Mr. Southey's service whenever he pleases to call for it.——Mr. S. proceeds to say that "if he had been told that Lord B. had turned Turk or Monk of La Trappe—had furnished a Harem or endowed a hospital he might have thought the account whichever it had been—*possible*—"—knowing Mr. Southey's beliefs in general—I have no objection to this addition to his creed of "possibilities"; there are very good precedents for both—King Solomon for the Harem—and Dean Swift for the hospital—but I have no disposition for either—having always found one woman (at a time) at least as much as any reasonable man could manage—and occasionally rather more—and as for the Hospital Mr. Southey and his Coadjutors have rendered their whole Country one of *Incurables* already.——"He might have spoken of me too as of Baron Gerambe¹—the Green Man² —the Indian Jugglers—or any other Figurante of the time being."— Good Company!—very good Company still!—For Baron Gerambe was at one time a great and especial favourite of Carlton palace,—the Green Man I do not recollect—unless it was Lord Erskine when invested with the Order of the Thistle—and the Indian Jugglers we have all seen or heard of.—But *why* with the *Jugglers*?—does Mr. S. recollect what a *Juggler* is?—is he not one who *shifts—turns—plays tricks*—deceives and swallows *strange substances*?—has not Mr. Southey himself practiced a little in the same line?—to be sure his own words (which he has gulped down) are not quite so sharp as a sword—but I should think that they were equally indigestible—and yet the Laureate has contrived to swallow the Jacobin without any detriment except a little occasional Sickness.——

Mr. S. "once and once only in connexion with Switzerland alluded to Ld. B."—in an article in the Quarterly Review—which as it was then curtailed in the press, he now adds,——"The Jungfrau was the scene where Ld. B's Manfred met the Devil and bullied him ["] &c. &c.— exactly so—"Resist the Devil and he will flee from you"³ are the words of the Sacred book which Mr. Southey has often in his mouth— like most others who make it rarely the rule of their conduct.——

¹ François Ferdinand, Baron de Geramb (1772–1848), an adventurer and soldier, became a Trappist monk in 1817.
² A character in old folk plays who set off fireworks.
³ *Epistle of James*, IV, 7.

Apparently Mr. S. has not been equally successful against the Tempter —in his political resistance.——The Epithets which he accuses me of lavishing upon him—are not mine—but proceeded from the tribunals and the Senate of his Great Britain.——The Chief Judge of the Kingdom—Lord Eldon—the Great legal oracle of Mr. Southey's own party—proclaimed Wat Tyler a blasphemous and seditious work from the Bench.[4]—The upright Member for Norwich—William Smith—denounced him from his place in parliament—as a "rancorous renegado"—and lately Mr. Southey has compared *himself* in the present paper to "the Hangman" an office to which the greatest criminals are usually promoted by way of earning their pardon—but this is the first time since the days of "Tony Fire the faggot"[5] that I ever heard of it's being volunteered.—He talks of "branding irons" and "Gibbets" and his own dealings therewith in a manner which would have secured him the admiration of George Selwyn,[6]—but which—if it were not nonsense (as it is in the present instance) could be something worse—than even Wat Tyler.—

With regard to Mr. Southey's story of the party of "my friends" who inscribed "Atheist" after their names[7]—in some album in Switzerland—it may be true or it may be not—⟨I was not . . . there on this occasion—and I [did not?] . . . to add that if I had, no such inscription would have taken place.—⟩ I was not present—nor should I have made such an adjunct to mine—if I had.—If Mr. Southey's [sic] supposes that *this* is the Calumny to which I alluded—he is mistaken—it was of a much baser complexion—and particularly when Mr. Southey made himself it's organ—because it regarded a lady to whose Mother Mr. Southey once professed himself passionately attached.[8]—Mr. S. "says that he leaves the many opprobrious appellations which Ld. B has bestowed upon him—as he finds them—with the praises which he has bestowed upon himself."—*I* did not *"bestow"* those "appellations"—I merely repeated what many men say—and

4 In 1794, when Southey was enthusiastic about the French Revolution, he wrote a poetic drama called *Wat Tyler*. It was dug out and published in 1817 piratically to expose Southey's early jacobinical views when he had become poet laureate and defender of Tory policies. See Byron's letter to Murray, May 9, 1817 (Vol. 5, p. 220).

5 In Scott's *Kenilworth*.

6 George Selwyn (1719–1791), politician and wit, was fond of attending executions.

7 In the summer of 1816, on his trip to Chamouni, Shelley wrote in Greek after his name in an inn album the word "Atheist". Byron later saw the inscription and erased the word in order to save Shelley's reputation among English travellers, but not before Southey had seen it or heard of it.

8 See Nov. 11, 1818, to Hobhouse (Vol. 6, p. 76).

every one knows annexed to a short list of such of Mr. Southey's own works—as have (together with his conduct) occasioned the stigma from the bench and from the Senate.——To this I added what many *do* know—but I have no particular wish to repeat till absolutely necessary—that I could vindicate my own claim by more than one action to having as far as lay in my power—done my best to benefit my fellow creatures.—

Mr. Southey conceives that "Ld. B's present exacerbation is "evidently produced by his preface to the Vision of Judgement[9]—and not by any hearsay reports of his conversation—some years ago in Switzerland".—He is wrong as usual; my feeling upon the subject of the Calumnies alluded to—was exprest in a work intended for publication & written above a year before the "Vision of Judgement" appeared, & it was only *not* published at the representation of some of my friends that he was not worth the ⟨trouble⟩ printing.—If I have since deviated from that intention it was rather because I had some curiosity to know by whom the "Satanic School" is meant—than from thinking that any thing of Mr. Southey's was more worthy notice than usual.—And now—what is the "Satanic School?" who are the Scholars?—Mr. Southey says that I am their Coryphaeus and Goliath—but who are the Philistines?—I have no school nor Scholars—nor Gath nor Askalon that I know of—my poetical friends are poets upon their own system not on mine.——

As far as I recollect I have had no imitators—& certainly no coadjutors.——The words of Mr. Southey's preface—which he accuses me of witholding [*sic*]—I have no opportunity of quoting—for the book was lost in the passage of my library into Tuscany from Romagna —and it is to the general tenor of his preface that I necessarily refer.— Mr. Southey proceeds to state—"what he has *not* scribbled"—and endeavours to *imply*—(for he does not assert it) that what *he* has *not* done—*I* have.—I presume that "by the libels upon my friends and acquaintances—recalled in a better mood of mind, and then reissued—when the evil Spirit &c."—he alludes to "English Bards".— Now of all the persons mentioned in that juvenile work—there was only *one* with whom I had the slightest personal acquaintance—at the time of it's composition—how the rest became my acquaintances afterwards, I have already stated in my letter upon Mr. Bowles's Pope.—But *"re-issued*!!!" why—my last act and deed on leaving

[9] In his preface to *A Vision of Judgement*, his laureate tribute to George III written on the King's death, Southey referred obliquely to Byron as the leader of the "Satanic School" of poetry.

England—after rejecting every offer of the booksellers—was to leave with my publisher Mr. Murray an express Power of Attorney to prevent the re-publication;—this power has been acted upon in a court of Justice in England—& that it has been evaded by the Irish or defied by the foreign booksellers—is no fault of mine, nor as far as I know—of Mr. Murray.—Mr. S. is here guilty of a gross and intentional falsehood.——Upon the rest of his paragraph I have to observe that in common I believe with most other writers I *have* published works to which I did not put my name on the title-page— but *none* which I dare not avow—or for which I am unwilling to consider myself responsible.—With regard to booksellers and *piracies*— &c. Mr. Southey may be as well and better acquainted with them than I am.—Whenever my publisher calls upon *me* with any well-founded legal opinion that the proceedings would be attended with success— my name shall be at his service. But I rather imagine that it was the omission of his *own* name which led to the piracy in question.—Why he did so—I neither know—nor care to know—why I omitted my own—could be from no apprehension of the personal consequences of a work generally recognized as mine—and which I never would deny to any person whom it could concern but from a motive which could be easily explained if it regarded either the public or my private character—and was not a mere point of *feeling*.—Of the rest of his paragraph the first sentence—if (and this "if" is not intended for a peace-maker) intended for *me*, is a falsehood.—In the latter sentence— in which Mr. S. declares that he has never written anything which can do harm—I agree with him,—his Works are of that description which do about as much Good as Mischief.—

In the penultimate sentence of his paper Mr. Southey gloriously compares himself to the Hangman—and adopts the language of his profession——"*He* has fastened my name upon the Gibbet!—take it down who can!—" I shall not disturb his own Similie of his Writing-desk—but merely add without Metaphor—that—when his person is annexed to this self-chosen type of his performances—in the coming and (I think) inevitable ⟨revolution⟩ Reformation of our Country—I will either cut him down—or (if possible) prevent his Suspension.— Such is my regard for Poesy even of a Laureate, that as Johnson said of Dr. D[odd][10]—"Sir, I should not have liked that one of our Club—

---

[10] The Rev. William Dodd was executed for forgery. Johnson attempted to obtain his pardon. When told that Dodd once wished to become a member of the Literary Club, Dr. Johnson replied: "I should be sorry if any of our club were hanged. I will not say but some of them deserve it." (Boswell, *Life of Samuel Johnson*, Oxford Edition, II, 213.)

had been hanged."———Mr. Southey declares that he "Abhors personalities"—so do I—cannot we settle our little affairs without troubling the public further?—I am as tired of this war of words as he can be—and shall be happy to reduce it to a more tangible ⟨compass⟩ decision—when—where—and how he pleases.—It is a pity that we are not nearer—but I will reduce the distance—if he will only assure me privately that he will not decline a meeting.—To any one but himself such a hint would be unnecessary.[11]——

I have the honour to be & [scrawl]

[TO DOUGLAS KINNAIRD]   *Pisa. F[ebruar]y 6th. 1822*

My dear Douglas/—"Try back the deep lane"[1] till we find a publisher for "the Vision"—and if none such is to be found—— *print* fifty copies (at *my expence*) distribute them amongst my acquaintances—and you will soon see that the booksellers *will* publish them—even if we opposed them.—That they are now afraid—is natural—but I do not see that I ought to give way on that account.—I know nothing of Rivington's remonstrance by the "eminent Churchman"[2] but I suppose he wants a living[.] I only heard of a preacher at Kentish town against Cain[3]—The same outcry was raised against Priestley—Hume—Gibbon—Voltaire—and all the men who ever dared put tithes to the question.———I wrote to you some time ago with and about "the Deluge"[4] & Werner (which I sent to Moore) and proposed Galignani as an experiment—(always under submission to yr.

[11] Byron did not send this letter and later gave it to the Countess Teresa Guiccioli. She had it in her possession in 1832 when she visited England. John Murray tried to get it for his 17-volume edition of Byron's works, and Lady Blessington and her publisher also tried to get her to consent to publication, but she refused, thinking it would not enhance Byron's reputation. It was first published in the *Keats-Shelley Journal*, Vol. III (Winter, 1954), pp. 33–38, by C. L. Cline.

[1] A hunting term, still used, when the fox, to outwit the hounds, has turned back on his own trail through some deep cover. Byron probably meant to try some of the less known publishers.

[2] Francis and Charles Rivington published in 1822 *A Remonstrance addressed to Mr. John Murray respecting a recent Publication*. The writer, who signed himself "Oxoniensis", protested against the publication of Byron's *Cain*.

[3] According to Major Byron, the forger, the Rev. Johnstone Grant preached against *Cain* at Kentish Town. (Major Byron, *Inedited Works of Lord Byron*, p. 93.) Prothero cites a printed sermon by the Rev. John Styles, who preached in Holland Chapel, Kennington [Kensington?], which describes Byron as a "denaturalized being, who, having exhausted every species of sensual gratification, and drained the cup of sin to its bitterest dregs, is resolved to show that he is no longer human, even in his frailties, but a cool, unconcerned fiend." (*LJ*, VI, 10.)

[4] *Heaven and Earth*.

Judgment in business matters) recommending you to forward all in your hands & all (unpublished) in Mr. Murray's hands (the translation from Pulci &c.—the Po &c.) to Moore at Paris—17 Rue d'Anjou— St. Honoré.———Murray (who is I suppose heartily alarmed) will I dare say give them up—(and the connection) very willingly.—I have written (civilly but coldly) to avise him thereof.——

What you say of Hobhouse—I had already anticipated by writing to him a letter which will settle the matter—and of course amicably.— As to any quarrel between him & me—(unless preceded by some very gross overt act) I should look upon it as out of the question after our long and not barren (on his part) friendship.—But I was hurt & the more so—as I have been ever very cautious in touching *him up* on literary matters.—For instance on his row with Canning—on which perhaps I might have differed from him—I kept total silence— because I thought that I might annoy him.—As to the ballad which he harps upon[5]—*he* has written half a dozen at different times on me,—and one I remember in which he quizzed both *you* and *me*—(in 1816) now—did *I* ever make words or fuss about it?—it was the deliberate and wrothful—*seriousness* of his criticism of the poem[6]— which vexed me—and the extreme unguardedness of [his] expressions. —But it is over.—I wish I was out of the funds for all your security— but I suppose I must bear the delay.—

yrs. ever & truly [scrawl]

P.S.—I have just got Southey's pretended reply—to which I am surprized that you do not allude—what remains to be done ⟨had I not better⟩ is to call him out—the question is—would he come? for if he would not—the whole thing would appear ridiculous—if I were to take a long & expensive journey to no purpose.——You must be my Second—and as such I wish to consult you.—Respond.——I apply to you as a Caranza[7]—one well versed in the duello—or mono-machie.[8]—Of course I should come to England as privately as possible —and leave it (supposing that I was the survivor) the same,—having

---

[5] "My Boy Hobby O".

[6] Byron was offended by a letter Hobhouse wrote to him about *Cain* which he thought would ruin Byron's reputation because of its attack on accepted religious views.

[7] Byron probably had in mind Jerónimo Carranza, a famous Spanish swordsman, who was made governor of Honduras in 1589.

[8] The Baron of Bradwardine (*Waverley*, Chap. 12) says of himself that he is "not wholly unskilled in the dependencies and punctilios of the duello or mono-machie."

no other object which could draw me to that country—except to settle quarrels accumulated during my absence.——9

[TO JOHN HAY]¹   *Pisa. F[ebruar]y 6th. 1822*

My dear Hay/—I am really overpowered by your Caccia²—which is too splendid—and I shall distribute it amongst our friends—with yr. remembrances.—I am sorry that I must decline my *own* proposition —and your kindness about the shooting at Bolgheri³—as I have got a little world of business on my hands from England &c.—but I shall be more glad to see you again—than I could have been in any success in sporting.—[name illegible] is not much improved in practice—and still less in health—he has had bilious attacks—partly owing I believe to waltzing with Mrs. [name crossed out]—and partly with my serving him up with blue ruin—(at Midnight) after a foundation of Madeira & Claret at dinner one day.——He hath left off wine—but still sticks to elderly gentlemen.——Excuse haste—& believe me ever & truly

yrs.
BYRON

[TO ROBERT SOUTHEY]   *Pisa. F[ebruar]y 7th. 1822*

Sir/—My friend the Honourable Douglas Kinnaird will deliver to you a message from me, to which an answer is requested. I have the honour to be

your very obedt. humble Servt.
BYRON¹

⁹ This letter and those of Feb. 19 and 23 to Kinnaird were first published in *The Keepsake* in 1830 and copied by Moore in this garbled form as one letter dated Feb. 6, 1822.

¹ John Hay, a Scotsman who came from Kelso, Roxburghshire, had known Byron as early as 1808 when they entered into a wager, Byron accepting one pound and agreeing to forfeit £50 (Hay later claimed it was £100) if he married. On his marriage in 1815, Byron paid his forfeit. Hay was related distantly to Byron's boyhood love Mary Duff. Hay had been hunting in the Maremma and asked Byron to join him, which he had promised to do but now withdrew his promise.

² The kill or game caught. Hay had sent a wild boar, portions of which Byron passed around among his friends. On January 20, Williams recorded in his diary that he had dined with the Shelleys on wild boar sent by Hay from the Maremma.

³ An estate near Leghorn, known for its shooting.

¹ Byron sent this challenge to Douglas Kinnaird who never delivered it.

Dear Sir/—Attacks upon me were to be expected—but I perceive one upon *you*[1] in the papers which I confess that I did not expect.— How—or in what manner *you* can be considered responsible for what *I* publish—I am at a loss to conceive.——If "Cain" be "blasphemous" —Paradise lost is blasphemous—and the very words of the Oxford Gentleman—"Evil be thou my Good" are from that very poem—from the mouth of Satan,—and is there anything more in that of Lucifer in the Mystery?——Cain is nothing more than a drama—not a piece of argument—if Lucifer and Cain speak as the first Murderer and the first Rebel may be supposed to speak—surely all the rest of the personages talk also according to their characters—and the stronger passions have ever been permitted to the drama.—I have even avoided introducing the Deity—as in the Scriptures—(though Milton does and not very wisely either) but have adopted his Angel as sent to Cain instead—on purpose to avoid shocking any feelings on the subject by falling short—of what all uninspired men must fall short in—viz—giving an adequate notion of the effect of the presence of Jehovah.——The Old Mysteries introduced him liberally enough— and all this is avoided in the New one.——

The attempt to *bully you*—because they think it won't succeed with me seems to me as atrocious an attempt as ever disgraced the times.— What? when Gibbon's—Hume's—Priestley's and Drummond's publishers have been allowed to rest in peace for seventy years—are *you* to be singled out for a work of *fiction* not of history or argument?— there must be something at the bottom of this—some private enemy of your own—it is otherwise incredible.——I can only say—"Me— me adsum qui feci"[2] that any proceedings directed against you I beg may be transferred to me—who am willing & *ought* to endure them all—that if you have lost money by the publication—I will refund— any—or all of the Copyright—that I desire you will say—that both *you* and *Mr. Gifford* remonstrated against the publication—as also Mr. Hobhouse—that *I* alone occasioned it—& I alone am the person who either legally or otherwise should bear the burthen.——If they prosecute—I will come to England—that is, if by Meeting it in my own person—I can save yours.——Let me know—you shan't suffer

---

[1] At the end of his *Remonstrance* against *Cain* "Oxoniensis" attacked Murray as its publisher. See Smiles, II. 427.

[2] Virgil, *Æneid*, IX, 427.

for me—if I can help it.—Make any use of this letter which you please.—

yrs. ever
BYRON

P.S.—You will now perceive that it was as well for you—that I have decided upon changing my publisher—though *that* was not my motive—but dissatisfaction at one or two things in your conduct—of no great moment perhaps even *then*. But now—all such things disappear in my regret at having been unintentionally the means of getting you into a scrape.——Be assured that no momentary irritation (at real or supposed omissions—or commissions) shall ever prevent me from doing you justice where you deserve it—or that I will allow you (if I can avoid it) to participate in any odium or persecution—which ought to fall on me only.——I had been laughing with some of my correspondents at the rumours &c. till I saw this assault upon *you*—and I should at that too—if I did not think that it may perhaps hurt your feelings or your business.——When you re-publish (if you do so) the Foscari &c. &c., to the note upon Southey—add Mr. Southey's *answer*—(which was in the papers) this is but fair play, and—I do not desire it—out of an affected contempt.——What my rejoinder to him will be is another concern—and is not for publication. Let me have your answer—remember me to Gifford—& do not forget to state that both you and he objected to publishing "Cain" in it's present form. ——

As for what the Clergyman says of "Don Juan" you have brought it upon yourself by your absurd half and half prudery—which I always foresaw—would bother you at last.—An author's *not* putting his name—is nothing—it has been always the custom to publish a thousand anonymous things—but *who* ever heard before of a *publisher* affecting such a Masquerade as yours was?—However—now—you may print my name to the "Juans" if you like it—though it is of the latest to be of use to you.——I always stated to you—that *my* only objection was in case of the law deciding against you—that they would annihilate my guardianship of the Child. But now (as you really seem in a damned scrape) they may do what they like with me; so that I can get you out of it——but—Cheer up—though I have "led my ragamuffins where they are well peppered"[3] I will stick by them as long as they will keep the field.——I write to you about all this row of bad passions —and absurdities—with the *Summer* Moon (for here our Winter

---

[3] *Henry IV*, Part I, Act V, scene 1.

is clearer than your Dog days) lighting the winding Arno with all her buildings and bridges—so quiet & still—what nothings we are! before the least of these Stars!—

[TO HENRY DUNN]   *F[ebruar]y 9th. 1822*

Sir/—The pistols are come in as *bad* a state as before[1]—one of them still sticks at half *cock* as before—when you pull gently—and if you don't pull gently—it is useless to pretend to take an aim.———They are sent back—pray see to this.——

yrs.
BYRON

[TO DOUGLAS KINNAIRD]   *Pisa. F[ebruar]y 17th. 1822*

My dear Douglas/—I have long ago written to you (in 1818) that in case of mortality on ye. part of Lady Noel,[1] Sir Francis Burdett would be my selection as referee, and I request you with all respect to propose to him the office. If he declines (which I hope that he will not)—then Earl Grey.——The next business is my wish that you would *immediately insure Lady Byron's* life for me—for *ten thousand pounds*—or (if the expence seems too great to you) for *six thousand* pounds—that in case of her demise—as the *Marital* is only a *life* interest—there may be some provision to compensate for the diminution of income, and provide for my children—as you will observe that Lady B's daughter only takes in *default* of *male* issue by the Curzons and Shirleys. Do *not* neglect *this*; but act *immediately*;—I will either repay you in your own Circulars (all whilk arrived safely & welcomely) or you may deduct it from our next account. I shall be very uneasy till I hear that you have done this by next post—as otherwise—the whole prospect rests upon the respiration of her Ladyship & my children may be after all no great gainers.—

With regard to the settlement of the property,—I have named my referee, but I have no wish to press Sir Ralph or his offspring hard;—for example—the Mansion-house (which rests in abeyance for the Umpires

---

[1] See p. 75.
[1] Lady Noel, Lady Byron's mother, died on January 28, 1822, and news of it reached Byron on February 15. By terms of the separation settlement, the income from the Wentworth estates, which Lady Noel had inherited, estimated at £10,000 a year (but actually less than £7,000) was to be divided by arbitrators at Lady Noel's death, one to be appointed by each party.

in this boxing-match to award to time) is no object to me living abroad—and with no wish to return to your agreeable country.—I will wave any pretension to it—or take a moderate equivalent—whichever you think proper—I have no desire but to act as a Gentleman should do—without any real enmity, or affected generosity towards those who have not set me a very violent example of forbearance.—Enclosed are letters from Mr. Hanson (and another Solicitor) on some Rochdale business—by which it seems that I may obtain *two thousand* pounds more or less—for permission to the town to take toll for the new Market place.—I will accept whatever you and he deem fair & reasonable—or I will be as unreasonable as you please.—Will you request Sir Francis Burdett to accept my nomination—he knows Leicestershire—and he knows Lawyers—and he is a man of the loftiest talents and integrity, with whom I have lived a little & for whom I have the highest esteem.—Will not my address through you suffice—without my writing to him in person.——Believe me ever & very truly

yours most affectionately and (since it must be so)

NOEL BYRON[2]

[TO JOHN HANSON]   *Pisa. F[ebruar]y 17th. 1822*

My dear Sir—By this post I have written to Mr Douglas K[innair]d to name Sir Francis Burdett for my referee in the first instance—and Earl Grey in the event of Sir Francis's declining the nomination.—Sir Francis knows Leicestershire and the property—is a friend of mine—tolerably opinionated—and a man of talents and integrity.—I trust that he will accept the trust.—I have also requested Mr. Kinnaird to insure Lady Byron's life for me for ten thousand pounds—which is necessary on account of my having the life interest in *her* only.—Do not omit to urge this to him—I will pay him either by a deduction from my present Bankers account with the house of Ransom & Co.—or by the same from the first balance in my favour.—I have also stated to him the proposition for the Rochdale Market-tolls and request you and him to make the best bargain you can for me.—I should hope that my presence in England is not now requisite, as I could wish to have things settled & my remaining debts liquidated before re-visiting that country.—You will of course put my referee in possession of all the

[2] By terms of the will Byron was to take the Noel arms and he signed himself here for the first time "Noel Byron". He continued to use that signature, or the initials "N.B." for the rest of his life.

information and claims upon my part to a just portion of my right in the estate.—I am very glad to hear such good news of your family—and especially of your hopes of becoming a Grandfather again—a *young* one you are by the way. Believe me ever & very truly yours

NOEL BYRON

Send me out a Seal and directions about the *Noel* arms—and how I am to adopt or quarter them?

P.S.—You will of course have a proper statement in the papers to prevent mistakes—Send me licence.—I need not request you to write to me with report of progress.—Remember me to Charles and all your family.——

[TO COUNTESS TERESA GUICCIOLI]   [*After Feb. 17, 1822*]

A[mor] M[io]—Molto volontieri ma vieni *accompagnata* da Pierino o Papa.—

tutto tuo
N B

P.S.—Retirate il Cocchiere tuo—almeno per ora.

[TRANSLATION]   [*After Feb. 17, 1822*]

My Love—Very willingly, but come *accompanied* by Pierino or Papa.—

Completely yours,
N B

P.S.—Take back your coachman—at least for now.[1]

[TO DOUGLAS KINNAIRD]   *Pisa. Feb[ruar]y 19th. 1822*

My dear Douglas—By last post yr. letter was answered at some length;—I also wrote to Mr. Hanson—and to Sir Francis Burdett requesting the latter to accept my nomination of referee in the case of Wife versus Husband on the score of Monies to be divided.—I also pressed and press upon *you*, (my Attorno of power) that Ly. B's life must be forthwith ensured for ten thousand pounds—by which I can—(in case of accidents) pay my creditors—while if she lives, and I live—I will set aside a sum in proportion to my share of the carrion, to pay

---

[1] Translated by Ricki B. Herzfeld.

the crows who hover about it; in two, three, or more years. I will either reimburse to you the expence of insurance in your own circulars —or by such deduction from our next account—as may liquidate the same; whichever you please—but pray—*insure her* life;—I have so little confidence of any Good coming from such a quarter—that I have been rather deprest in spirit than otherwise since the intelligence that I had an enemy the less in this world.——By the same post I also transmitted to you a letter of Mr. Hanson upon some Rochdale *toll* business, from which there are Monies in prospect—*he* says *two* thousand pounds—but supposing it to be *one only*; or even *one hundred*; still—they be *monies*—and I have lived long enough to have an ⟨infinite⟩ exceeding respect for the smallest current coin of any realm) or the least sum which, though I may not want it myself, may at least do something for my children, or for others who may want it more than me.—

They say "Knowledge is power"—I used to think so, but they meant *"Money"*—who said so—& when Socrates declared "that all that he knew was that he knew nothing"—he merely intended to declare that he had not a drachma in the Athenian World.——The principal points for the consideration of my referee—besides those more technical ones (wherewithal Mr. Hanson should possess him) are —*firstly*—the large Settlement (Sixty thousand pounds, i.e. ten thousand pounds more than I was advised to make upon the Miss Milbanke)—made by me upon this female;—*secondly*—the comparative smallness of her then fortune—(twenty thousand pounds—and *that* never paid) when surely as a young man with an old title—of a fortune independent enough at that time (as Newstead would have made me had the purchaser kept to his bargain) with some name and fame in the world, I might have pretended to no worse a match than Miss Milbanke anywhere—and in England to a much better whether you take into the balance [:] fortune—person—or connection.—Thirdly—my leaving both her father Sir Ralph, and her Uncle Lord Wentworth (notwithstanding that I was again strongly advised to the contrary—) perfectly free to leave their property as they liked—instead of requiring a previous settlement upon her; —thereby showing (what was true) that I did not wed her for her expectations, and (for anything I know) I may be as much disappointed in them—as in any comfort which came with her.—

But—all this at *that* time—is surely not to operate *now* against me in the mind of my referee;—after I have been made the victim of this woman's family—and have been absolutely ruined in reputation, and anything but a gainer in Fortune by the match hitherto.—I certainly did by no means marry her for her fortune, but if, after having undergone what I have, "Fortune (like Honour) comes unlooked for;"—I feel by no means disposed to abandon my *just* claim to my just share;—at the same time neither desiring nor requiring more than is fair and honourable.—And so there is a short end to a long chapter.—Let me be answered by you [in] course of post.

yrs. ever & truly
NOEL BYRON

P.S.—I wrote to you some time before this date on Southey's business—(to call him out) which is not to be superseded by *this*, recollect; I shall be very willing to come to England to meet him—but I do not see any reason why I should go to be bored about the law business of the new dispute between my wife & her husband.— Recollect too that She has her father's fortune in complete reversion to herself—and that I have merely *her life* interest in her Uncle's.—— With regard to the Mansion house—I have as little wish to inhabit, as to dispute about it.—*That* may be either waved, or given up for a moderate equivalent, whichever my referee pleases to think properest. —If there be any *Church* patronage—*stickle* for it *obstinately*; I should like to prefer a Clergyman;—Also—I should like to know the appropriation of any timbers which are to be felled—& how *vested*—& whether I have any interest in the *interest* of the same. I think the Will directed such produce to be vested somewhere for some purpose or other—but what I forget.—

[TO THOMAS MOORE]   *Pisa, February 19th, 1822*

I am rather surprised not to have had an answer to my letter and packets. Lady Noel is dead, and it is not impossible that I may have to go to England to settle the division of the Wentworth property, and what portion Lady B. is to have out of it; all which was left undecided by the articles of separation. But I hope not, if it can be done without,— and I have written to Sir Francis Burdett to be my referee, as he knows the property.

Continue to address here, as I shall not go if I can avoid it—at least, not on that account. But I may on another; for I wrote to Douglas Kinnaird to convey a message of invitation to Mr. Southey to meet me, either in England, or (as less liable to interruption) on the coast of France. This was about a fortnight ago, and I have not yet had time to have the answer. However, you shall have due notice; therefore continue to address to Pisa.

My agents and trustees have written to me to desire that I would take the name directly so that I am,

Yours very truly and affectionately,
NOEL BYRON

P.S.—I have had no news from England, except on business; and merely know, from some abuse in that faithful *ex* and *de*-tractor Galignani, that the clergy are up against "Cain." There is (if I am not mistaken) some good church preferment on the Wentworth estates; and I will show them what a good Christian I am, by patronising and preferring the most pious of their order, should opportunity occur.

M[urray] and I are but little in correspondence, and I know nothing of literary matters at present. I have been writing on business only lately. What are *you* about? Be assured that there is no such coalition as you apprehend.[1]

[TO THOMAS MOORE]   *Pisa, February 20th, 1822*

Your letter arrived since I wrote the enclosed.[1] It is not likely, as I have appointed agents and arbitrators for the Noel estates, that I should proceed to England on that account,—though I may upon another, within stated. At any rate, *continue* you to address here till you hear further from me. I could wish *you* still to arrange for me, either with a London or Paris publisher, for the things, etc. I shall not quarrel with any arrangement you may please to make.

I have appointed Sir Francis Burdett my arbitrator to decide on Lady Byron's allowance out of the Noel estates, which are estimated at seven thousand a year, and *rents* very well paid,—a rare thing at this time. It is, however, owing to their *consisting* chiefly in pasture lands, and therefore less affected by corn bills, etc., than property in tillage.

Believe me yours ever most affectionately,
NOEL BYRON

Between my own property in the funds, and my wife's in land, I do not know which *side* to cry out on in politics.

[1] Moore had written that he had heard of Leigh Hunt's going to Italy to join Byron and Shelley in joint contributions to what he then believed to be *The Examiner*, and warned Byron that his reputation would suffer from such a collaboration.
[1] Byron's letter of Feb. 19 to Moore was enclosed in this.

There is nothing against the immortality of the soul in "Cain" that I recollect.[2] I hold no such opinions;—but, in a drama, the first rebel and the first murderer must be made to talk according to their characters. However, the parsons are all preaching at it, from Kentish Town and Oxford to Pisa,—the scoundrels of priests, who do more harm to religion than all the infidels that ever forgot their catechisms!

I have not seen Lady Noel's death announced in Galignani.—How is that?

[TO DOUGLAS KINNAIRD]   *Pisa. Feb[ruar]y 20th. 1822*

My dear Douglas/—You will be glad to find by my two preceding letters (& also by a third to Sir Francis himself) that I had anticipated your recommendation & appointed Sir Francis Burdett my arbitrator:— I enclose the nomination in form.—My instructions are already touched upon in my two letters to you.—They may be simplified as follows. —The possession of the Estates to be claimed for me—paying Lady Byron a proper annuity from the same.—Mr. Hanson has instructions to acquaint the Arbitrator with all points of information & interest on my behalf.—I have no objection to Sir Ralph occupying the Mansion house during his lifetime—but the *option* of occupying it after his demise—to *revert* to or remain with *me*—though it is not probable that I should disturb Lady B's residence there at any period.—In the event of the estates rising in value I should have no objection to in- creasing Lady B's allowance in proportion.——The Church prefer- ment—& manor to remain with me—or at least an *equal right* thereon. I wish to know too—about the felling of timber and vesting the monies arising from such—what is the proper course? or if there are any such?— I recollect hearing of something of the kind some years ago.——I wish my Arbitrator to see Mr. Hanson & to give him a fair *hearing* upon all points which he thinks proper to be stated—leaving of course to Sir Francis to give them what weight—he thinks proper.——I am not aware of more to be added at present.——I wrote to you about the Rochdale *toll*-business a few days ago—& I now enclose two other letters of Mr. Hanson—as a sort of memorandum on the Noel estate business—which I particularly recommend to your attention because his opinions upon it coincide with mine. If I see that what I consider my *rights* are properly adjusted—of course I may not think it unfair to increase Lady B's allowance—or to do what is handsome in all respects

[2] Writing of *Cain* Moore had protested against giving up the "*poetry* of religion" and the "dream of immortality".

111

in that & other matters.—Tell Burdett that if he makes me an adequate landholder I will come & have a touch for reform in the House with him —that is to say in the House of Peers.——I still think that you should get me out of the Funds.—With regard to the M.S.S I wrote some [time] ago—requesting you to get them from Murray—& to forward the whole—to Mr. Moore at Paris.—Remember me to Hobhouse and to all friends—& believe me ever & truly

yours
Noel Byron

P.S.—*Above all do not forget or omit to insure* Lady Byron's life for me for ten thousand pounds *immediately.*

[TO JOHN HANSON]   *Pisa. Fy. 20th. 1822*

Dear Sir/—I wrote to you two posts ago.—Sir Francis Burdett is my Arbitrator—at least I have enclosed the nomination by this post to Mr. Douglas Kinnaird—according to the form transmitted in your letter.—Sir Francis is my friend—an honest and able man—who knows Leicestershire and *lawyers* sufficiently to be no unfit match for Mr. Shadwell.—I prefer him as a Man of large property & consideration in the country—together with some interest in the county where the Noel estates are situated.——As my opinions coincide with yours upon that subject—I have written to Mr. Kinnaird to request that *you* may be consulted upon all the points of law &c. &c. and I now add to yourself my request that you will have an interview with Sir Francis (if he accepts the nomination) to put him in possession of all requisite points of interest and information.——As I believe I wrote to you at some length two posts ago—I shall only repeat that I leave to you to decide with Mr. K[innaird] what sum is to be taken for the Rochdale tolls &c. and to request you to re-iterate my desire to Mr. Kinnaird to *insure* Lady Byron's life for *ten* thousand pounds—that in case of accidents I may have some compensation, to enable me to leave that sum to my children, or dispose of it otherwise for their or my own advantage.——I have received the Noel pedigree—Has Mr. N. Curzon any male issue?—when I left England—he was unmarried.—— If the business can be settled without a journey to England—I should prefer it—and this I think it *may*—by your pressing upon the Arbitrator —what you have stated to me [.]

yours ever & very truly
Noel Byron

P.S.—Get the Crown license as soon as possible and convenient.—
My dispositions are very simple and succinct—viz. to claim possession
of the estates—making Lady Byron a fair allowance by way of Annuity.—I have no objection to Sir Ralph's occupying the house during
his life time—but *then* at his demise the *option* to remain with me
whether I will reside there or no.—All *Church* patronage—the *Manor*
&c. to remain with me—also I wish to know how monies for felling
timber &c. are to be vested & employed?

[TO DOUGLAS KINNAIRD (*a*)]   *Pisa. F[ebruar]y 23d, 1822*

My dear Douglas/—I have already answered yr. letters.—The
Circulars are arrived and circulating like the Vortices (or Vortex's) of
DesCartes.—Still I have a due care of the needful,—& keep*s* a look
out ahead. I have written to you three times since the announcement of
the change.——I refer you to my letters—(three in number) [,] to
Mr. Hanson's (which I have enclosed as they coincide with my own
opinions) [,] to my note to Sir Francis of request that he would be my
arbitrator—for my own thoughts upon the subject.——As my notions
upon the score of monies coincide with yours and all men's who have
lived to see that every guinea is a philosopher's stone—or at least his
touch-stone—you will doubt me the less when I pronounce my firm
belief that Cash is Virtue.——I have been endeavouring to square my
conduct to this maxim—which may account for my late anxieties upon
all topics of £.S.D.—And now I do again desire and entreat and
request you to ensure the Lady Byron's life (for me) for ten thousand
pounds—as the mere life interest in *her* life—renders this necessary—
at least for the first three years—till I can clear off all the remaining
demands.——And again—I do require you to extricate my own proper
property from the funds—in which I do not trust notwithstanding their
present Apparitions.——

Though a good many of your circulars will be come round again to
you—yet I cannot reproach myself with much expenditure as I have
lately drawn on account of the high exchange.—My only extra
expence (and it is more than I have spent upon myself) is a loan to
Leigh Hunt of two hundred & fifty pounds—and fifty pounds worth of
furniture I have bought for him—and a boat which I am building for
myself at Genoa—which will cost a hundred or more.——With
regard to L. Hunt—he stuck by me through thick & thin—when all
shook, and some shuffled in 1816.—He never asked me for a loan till
now.—I am very willing to accommodate a man to whom I have

obligations.—He is now at Plymouth—waiting for a ship to sail for Italy.——But to return—I am determined to have all the monies I can—whether by my own funds or succession—or lawsuit—or wife—or M.S.S. or any lawful means whatsoever.——I will pay (though with the sincerest reluctance) my remaining creditors & my man of Law, by installments from the award of the Arbitrators or from the ten thousand £ to be insured on her Ladyship's vitality—in case that I should survive her.—I recommend to you the notice in one of Mr. Hanson's letters on the demand of monies for the Rochdale tolls of Market.——And above all I recommend my interest to Sir Francis B[u]r[de]tt and to your honourable Worship——Recollect too that I expect some monies for the various M.S.S. (no matter what) and in short—"Rem—quocunque modo *Rem.*"¹ the noble feeling of cupidity grows upon us with our years—believe me

yrs. ever & truly
NOEL BYRON

[TO DOUGLAS KINNAIRD (*b*)]   [*Feb. 23, 1822?*]¹

P.S.—I give you "Carte Blanche" in Southey's business.—If you agree with me that he ought to be called to account—I beg you to convey my invitation to meet when & where he may appoint—to settle this with him & his friend—and to let me know in as few posts as possible—that I may join you.——This will (or ought) to prevent unnecessary delay.——I wish to observe that if I come to England with this object *before* my message is delivered and the preliminaries fixed, my arrival would transpire in the interim of the arrangement—whereas if all is settled before hand—we may bring the affair to a decision on the day of my landing.—Better on the coast of France—as less liable to interruption or publicity—but I presume Mr. S. is too great a patriot to come off the soil for such a proposal.—The grounds are, that after the language he has both used and provoked—this is the only honourable way of deciding the business.——I enclose your credentials in a note to Mr. Southey.²——I require satisfaction for his

¹ Horace, *Epistles* I, i, 65–66 "Rem, facias rem; Si possis recte, si non, quocunque modo rem" ("Get money, get money; honestly if you can, if not, by any means get money.")

¹ This postscript probably belongs to the preceding letter. Byron has written on the cover "1822 Pisa Feby 23," and the post mark indicating the time of its arrival in England is March 11.

² This is the note dated Feb. 7, 1822 addressed to Southey, which Byron apparently held for two weeks before sending it to Kinnaird.

expressions in his letter in the Newspapers,—that will be the tenor of the Message—as you are well aware.—Of course you will suspend the publication of "the Vision" till we know whether the business can be settled in a more proper manner.——

[TO JOHN HANSON]   *Pisa. Fy. 27th. 1822*

Dear Sir/—I had already named Sir Francis Burdett before I received Mr. K[innair]d's suggestion.—It was my own choice, years ago. —I have great confidence in his uprightness—his integrity—& his personal regard for me.—He also knows the property—from being much in Leicestershire.—I am glad that *they too* will name a man not in the profession of the law—as it is less liable [to ob- ?]jection on their *own* account & more amicable & open, & not as if we were seeking out for matters of cavil & lawsuit.—I refer you to my answers to your letters (three in number) by last three posts—but I request you to press upon Mr. K[innair]d my request that he would immediately *insure* Lady Byron's *life* for me—for *ten* thousand pounds—since I have only a life interest in the property.—If ten thousand be too costly (which it hardly can as far as I recollect) then say for *eight* or *six* thousand pounds but *no lower.*—Do not omit this I request you earnestly.—I am glad to hear good news of your family and of yourself always.—Send me a Seal with the new arms—& a smaller one with the Coronet and initials of *N B* upon it for notes &c. &c. Believe me

yours ever & truly
NOEL BYRON

[TO THOMAS MOORE]   *Pisa, February 28th, 1822*

I begin to think that the packet (a heavy one) of five acts of "Werner," &c., can hardly have reached you, for your letter of last week (which I answered) did not allude to it, and yet I insured it at the post-office here.

I have no direct news from England, except on the Noel business, which is proceeding quietly, as I have appointed a gentleman (Sir F. Burdett) for my arbitrator. They, too, have said that they will recall the *lawyer* whom *they* had chosen, and will name a gentleman too. This is better, as the arrangement of the estates and of Lady B.'s allowance will thus be settled without quibbling. My lawyers are taking out a licence for the name and arms, which it seems I am to endue.

By another, and indirect, quarter, I hear that "Cain" has been pirated, and that the Chancellor has refused to give Murray any redress. Also, that G. R. (*your* friend "Ben")[1] has expressed great personal indignation at the said poem. All this is curious enough, I think,—after allowing Priestley, Hume, and Gibbon, and Bolingbroke, and Voltaire to be published, without depriving the booksellers of their rights. I heard from Rome a day or two ago, and, with what truth I know not, that * * *.

Yours, etc.

[TO ?] *F[ebruar]y [29th.?] 1822*

Sir/—Will you excuse my not waiting upon you—I am only just up —unshaved & in my dressing gown—but I will see you at two if not inconvenient to you.—The Bills of mine are *Ransom's*—late partners with Morland—and therefore I am not aware whether it would be the same to Mr. Webb to negociate them.—But I am obliged to Mr. W's civility—and regret the trouble.—

yr. obedt. Sert.
BYRON

[TO F.C. ARMSTRONG][1] *[March, 1822]*

Sir,—I have to acknowledge the honour of your letter.—It would have given me pleasure to have treated with you for your yacht—but I have already had one built at Genoa—under the direction of Capt. Wright and Capt. Roberts R. N. who have had the goodness to super-intend her progress.—This renders any further trouble to you—Sir, unnecessary—but I am not the less obliged by your offer—and have the honour to be

your very obedt. humble Servt.
NOEL BYRON

[TO THOMAS MOORE] *Pisa, March 1st, 1822*

As I still have no news of my "Werner,"[1] etc., packet, sent to you on the 29th of January, I continue to bore you (for the fifth time, I believe)

[1] Byron refers to Moore's "Epistle from Tom Crib to Big Ben", regarding the Regent's ignoble role in the transportation of Napoleon to St. Helena. In the poem the Regent (later George IV) is Big Ben who treads on a man who is down.

[1] Unidentified.

[1] Byron had sent his drama *Werner* to Moore in Paris in the hope that he could find a publisher for it there. He was then dissatisfied with Murray as a publisher,

to know whether it has *not* miscarried. As it was fairly copied out, it will be vexatious if it be lost. Indeed, I insured it at the post-office to make them take more care, and directed it regularly to you at Paris.

In the impartial Galignani I perceive an extract from Blackwood's Magazine,[2] in which it is said that there are people who have discovered that you and I are no poets. With regard to one of us, I know that this north-west passage to *my* magnetic pole had been long discovered by some sages, and I leave them the full benefit of their penetration. I think, as Gibbon says of his History, "that perhaps, a hundred years hence it may still continue to be abused." However, I am far from pretending to compete or compare with that illustrious literary character.

But, with regard to *you*, I thought that you had always been allowed to be *a poet*, even by the stupid as well as the envious—a bad one, to be sure—immoral, florid, Asiatic, and diabolically popular,—but still always a poet, *nem. con.* This discovery, therefore, has to me all the grace of novelty, as well as of consolation (according to Rochefoucault), to find myself *no*-poetised in such good company. I am content to "err with Plato;"[3] and can assure you very sincerely, that I would rather be received a *non*-poet with you, than be crowned with all the bays of the (*yet*-uncrowned) Lakers in their society. I believe you think better of these worthies than I do. I know them. * * * * * * * * * * * * *

As for Southey, the answer to my proposition of a meeting is not yet come. I sent the message, with a short note, to him through Douglas Kinnaird, and Douglas's response is not arrived. If he accepts, I shall have to go to England; but if not, I do not think the Noel affairs will take me there, as the arbitrators can settle them without my presence, and there do not seem to be any difficulties. The license for the new name and armorial bearings will be taken out by the regular application, in such cases, to the Crown, and sent to me.

Is there a hope of seeing you in Italy again ever? What are you doing?—*bored* by me, I know; but I have explained *why* before. I have no correspondence now with London, except through relations and lawyers and one or two friends. My greatest friend, Lord Clare, is at

---

but soon after a letter from Murray "melted" him and he asked Moore to send the manuscript to his London publisher. It appeared on November 23, 1822, the last of Byron's works to be published by Murray.

[2] An article on Moore's *Irish Melodies* in *Blackwood's Edinburgh Magazine* (Jan. 1822, pp. 62–67) belittled Byron along with Moore, saying of the former that he had "gutted himself, body and soul, for all the world to walk in and see the show".

[3] Cicero, *Tusculanae Disputationes* 1, XVII, 39: "Errare, mehercule, malo cum Platone."

Rome: we met on the road, and our meeting was quite sentimental—
really pathetic on both sides.[4] I have always loved him better than any
male thing in the world.

[TO THOMAS MOORE]   *Pisa, March 4th, 1822*

Since I wrote the enclosed,[1] I have waited another post, and now
have your answer acknowledging the arrival of the packet—a troublesome one, I fear, to you in more ways than one, both from weight
external and internal.

The unpublished things in your hands, in Douglas K.'s, and Mr.
John Murray's, are "Heaven and Earth, a lyrical kind of Drama upon
the Deluge, etc."; "Werner," *now with you*;—a translation of the
First Canto of the Morgante Maggiore;—*ditto* of an Episode in Dante;
—some stanzas to the Po, June 1st, 1819;—Hints from Horace,
written in 1811, but a good deal, *since*, to be omitted; several prose
things, which may, perhaps, as well remain unpublished;—"The
Vision, &c., of Quevedo Redivivus," in verse.

Here you see is "more matter for a May morning;"[2] but how much
of this can be published is for consideration. The Quevedo (one of my
best in that line) has appalled the Row already, and must take its
chance at Paris, if at all. The new Mystery is less speculative than
"Cain," and very pious; besides, it is chiefly lyrical. The Morgante is
the *best* translation that ever was or will be made; and the rest are—
whatever you please to think them.

I am sorry you think Werner even *approaching* to any fitness for the
stage, which, with my notions upon it, is very far from my present
object. With regard to the publication, I have already explained that
I have no exorbitant expectations of either fame or profit in the present
instances; but wish them published because they are written, which is
the common feeling of all scribblers.

With respect to "Religion," can I never convince you that *I* have
no such opinions as the characters in that drama, which seems to have
frightened every body? Yet *they* are nothing to the expressions in
Goethe's Faust (which are ten times hardier), and not a whit more
bold than those of Milton's Satan. My ideas of a character may run
away with me: like all imaginative men, I, of course, embody myself

---

[4] See "Detached Thoughts", numbers 91 and 113.
[1] The previous letter (March 1) to Moore.
[2] *Twelfth Night*, Act. III, scene 4.

with the character while I *draw* it, but not a moment after the pen is from off the paper.

I am no enemy to religion, but the contrary. As a proof, I am educating my natural daughter a strict Catholic in a convent of Romagna; for I think people can never have *enough* of religion, if they are to have any. I incline, myself, very much to the Catholic doctrines; but if I am to write a drama, I must make my characters speak as I conceive them likely to argue.

As to poor Shelley,[3] who is another bugbear to you and the world, he is, to my knowledge, the *least* selfish and the mildest of men—a man who has made more sacrifices of his fortune and feelings for others than any I ever heard of. With his speculative opinions I have nothing in common, nor desire to have.

The truth is, my dear Moore, you live near the *stove* of society, where you are unavoidably influenced by its heat and its vapours. I did so once—and too much—and enough to give a colour to my whole future existence. As my success in society was *not* inconsiderable, I am surely not a prejudiced judge upon the subject, unless in its favour; but I think it, as now constituted, *fatal* to all great original undertakings of every kind. I never courted it *then*, when I was young and high in blood, and one of its "curled darlings;"[4] and do you think I would do so *now*, when I am living in a clearer atmosphere? One thing *only* might lead me back to it, and that is, to try once more if I could do any good in *politics*; but *not* in the petty politics I see now preying upon our miserable country.

Do not let me be misunderstood, however. If you speak your *own* opinions, they ever had, and will have, the greatest weight with *me*. But if you merely *echo* the "monde", (and it is difficult not to do so, being in its favour and its ferment,) I can only regret that you should ever repeat any thing to which I cannot pay attention.

But I am prosing. The gods go with you, and as much immortality of all kinds as may suit your present and all other existence.

Yours, &c.

---

[3] Byron apparently read to Shelley some of Moore's letters, including one in which he deprecated Shelley's influence on Byron's views, especially in *Cain*. Shelley wrote to Horace Smith on April 11, 1822: "Pray assure him [Moore] that I have not the smallest influence over Lord Byron, in this particular, and if I had, I certainly should employ it to eradicate from his great mind the delusions of Christianity, which, in spite of his reason, seem perpetually to recur . . . ."

[4] *Othello*, Act I, scene 2.

My dearest Augusta/—I write two words to acknowledge your letter.—I certainly felt a good deal surprized that *you* did not write immediately to announce that event[1]———but it was probably for some good *nursery* reason—that you did not.—I regret the pain which the privation must occasion to Sir R[alph] N[oel] & to Ly. B[yron]—but I shall not pretend to any violent grief for one with whom my acquaintance was neither long nor agreeable.—Still I bear her memory no malice.———I am a little affronted that Georgy should not write—it is proper that my nephews & nieces should cultivate some acquaintance with me—otherwise the interest I feel for them may diminish unavoidably from total estrangement. It has ever been my object (if I live long enough) to provide as far as I can for your children—as my daughter by Ly. B is rich enough already—& my natural daughter also will have a decent provision. I shall try what I can to save or accumulate some funds for this purpose (if Fortune be favourable) and should therefore like to *hear* now & then from my *"residee legatoos"* as I am not likely to *see* much of them for the present.—If it should seem odd that I do not prefer my *own* family—I think there are some reasons which will suggest themselves to you however—as it is quite impossible that any thing which reminds me of that unhappy connection with Ly. B's family—can excite the same *unmixed* feeling which exists where there are no divisions.

yrs. ever & truly
NOEL BYRON

The enclosed letter from Murray hath melted me; though I think it is against his own interest to wish that I should continue his connexion. You may, therefore, send him the packet of "Werner," which will save you all further trouble. And pray, *can you* forgive me for the bore and expense I have already put upon you? At least, *say* so—for I feel ashamed of having given you so much for such nonsense.

The fact is, I cannot *keep* my *resentments*, though violent enough in their onset. Besides, now that all the world are *at* Murray on my account, I neither can nor ought to leave him; unless, as I really thought, it were better for *him* that I should.

I have had no other news from England, except a letter from Barry

---

[1] The death of Lady Noel, Lady Byron's mother.

Cornwall,[1] the bard, and my old school-fellow. Though I have sickened you with letters lately, believe me.

Yours, &c.

P.S.—In your last letter you say, speaking of Shelley, that you would almost prefer the "damning bigot" to the "annihilating infidel." Shelley believes in immortality, however—but this by the way. Do you remember Frederick the Great's answer to the remonstrance of the villagers whose curate preached against the eternity of hell's torments? It was thus:—"If my faithful subjects of Schrausenhaussen prefer being eternally damned, let them."[2]

Of the two, I should think the long sleep better than the agonised vigil. But men, miserable as they are, cling so to any thing *like* life, that they probably would prefer damnation to quiet. Besides, they think themselves so *important* in the creation, that nothing less can satisfy their pride—the insects!

[TO JOHN MURRAY]   *Pisa. March 6th. 1822*

My dear Sir/—I have got your letter of ye. 19th. F[ebruar]y. You will have long ago received a letter from me (or should) declaring my opinion of the treatment *you* have met with about the recent publication. —I think it disgraceful to those who have persecuted you.——I make peace with you—though our war was for other reasons—than this same controversy.——I have written to Moore by this post to forward to you the tragedy of "Werner", which I sent to him to transmit to another publisher.——I shall not make or propose any present bargain about it or the new Mystery[1] till we see if they succeed.—If they don't sell—(which is not unlikely) you shan't pay—and I suppose this is fair play—if you choose to risk it.——Bartolini the celebrated Sculptor[2] wrote to me to desire to take my bust—I consented on condi-

---

[1] The pseudonym of Bryan Waller Proctor.

[2] Frederick the Great wrote to the Electress Marie-Antoine on May 3, 1768: "Not even the little Town of Neufchâtel but has had its troubles . . . A Parson there had set forth in a sermon, that considering the immense mercy of God, the pains of Hell could not last forever. The Synod shouted murder at such scandal." Frederick said he settled the matter by decreeing: "Let the parsons, who make for themselves a cruel and barbarous God, be eternally damned, as they desire, and deserve; and let those parsons, who conceive God gentle and merciful, enjoy the plenitude of his mercy!" (Carlyle, *Frederick the Great*, Book XII, chap. 4).

[1] *Heaven and Earth.*

[2] The Italian sculptor Lorenzo Bartolini had written to Byron shortly after the poet's arrival in Pisa, and Byron commissioned him to make busts of himself and Teresa. When Edward Williams called on him on Jan. 3, 1822, Byron was sitting to Bartolini.

tion that he also took that of the Countess Guiccioli.—He has taken both—& I think it will be allowed that *Her's* is beautiful.—I shall make you a present of them both to show you that I don't bear malice—and as a compensation for the trouble and squabble you had about Thorwaldsen's.[3]——Of my own I can hardly speak, except that it is thought very like what I *now am*—which is different from what I was of course, since you saw me.—The Sculptor is a famous one & as it was done by *his own* particular request will be done well probably.——What is to be done about Taaffe and his Commentary? He will die,—if he is *not* published—he will be damned if he *is*—but that *he* don't mind. ⟨You⟩ We must publish him.—All the *row* about *me* has no otherwise affected me than by the attack upon yourself—which is ungenerous in Church & State. But as all violence must in time have it's proportionate reaction—you will do better by & bye.

yrs. very truly
NOEL BYRON

Apply to Mr. Douglas Kin[nair]d for the proofs of the new Mystery.

[TO THOMAS MOORE]   *Pisa, March 8th, 1822*

You will have had enough of my letters by this time—yet one word in answer to your present missive. You are quite wrong in thinking that your "advice" had offended me;[1] but I have already replied (if not answered) on that point.

With regard to Murray as I really am the meekest and mildest of men since Moses (though the public and mine "excellent wife" cannot find it out), I had already pacified myself and subsided back to Albemarle-street, as my yesterday's *ye*pistle will have informed you. But I thought that I had explained my causes of bile—at least to you. Some instances of vacillation, occasional neglect, and troublesome sincerity, real or imagined, are sufficient to put your truly great author and man into a passion. But reflection, with some aid from hellebore, hath already cured me "pro tempore", and, if it had not, a request from you and Hobhouse would have come upon me like two out of the "tribus Anticyris,"[2]—with which, however, Horace despairs of purging a

---

[3] A misunderstanding caused Murray to think that the bust by Thorwaldsen was intended for him instead of Hobhouse.

[1] Moore's advice to avoid religious scepticism and the influence of Shelley.

[2] Horace, *Ars Poetica*, line 300: "For oh! he shines a bard confessed, be sure,/ Whose poll (which three Anticyras could not cure)/To barber Licinus was ne'er consigned!"

poet. I really feel ashamed of having bored you so frequently and fully of late. But what could I do? You are a friend—an absent one, alas!—and as I trust no one more, I trouble you in proportion.

This war of "Church and State" has astonished me more than it disturbs; for I really thought "Cain" a speculative and hardy, but still a harmless production. As I said before, I am really a great admirer of tangible religion; and am breeding one of my daughters a Catholic, that she may have her hands full. It is by far the most elegant worship, hardly excepting the Greek mythology. What with incense, pictures, statues, altars, shrines, relics, and the real presence, confession, absolution,—there is something sensible to grasp at. Besides, it leaves no possibility of doubt; for those who swallow their Deity, really and truly, in transubstantiation, can hardly find any thing else otherwise than easy of digestion.

I am afraid that this sounds flippant, but I don't mean it to be so; only my turn of mind is so given to taking things in the absurd point of view, that it breaks out in spite of me every now and then. Still, I do assure you that I am a very good Christian. Whether you will believe me in this, I do not know; but I trust you will take my word for being

Very truly and affectionately yours, &c.

P.S.—Do tell Murray that one of the conditions of peace is, that he publisheth (or obtaineth a publisher for * * * [Taaffe]'s Commentary on Dante, against which there appears in the trade an unaccountable repugnance. It will make the man so exuberantly happy. He dines with me and half-a-dozen English to-day; and I have not the heart to tell him how the bibliopolar world shrink from his Commentary;—and yet it is full of the most orthodox religion and morality. In short, I made it a point that he shall be in print. He is such a good-natured, heavy * * Christian, that we must give him a shove through the press. He naturally thirsts to be an author, and has been the happiest of men for these two months, printing, correcting, collating, dating, anticipating, and adding to his treasures of learning. Besides, he has had another fall from his horse into a ditch the other day, while riding out with me into the country.

[TO JOHN CAM HOBHOUSE]   *Pisa. March 9th. 1822*

My dear Hobhouse/—"If I am of age let me have my fortin"[1]—why did you not write to me before?—Now that the old Lady is gone—I

---

[1] Goldsmith, *She Stoops to Conquer*, Act II: Tony Lumpkin: "If I'm a man let me have my fortin'."

123

forgive her memory which is perhaps more than she would have done by mine.—I had already forgiven Murray before I received your epistle—so that I cannot assume the merit of complying with your request.——I dare say you are quite right—and it seems that you were not far wrong about that 'ere "Cain"—which must be a Rochfoucault [sic] consolation for you.—I will however make one remark which is that your letter gave me far more pain—than all this outcry—which has had no great effect, at least, upon myself.—My wrath with Murray arose from previous considerations long before the publication of the plays,—but—as I have graciously accorded a pardon to my own Interest, you may be spared the recapitulation of an author's irritabilities,——To Douglas K[innair]d I have written various letters on business—also to Spooney [Hanson]—also to Sir Francis Burdett—asking him to arbitrate on my behoof and behalf.——I also wish to press upon Douglas K[innair]d *two* things—the one—to insure Lady B's life for me for *ten* thousand pounds—(as I partake only her life interest in the property) in case of accident—for the first two or three years,—& the other to extricate my *own* property from the *fundivorous* speculation of the three per Cents Consols.——For nearly three years have I been urging him to this—but my Potestas of Attorno—is somewhat despotic—and rather governs than obeys.—Also have I written upon various questions to the Attorno Spooney who is busy of course with the prospect of a Succession to his Client—and consequently an increase of the "fee"—for which Lawyer Scout[2] himself had not a greater respect,—than Solicitor H[anson].——

The papers tell me your "whereabouts" in politics—and also give a "sheet of speech" occasionally of you & your yoke-fellow. I am all for the Agricultural interest now that I am likely to have the land of other people—at least during their life time.—I highly approve of the Ministerial measures however though I don't understand them.—Still like the Bailiff in "Amelia"[3] I love liberty, though I must say with the Butler in the Vicar of Wakefield—that you seem to be taking kindly to the "saddles of wooden shoes"[4] of which Ld. Londonderry appears to be the national Hoby.[5]—How very odd that you should all be governed by a man who can neither think nor speak English.[6] "Did I ever! no! I

[2] Fielding, *Joseph Andrews*, Book IV, chap. 3.

[3] In Fielding's humanitarian-sentimental novel, *Amelia*.

[4] *Vicar of Wakefield*, Chap. 19: "What, give up liberty, property, and as the Gazette says, lie down to be saddled with wooden shoes".

[5] Hoby was a fashionable London bootmaker.

[6] Robert Stewart, Viscount Castlereagh (he became the 2nd. Marquess of Londonderry in 1821), was British Foreign Secretary in the Tory government

never" &c. &c.—My head aches considerably from a Symposium of yesterday—which closed with a Midnight of rather more Brantwein— and water—than ⟨elements of which are in a⟩ agrees with me this morning.—But in general I am temperate—taking only a pint of light Clary wines at my *one* meal.—Go on and prosper,

yrs. ever & truly affect[ionat]e

NOEL BYRON

[TO JOHN MURRAY]   *Pisa. March 15th. 1822*

Dear Sir/—I am glad that you and your friends approve of my letter of the 8th. Ult.o[1]—you may give it what publicity you think proper in the circumstances.—I have since written to you twice or thrice.——Besides the M.S.S. you are aware of another in your own possession or Mr. D. Kinnaird's—there is a drama in five acts now in the care of Mr. Moore which he will forward.—I think of publishing it & the new Mystery in one volume—the "Vision of Judgement" anonymously and *secretly*—as *it* will be *pirated* of course & remedy refused according to law and lawyers.—Also the Pulci in the same way.—The translation from Dante and the lines to the Po may be published with the Mystery and Tragedy.—For all or any of these it may be as well to make no positive agreement till you can pronounce upon their success or other-wise after publication.——As to "a poem in the old way to interest the women"—as you call it; I shall attempt of that kind nothing further.— I follow the bias of my own mind without considering whether women or men are or are not to be pleased.—But this is nothing to my publisher —who must judge and act according to popularity.—Therefore let the things take their chance—if *they pay* you will pay me in proportion— and if they don't—I must.

The Noel affairs I hope will *not* take me to England—I have no desire to revisit that country—unless it be to keep you out of a prison— (if this can be effected by my taking your place) or perhaps to get my-self into one by exacting satisfaction from one or two persons who take advantage of my absence to abuse me.——Further than this—I have

---

from 1812 to 1822. He was an enemy to all liberal movements in England and abroad. Byron wrote harshly of him on many occasions, as for example in the Dedi-cation to *Don Juan*, and in the Preface to Cantos VI, VII, and VIII. In the latter he said: "It is the first time indeed since the Normans that England has been insulted by a *minister* (at least) who could not speak English, and that Parliament permitted itself to be dictated to in the language of Mrs. Malaprop."

[1] The letter in which Byron protested against the unfairness of attacks on Murray for publishing *Cain*.

no business nor connection with England nor desire to have *out* of my own family & friends—to whom I wish all prosperity[.] Indeed I have lived upon the whole so little in England—(about five years [since] I was one and twenty) that my habits are too continental, and your climate would please me as little as the Society.—I saw the Chancellor's report in a French paper.—Pray why don't they prosecute the translation of *Lucretius* or the original with it's

"Primus in orbe Deos fecit Timor."[2]

or

"Tantum Religio potuit suadere Malorum."[3]—

I have only seen one review of the book and that was in Galignani's magazine quoted from the Monthly.—It was very favourable to the plays—as Compositions.——You must really get something done for Mr. Taaffe's Commentary.—What can I say to him?

yrs. ever & truly
NOEL BYRON

[TO W. H. REINGAMUN?]   *Pisa. March 20th. 1822*

Sir/—Signor [Balatreri?] has misunderstood me—I did not require the tickets for *all* the Classes (4 being already drawn) but for those classes which *remain to be drawn.*—Upon those conditions viz—for the *remaining* classes I am content to take the tickets you have sent to me.—Have you received the money for the [*Wocroll?*] and [*Marlbrighetto?*] tickets?—*I* have paid Sr. Balatreri & desired him to honour your draft.—Please to draw on him for the balance of the Frankfort tickets.—I enclose as you desire the 30 F[ranc]s prize ticket, and have the honour to be your very obedt. & obliged humble St.

NOEL BYRON
Pair d'Angleterre

[TO JOHN HANSON]   *Pisa. March 22d. 1822*

Dear Sir/—I greatly approve of the steps you have taken as indicated in your various letters—*all* of which I have reason to think have been received safely.—I have written to you about three or four times but do not precisely recollect the number.—You [are] too sanguine about

---

[2] Statius, *Thebais*, iii, 661: "It was fear first created gods in the world."

[3] Lucretius, *De Rerum Natura*, I, 101: "So potent was religion in persuading to evil deeds."

126

Deardon & the Rochdale affairs—I doubt.—The decision in the Exchequer extinguished any further hopes on that point—for the Chancellor is no friend of mine and may probably decide according to his feelings.—As to the tolls you will I presume make the best bargain we can.—Press the *points* you mention of the "Mansion &c." on the mind of the Arbitrator.——I regret what you say of the "Portrait" &c. &c.[1]—as some steps must be taken to prevent the Child's mind from being prejudiced against her father—and I beg of you to inform me what can *legally* be done to direct her education so as to prevent her being brought up in a hostile state towards me.[2]——I have no wish to pretend to educate her *myself* as she is a *daughter*—but if her mother's friends are to instil hostile feelings into her head—the Chancellor must be called upon to name a proper third person or Guardian to have her properly educated by.—Let me hear from you soon.

yrs. ever & truly
NOEL BYRON

P.S.—Would not Deardon think you come to some terms without going through with the Appeal?

P.S. 2d.—I am told that there are some erroneous paragraphs on the subject of the Noel business in the papers; I trust that you will cause such to be corrected and my right in the settlement truly stated.

[TO DOUGLAS KINNAIRD]   *Pisa. March 22d. 1822*

My dear Douglas/—I presume to hope that by this time you will have ensured Lady B's life "absolutely" without waiting for further advices from myself.—I enclose you two letters from Hanson—to which I pray your attention & consideration as far [as] you think that he gives sound Counsel.—I regret this portrait whim of Lady Noel's because it *shows* a posthumous protraction of no very good feelings on her part.—You must advise Dr. Lushington & Ly. B. from me that I came to this discussion of interests with every conciliatory disposition to settle things amicably—as far as the *Separation* would allow—but that I will *not* wittingly have my daughter prejudiced against her

[1] When Lady Noel's will was proved at Doctor's Commons on Feb. 22, 1822, Hanson learned that she left to the Trustees a portrait of Byron with directions that it was not to be shown to his daughter Ada until she was twenty-one, and then only with her mother's consent if Lady Byron was still alive.

[2] Ada did not see her father's handwriting until she was grown up and married, when she called at John Murray's and was given the manuscript of one of his poems (*Beppo*). (*LBC*, II, 219.)

father.—We must have something about her settled in Chancery—or I must have an assurance from their part—that her Mind is not to be biassed against me. I must also stipulate that Mrs. Clermont is *not* to be about her person.[1]——If these points are not accorded I must come to England & bring the matter before a Court of law—as far as regards her education and my paternal rights to direct it.—I have *otherwise* no wish to remove her from the mother.—

yrs. ever & truly
NOEL BYRON

P.S.—I hear of some erroneous paragraphs in the foreign papers (taken from the English) on the Noel business.—I trust that you will see all such corrected. It is more honourable for all parties that the real [temper?] of the settlement should be fully comprehended and explained. I also recommend to your consideration what Mr. Hanson says of "the Mansion" &c.——Would not Deardon (think you?) come to some arrangement about Rochdale without going through with the Appeal?—Still it ought to go *on* in the interim.—*not* to lose time—if he refuses an arbitration.——*The Funds*! *The Funds*! The Funds!

[TO JOHN HAY] *March 25th. 1822*

My dear Hay/—We are just returned from riding—well armed of course—as the wounded man[1] was a favourite bully of the Students and soldiers.—No interruption has yet been experienced.—I am sorry for the fellow—& should have been wretched but for the gross and murderous provocation he had given—but people are not to be cut down unarmed without some retaliation.—He is said to be in danger but with what truth in this country of fiction it is not easy to discover.— —I trust that you will only suffer a temporary inconvenience from this assassination. [sentence crossed out] What are the books you want—I did not know that you were visible or I should have called upon you.—

yrs. truly
N B

[1] Mary Anne Clermont, the maid and confidant of Lady Noel, who, Byron believed, was largely responsible for his wife's hard intransigence during the separation proceedings.

[1] Sergeant-Major Stefani Masi of the Tuscan Royal Light Horse had jostled Byron and his companions during their ride out of Pisa on March 24, and in the altercation that followed Shelley and John Hay were slightly wounded and Masi was severely but not mortally stabbed. The story of the complicated affray is told in detail by C. L. Cline in *Byron, Shelley and their Pisan Circle*, Chapter 6.

[TO JOHN TAAFFE]   *March 26th. 1822*

Dear Taaffe/—I write a word of [in?] haste in answer let me know
the truth as soon as possible—[1]

                                                    yrs. truly &c.
                                                          N B

[TO E. J. DAWKINS (*a*)][1]   *Pisa, March 27, 1822*

Sir,—I take the liberty of transmitting to you the statements, as
delivered to the police, of an extraordinary affair which occurred here
on Sunday last. This will not, it is to be hoped, be considered an in-
trusion, as several British subjects have been insulted and some wounded
on the occasion, besides being arrested at the gate of the city without
proper authority or reasonable cause.

With regard to the subsequent immediate occurrence of the aggressor's wound, there is little that I can add to the enclosed statements.
The testimony of an impartial eye-witness, Dr. Crawford, with whom
I had not the honour of a personal acquaintance, will inform you as much
as I know myself.

It is proper to add that I conceived the man to have been an officer, as
he was well dressed, with scaled epaulettes, and not ill-mounted, and
not a serjeant-major (the son of a washerwoman, it is said) as he turns
out to be.

When I accosted him a second time, on the Lung' Arno, he called
out to me with a menacing gesture, "Are you content?" I (still ignorant
of what had passed under the gateway, having ridden through the
guard to order my steward to go to the police) answered. "No; I want
your name and address." He then held out his hand, which I took, not
understanding whether he intended it as a pledge of his hostility or of
his repentence, at the same time stating his name.

The rest of the facts appear to have been as within stated, as far as my
knowledge goes. Two of my servants (both Italians) are detained on
suspicion of having wounded him. Of this I know no more than the
enclosed papers vouch, and can only say that, notwithstanding the

[1] The members of Byron's Pisan circle were annoyed with Taaffe because he was
reluctant to give a deposition in the Masi affair, although he was the one jostled
by the sergeant. He feared getting into trouble with the authorities, for he had
friends in high places in Tuscan society.
[1] Dawkins was the British *Chargé d'Affaires* at Florence, to whom Byron sent
copies of the depositions on the Masi affair, hoping that he would use his influence
to present the case of his English compatriots to the Tuscan authorities, and also
prevent false reports from getting back to England.

atrocious aggression (of the particulars of which I was at the moment ignorant), the act was as completely disapproved of by me as it was totally unauthorized, either directly or indirectly.

It neither is nor has been my wish to prevent or evade the fullest investigation of the business; had it been so, it would have been easy to have either left the place myself or to have removed any suspected person from it, the police having taken no steps whatever till this afternoon—three days after the fact.

I have the honour, etc.
NOEL BYRON

[TO EDWARD DAWKINS? (*b*)]   [*March 27? 1822*]

[At top of letter of Taaffe to Byron, reporting that Masi's wound was not serious.]

It is proper to observe that the following note proved incorrect the man being *dangerously* wounded (and still said to be so) but this does not alter his previous behaviour.

N B

[TO DOUGLAS KINNAIRD]   *Pisa. March 28th. 1822*

Dear K/—To prevent misstatements I send you authentic copies of some circumstances which occurred on Sunday last.——You can use them according to the circumstances related by others; if there is anything stated incorrectly in the papers these will serve to rectify them by.—You must get them translated by a very careful hand.——They are the same papers directed to the Government here & our Ambassador at Florence. The Aggressor is dangerously wounded & still in danger —(they say) two of my Servants both Italians are arrested on suspicion.—I need hardly add that *I* neither approved nor sanctioned directly nor indirectly—their summary mode of acting—notwithstanding the atrocious brutality of the Dragoon's whole conduct—of part of which (his sabring those arrested at the gate) I was ignorant having rode through the Guard to send my Steward to the police.—I did not dismount—but rode back to the Gate with only a stick in my hand—and expecting merely to find the party detained.—On my way I met the Aggressor—the papers enclosed will inform you of the rest.—

yrs. truly & ever
NOEL BYRON

[TO SIR WALTER SCOTT]   [*March 28th. 1822?*]

[Note following copy of Taaffe's deposition to the Governor of Pisa]

Nota bene—This deposition of Mr. John Taaffe—who began the quarrel—and then tried to back out of it for fear of the Pisans—hath acquired for the said John Taaffe the name & designation of *Falstaaffe*. He hath since recanted a part of his said statement to the English Minister—and now admits that he did think himself affronted &c.

[TO JOHN TAAFFE (*a*)]   [*March 28, 1822 ?*]

Dear Sir/—I have not sent the papers to England but to the B[ritish] Minister at Florence by *express*. I beg leave to observe that your deposition is absolutely necessary & not to be dispensed with & must add my wonder that you should wish to recall your word upon the occasion.

                                                    Yrs. &c.
                                                    N B

[TO JOHN TAAFFE (*b*)]   *March 28th. 1822*

If you can make it convenient to see me this evening I am at home & will state to you my opinion on your note & the enclosed paper.— Of course you are the best judge of what concerns yourself.

                                                    yrs. &c.
                                                    N B

P.S.—One of the Servants ⟨The Coachman⟩ has been released at least for the present.—

[TO JOHN TAAFFE]   *April [i.e. March] 29, 1822*

Sir/—I have been informed that you thought proper without consulting me or any of the party to give Lord Bradford a written statement of the late affair here at the same time declining to comply with his Lordship's request to apply to *me* for one.—

Did you do this or not?—

An early answer will oblige

                                                    Yr. obedt. Servt.
                                                    NOEL BYRON

Dear Sir/—I have to acknowledge the receipt of several books &c. which I will acknowledge more at length shortly.—I am very much occupied at present with a squabble between some English (myself for one) and some Soldiers of the Guard at the Gate and a dragoon who wanted to arrest us.—Some have been wounded—the dragoon severely—but now recovering.—The matter is before the British Minister at Florence and of course I cannot send an ex parte statement—till I see what he says further.—His letter to me has been very handsome & obliging.— —

                 yrs. ever & truly
                   N B

[TO EDWARD J. DAWKINS]   *Pisa. March 31st. 1822*

Sir—I beg leave to acknowledge your very obliging letter—the more so—as I have not the honour of your personal acquaintance—and have no great claim to the favour of diplomatists from my political opinions.— —It is indeed necessary for me that this business should have a full & free investigation—for I have no pretensions to popularity abroad or at home—and I know not what story the Public in the first confusion—may be pleased to make of it.— —Two servants have been detained—one since released,—and a Servant of the Countess Guiccioli's confined in his stead—the rest of my Servants and various others have been examined—but I am rather surprized that they have not yet called upon Dr. Crawford whose evidence is essential—but who probably will not remain much longer at Pisa.—To the steps which the Government have taken I have nothing to object—but I wish to allude to some that they have *not* yet taken.— —

The Man is pronounced out of danger (as far as I can learn) and I employed an English physician Dr. Todd to visit him & report upon his progress—towards recovery; this being the case is it not proper that they should investigate the conduct of this person as well as the consequence of that conduct?—He is not an officer or a Gentleman—though his dress differed from that of the former only by the bars on his sleeve—which as I am no great Connoisseur in uniforms I did not recognize or distinguish,—and had he been either of the above—he forfeited all pretensions to the name by his conduct in sabring those who were already arrested by the Guards & unarmed and defenseless.—I should wish to know whether—delivering a card to a man who insults you justifies *him* in arresting you—or your companions—or whether

I broke any law in resisting that arrest—which I did not do by any violence—but merely by riding through the Guard when they surrounded me with arms in their hands.—But even had they cut me down —was that any reason to assault those who had *not* opposed their detension?——

With regard to what passed afterwards the evidence is before your Excellency.—I do not present these *questions* to be answered by *you*—but merely as suggestions upon which you will form your own judgement—whether this Man was or was not grossly culpable in the first instance. I gave him no ill language—nor menaced him by gesture or threat—I merely asked him his name (which he did not give till I met him on the Lungarno the second time) and I neither saw nor heard such from the others.—When I gave him my address—— always ignorant that he was not an Officer—I certainly did not expect him to call out the Guard in reply. But I am troubling you at too great a length—and what vexes me is that I fear that I must trouble you still further. I had at first thought of sending the enclosed accounts to England—but as this would appear an ex parte statement— I could wish that whatever account is to be given came through your Excellency—that it [sic] is to say—if my request is not improper.—Of course the Statement must be what appears just to you, I have no wish that anything as far as I am concerned should be modified or concealed. ——I add a testimony of Mr. Taaffe's—upon which you will form your judgement also.—There is a note of mine appended to it.[1]—I have the honour to be most respectfully your Excellency's obliged & obedt. humble Servt.

Noel Byron

[to john taaffe] [*April, 1822?*]

P.S.—That Mr. Dawkins will see justice come on both sides—I do not doubt—but even if he should not—I will have the business

---

[1] Taaffe's statement denied that the dragoon had touched him in passing or that he had been offended by his behaviour. He also denied that he had taken part in the fracas that followed or had witnessed any significant part of it. Before sending another copy to Kinnaird, Byron wrote at the end of the statement:
"This being Mr. Taaffe's testimony as to his own impressions I cannot and do not wish to controvert them—as he must be the best judge of his own feelings.—But I must declare that the impression of the moment on my mind—from the *words*— the *tone*—the *starting* of his *horse*—and the nearness and rapidity with which the dragoon rushed past him—was—that he had received and *felt* that he had received an insult. With regard to the rest as I saw no more of him till some time after the close of the whole business—I have nothing to observe."—(Cline, pp. 115–116.)

brought before parliament.—I should like to know if unarmed men are to be cut down at City gates with impunity.—Now that the fellow is recovered he ought to be looked to.—

[TO DOUGLAS KINNAIRD]   *Pisa. April 2d. 1822*

My dear Douglas/—You ask me if I should like 4 per Cent? I should prefer five—but will take what is to be had (with your approbation) on *safe* security which is the principal point.———I cannot make this a long letter (luckily for you) for I am a good deal occupied about a very unpleasant squabble between some soldiers of the Guard at the Gate a drunken or brutal dragoon—and some English Gentlemen including myself.—The result was that they tried to arrest us—I broke through with another—an Englishman was wounded—and the dragoon (supposed by a servant) stabbed in a very dangerous way in the full street before thousands of people as he was galloping along after sabring the unarmed people already in arrest.—The fellow is however declared out of danger—and the wounded Englishman is well also.———This is the sum—but the particular depositions I reserve till I hear again from our Minister at Florence who has sent me one very polite answer to the papers which I forwarded to him, that the statement may not appear garbled or premature.——

You may suppose the row—a sort of miniature Manchester business[1] —except that the military aggressor has not in this instance escaped with impunity.—It is a strange instance of the fallibility of human testimony—that with thousands of witnesses—they have not been able to identify the man who wounded the Drago[o]n—nor even the weapon —for some said a pistol—an air-Gun—a stiletto—or lance—and a pitchfork.——Mr. Dawkins our Minister—says that I am acquitted of any suspicion of having sanctioned or approved or suggested the act of which his assailant is accused.—The fact was we (at least I) mistook the fellow for an Officer.—He is a Sergeant Major—but I am no great tailor in uniforms.—He rode against one of the party—& I rode up to ask him what he meant.—He blustered & bullied &c. &c. & thence the whole affair.—After I had given him my card—he called to the Guard to arrest us—&c. &c. & so forth as alluded to above.—I have just had the annexed letter from the English Minister.

yrs. ever & truly
N B

[1] A reference to the "Reform" riot in St. Peter's Field, Manchester, on 16 August, 1819, when the soldiers attacked unarmed men.

P.S.—I have just had Mr. Dawkins the E[nglish] Minister's second answer of which I enclose a copy as well as of the first—I leave to your own discretion whether it will be proper to quote more from his letter than the passage exculpating me in the opinion of the Government here from having directly or indirectly sanctioned the act of which the Servants are suspected. The Man they have sworn to is not a Servant of mine but of Count Gamba's but there is every reason to suppose that he is *not* the real assailant.[2]———You will judge for yourself as to what statement will be proper & requisite on the occasion.——

April 5th. 1822

[TO EDWARD J. DAWKINS]   *Pisa. April 4th. 1822*

Sir/—Captain Hay has requested me for the honour of a letter of introduction to your Excellency.——It may well be deemed a liberty in me—who have not had that honour myself, to venture on the presentation of another.—But as he is the most injured party in the late business, —& can give any details which may be further necessary for it's elucidation—I hazard being deemed intrusive—or perhaps worse. ——I have to acknowledge the receipt of your second letter—which is quite satisfactory as far as the business has hitherto gone.—I have no objection to any use you think proper being made of my letters.—I shall forward the returned documents by post to London tomorrow— as you say that you have no objection.—I have the honour to be with great respect & obligation

your most obedt. very humble Sert.
NOEL BYRON

[TO JOHN HAY]   *Pisa. April 6th. 1822*

My dear Hay/—Many thanks.—It seems just the thing or nearly so by the description.[1]—But if I take it for *six* months they ought to abate a good deal of the price.—If they don't I will only take it for one or two.—I shall send *Battuzzi* tomorrow to reconnoitre.——I am glad you like the pistols & [line crossed out]—It will give me great

2 See April 11, 1822, to Hobhouse, note 4.
1 Byron was looking for a summer house near the sea. This may well have been the Villa Dupuy, at Montenero near Leghorn, which he leased and where he took the Gambas in the middle of May. Hay was then in Leghorn. Byron addressed him in care of Mr. Dunn, the English merchant who was his business agent in that city.

pleasure to see you again here or elsewhere—and I beg you to believe me with a perfect exchange of good wishes[.]

yrs. ever & truly
N B

[TO JOHN HANSON]   *Pisa. April 8th. 1822*

Dear Sir/—It has been suggested to me that a legal authority (Mr. C. Butler) has said that it will be necessary to have an act of parliament for the assumption of the name of Noel.—Is this so? or not? I trust that the best advice has been taken.———I should be glad to know too why the arbitration is not proceeded upon as I have already appointed my referee and forwarded my sentiments on the subject to yourself and all others concerned in the direction of my affairs.—

yrs. ever & truly
NOEL BYRON

[TO JOHN MURRAY]   *Pisa. April 9th. 1822*

Dear Sir/—The busts will be sent when completed.[1]—They are already paid for &c.—Thank Mr. D'Israeli for his book[2]—and say that I shall write to him soon to acknowledge it's arrival more particularly.———Also the same to Mr. Luttrel.[3]———I believe the new Mystery is pious enough but if anything wants softening here & there [;] send me an extract—but *not* a [proof]—as I have already corrected it carefully.———Have you got "Werner" from Mr. Moore? —Your best way to publish the "Quevedo redivivus"[4] will be with some other bookseller's name—or as a *foreign* edition—& in such a *cheap* form—that the pirates cannot undersell you.—Mr. Douglas Kinnaird has the corrected proof in his hands, & will put it into yours upon your application to him.———I wish you would decide something about the publication of the Pulci &c.———I do not mean *terms* but the time of publication.———*My* lawyers say that the Act of Parliament is *not* necessary for the name of Noel but I have written to them & to

[1] The busts of Byron and the Countess Guiccioli by Bartolini.

[2] The third edition of Isaac D'Israeli's *The Literary Character*, published in 1822. Byron did not write the promised letter to the author until June 10th.

[3] Henry Luttrell published in 1820 his *Advice to Julia, a Letter in Rhyme*, which Byron much admired. A third edition was published in 1822.

[4] *The Vision of Judgment*, for which Byron used this as a pseudonym for the author.

my trustee Mr. D[ouglas] K[innaird] to get good advice thereanent.—
I have had a newspaper letter sent to me—which asks "who molested
you?" did you not say to me that they were prosecuting you?[5]—Let
me hear from you—

yrs. truly
NOEL BYRON

[TO DOUGLAS KINNAIRD]   *Pisa. April 9th. 1822*

My dear Douglas/—I hear that Mr. C. Butler (a lawyer I presume)
says that an act of parliament will be necessary to sanction the name of
Noel. I hope you have good advice thereupon that it may be done if
requisite without loss of time.———By thursday's post I addressed to
you a packet containing [various?] documents upon an affair which
occurred here not long ago.———At your leisure acknowledge the
same and believe me

yrs. ever & truly
NOEL BYRON

P.S.—Thank Sir Francis [Burdett] for his letter which I will acknowledge in a post or two.—In the mean time why don't you get on? with
the arbitration?

[TO CAPTAIN DANIEL ROBERTS][1]   *Pisa April 9, 1822*
[Added to letter from Trelawny to Roberts]

P.S.—Dear Sir/—Draw away—the first draft is (or ought to be)
honoured by this time—as I sent a hundred pound bill to Messrs
Webb this morning to answer it.———I hope the Schooner will be
Varmint[2] all over, & I should be more vexed that she should want
anything to render her neat and complete than [Page missing in MS.]

---

[5] For publishing *Cain.*
[1] Captain Daniel Roberts, R.N., a friend of Trelawny, who had travelled from
Geneva to Genoa with him, was an expert on boats and boat-building. Byron had
commissioned him through Trelawny to superintend the building of a boat in
Genoa.
[2] Trelawny had used this term in writing instructions to Roberts for the building
of a boat for Shelley and Williams, which was to be "a thorough *Varment* at *pulling*
and *sailing!*" (Trelawny to Roberts, Feb. 5, 1822. *Letters of Edward John Trelawny*, ed. Forman, p. 2.)

My dear Hobhouse/—I did not disapprove of your Philippic on Canning[1]—but thought it equally just and able—quite a piece of *permanent* Oratory—which will last longer than either of you.—But I heard (& did not allude to it—as you never did yourself) that you had written a pamphlet about him—which you refused to avow when he charged you therewith.—Now—I dare say I was wrong—but not knowing the circumstances I perhaps might be of opinion that you should have owned it—as it was personal.—Still however as I do not know the circumstances & was not consulted—I repeat that I can form no positive opinion—nor does it matter if I did—as you should be the best judge of your own decorum—& will have had better advice than mine upon all such subjects.———"Precarious!" my Lady's "health precarious!"—Oons! what do you mean?—Must I be reduced to marry Mrs. Coutts[2] then in case of widow*er*hood?—you would see that my second match would be an excellent one—as somebody would be sure to take me because all the world would say that she ought not.—Indeed my greatest obligation to Lady Noel Byron—or whatever her name is—is—that she has prevented me from marrying.——But

> How goes the Arbitration
> Upon this separation?
> I trust my friend Burdett
> Will know how to word it—
> In dividing the Acres
> With the Baron Dacres.[3]—

Enclosed I send you—(they are already sent to Douglas K[innair]d) the depositions on a squabble between some English and Soldiers (horse and foot) in which there was some cutting and slashing about a fortnight ago.—I wish to know what you think of it.——

yrs. ever & truly
N B

P.S.—Observe that I mistook the fellow for an *Officer* as he was well dressed & mounted &c.——copies of these depositions &c.

---

[1] See May 19, 1821, to Murray, note 8. (Vol. 8, p. 120).

[2] The widow of Thomas Coutts, the wealthy banker, had been a popular actress named Harriet Mellon. Coutts had married her after the death of his first wife in 1815. Coutts died on Feb. 24, 1822. His youngest daughter Sophia, by his first wife, was married to Sir Francis Burdett, Byron's friend who had become his arbitrator for the settlement of the Wentworth estate after the death of Lady Noel.

[3] Lord Dacre was arbitrator for Lady Byron in the division of the estates.

were forwarded to Douglas K[innair]d a week ago, they have still detained a Servant of mine[4]—and a Servant of Count Gamba's on suspicion—but they cannot even make out with what weapon the Drago[o]n was perforated.—Some said—a pistol—an air gun—or sabre—a stiletto—a pitchfork—a lance—and all this in presence of thousands of people! Pretty evidence of crowds.—The ragamuffin is at last out of danger—but he was smartly touched at the outset.—— Though he richly deserved it—I am glad that he did not go off—but recovered though after several changes.——There is now an opportunity of studying Etruscan jurisprudence—which however *you* know already.—

[TO EDWARD J. DAWKINS]   *Pisa. April 12th. 1822*

Sir.—I have received a letter from Capt. Hay—who requests me (I presume with your permission) to address my answer under cover to you.——As the letter is entirely upon the late squabble—I send it open—if you think it worth the trouble of your perusal.—Indeed, it refers to matters which must be submitted to your attention.—I have the honour to be with great consideration and esteem

your obliged & obedt. humble Sert.

NOEL BYRON

[TO JOHN HAY (*a*)]   *Pisa. April 12th. 1822*

My dear Hay/—I received your dispatch early this Morning.— Many thanks to Mr. Dawkins and to yourself.——The detenees[1] are treated with great rigour—they won't even allow them to receive any thing to eat but the prison allowance.—The Judge appears to have a better table—as he is allowed three Scudi a day—during the process— which is *thus* likely to be soon terminated!! Now—these poor devils are innocent, and I really believe that the [Court?] knows that neither of them was the suspected person.—It is a question (as you say Mr. Dawkins thinks that he could have the affair terminated) whether I to save any unjust surmises—should dissent from the steps being taken to

---

[4] Byron's servant "Tita" was arrested but finally released after they had shaved off his great beard. The man who actually stabbed Sergeant Masi was Byron's coachman Vincenzo Papi, who was also arrested but released. Byron later dismissed him for his violence in quarrelling with other servants.

[1] Byron's servant Giovanni Battista Falcieri ("Tita") and the Countess Guiccioli's servant Antonio Maluccelli had been arrested and held for some time without trial, though they were both innocent.

liberate these men.—With regard to my own conduct—I have given them all time (it is now three weeks) to examine & investigate hundreds of witnesses—and am willing to undergo any investigation they please—and at their own length.——Nobody has evaded or withdrawn from the pursuits of their process.——

I cannot contemplate the probable duration of the detention in the harshest confinement of these two innocent men—without great uneasiness on their account.—Every body says—& believes that it was another man who harpooned the Scoundrel—& yet upon this they have not acted.—I will give you an instance of their Spirit of Justice—the Procaccino was taken ill last night—the Priests told him that it was a judgement on him for having forsworn himself.—What he has sworn or forsworn I do not know—nor am I aware of the person of the man— but believe him to be the same who goes to Leghorn.——The Man is better—& says this himself of the priests, so Fletcher tells me.—I will agree to whatever Mr. Dawkins thinks proper—my own opinion inclines rather (& naturally) to the wish that these poor fellows should be out, for two things are sure—one—that they are innocent—& the other—that they have not fair play granted them.——I write in haste to save time—make my best respects to the Minister Mr. D[awkins] & believe me yours ever

N B

P.S.—Mr Taaffe's Statement can (I think) hurt no one but himself— a pretty fellow he is!—The Officers defend their Sergeant—(I am told) upon this principle—"that Mr Taaffe declared that he exculpated the Man—as he had not been even slightly moved by his original aggression."—Now—his *own* Statement contradicts this—for he admits that his horse was startled—and that he appealed to me upon the subject of the *rush* past him!—He also [saltornando?][2] adds that the dragoon was all in the wrong.—Besides I sent his first note *in English* (the morning after) to Mr. Dawkins which is decisive of his *then* opinion.——At all events I hope that these men will be allowed some victuals & decent treatment.——

[TO JOHN HAY (*b*)]   *April 12th. 1822*

Dear Hay/—I forgot to say in my letter—that I agree with you about the paper you wish to draw up—& will do what you like about it.

2 The word is difficult to read, but it looks like the Italian word meaning "skipping" or "turning about".

—No introduction to Douglas K[innair]d will be necessary—except mentioning my name to him—you will find that sufficient—& I had already written to him on the subject.

yrs. ever & truly

N B

Pisa. April 13th. 1822

My dear Douglas/—"Milk diet! and not insurable!"—it is to be presumed then that there will be more *Milk* than *Honey* (and *Gall* than either) from this new land of Canaan.—There are two questions which I would ask which will show you how much I know of my own affairs.—The one is—if the remaining ten thousand pounds of Lady B's original portion—comes to me—in case of her demise—or to whom? —or the whole—or a part only?—The other is—whether there being a daughter only—a part of the settlement (of my money) does not become released in case of her decease previous to mine.—I ask this— as essential to meet the debts—in case of her not surviving me.—I see that there is but very little to hope from that quarter (the Noel business) and I never expected that any good could come from a party— which seems engendered for my embarrassment in character—as well as fortune.——I have since your letter become indifferent to what the trustees may decide—as I merely looked to the insurance for any probability of advantage—in the liquidation of the remaining debts. ——It would be a foolish thing in me to marry again—& yet I would not answer for my not repeating such a folly—if a widower.—The Woman is no friend of mine—yet I should be sorry for her own sake —& for the Child's that she should go down to the Grave with a heart colder than her dust will ever be.———But enough of this subject.—— Mr Murray has not sent to me any defence—of "Cain"—but some attacks upon it.—I sent you last week packets of an affair that occurred here—of which you will have heard enough by this time.—I enclose you three more letters on the subject—which will enable you to judge still further for yourself.—I trust you are getting well

I am ever yours

N B

Pisa. April 13th. 1822

Dear Sir/—Your congratulations on the Noel accession—are somewhat premature, as Lady B. is on a "Milk diet"—from which it may be—that there will be a greater flow of *Milk* than *Honey* (& of *Gall* than either) from this new "land of Promise".—You might as well expect peace in the House of Atreus—as comfort—honour—or prosperity from the Union between those of Noel & Byron. Mr. K[innair]d writes that there has been an "excellent defence of 'Cain' against Oxoniensis" [;][1] you have sent me nothing but a not very excellent *off*ence of the same poem.—If there be such "a defender of the Faith"—you may send me his thirty nine articles,—as a counter-balance to some of your late communications.—Are you to publish or not what Moore and Mr. Kinnaird have in hand—& the Vision [of] Quevedo?—If you publish the latter in a very cheap edition so as to baffle the pirates by a low price—you will find that it will do.——The "Mystery" I look upon as good—and "Werner" too—and I expect that you will publish them speedily.—You need not put your name to *Quevedo*—but publish it as a foreign edition & let it take it's chance—& make it's way.—D[ouglas] K[innaird] has it still with the preface—I believe.——I refer you to him for documents on the late row here—I sent them a week ago.

yrs. ever
N B

[TO EDWARD J. DAWKINS]   *Pisa. April 16th. 1822*

Dear Sir.—Enclosed are the names of the Servants detained, as required.—I shall be delighted to know Collini[1] to whom I had the letter which he mentions, though I little thought that the first occasion I should have of availing myself of the introduction would be on an affair of carnage and cuttings of throats.—Whenever he comes he will find an apartment prepared for him in my house—where I hope that he will make himself at home.—Could you have the goodness to favour me with the account of proper and highest *fees* of Tuscan Counsel in such affairs?—I do not ask this from motives of economy or a wish to limit our friend's emoluments but from actual ignorance, and a fear of perhaps falling short of what is right—from that ignorance.—This is of course *"entre nous"*. With regard to *"my time* and *patience"* the one is about as little worth as the other—God help me!—but that is no

---

[1] See Feb. 8, 1822, to Murray, note 1. The defense was *A Letter to Sir Walter Scott, Bart., in answer to the Remonstrance of Oxoniensis on the publication of Cain, a Mystery, by Lord Byron.* By Harroviensis, 1822.

[1] Lorenzo Collini was an Italian lawyer from Florence whom Byron employed to represent him in legal matters connected with the Masi affair.

reason why yours should be further abused.—I trust that Collini's retainer will at least render further trouble to yourself unnecessary.—I believe that I need hardly repeat my acknowledgements and those of my countrymen for your extremely kind and handsome conduct throughout this business—If I were insensible to it—(which I trust that I am *not*—) I should not have the plea of ignorance for ingratitude —for besides what has occurred to my own knowledge—I hear of nothing else from Florence—(not only from Capt. Hay—but from several others) but of the highly zealous and effective conduct for which we are indebted to Mr. Dawkins.——

With regard to that illustrious deponent John Taaffe Jr. Esqre.— whose head is more Irish (apparently) than his heart—he did not *directly* give me to understand that he had a separate correspondence with you—and still less that *you* had sought it.—He merely said that you were his friend, in general, & that he had written to you on this subject.—To this nor to any other mode of communication—I could possibly have no objection—leaving his deposition to make it's proper impression upon a Man of honour.—What he means or meant I cannot pretend to guess—I can only judge of his paper from it's con- tents—and as a party I am not a competent Arbiter.———His whole language changed upon one morning—about three days after the event.—He came to me with a Cock and a Bull Story—about his having been to the Captain of the wounded man— (*totally without* the knowledge of and with the fullest disapprobation on it's being known— of *all* concerned) to speak about the Soldiery &c.—as they had threat- ened to besiege the house—and such like magnanimous menaces.—He added something to me—about the Man's (the Serjeant's) being ready to ask satisfaction if he got well—and if not—somebody or other for him.—Upon this—I immediately spoke with my friends—and we agreed that we would either give *singly* satisfaction to any *officer* of the regiment—or as we were six in number (including Mr. Taaffe the original Cause of the Scene—and an Italian Gentleman whose name I kept out of the paper as he is an exile on account of politics) would meet any *six officers* of the regiment—whichever they chose.—— I said to Mr. Taaffe "I suppose you would choose to make one".—To this he answered that he could make no such thing—neither *singly* nor *sixthly*—that *he* was *not* offended—*never* had been—&c. &c. &c. though before he had used a different tone.—He became so tiresome and *tedious* & contradictory of *himself* & his *first* accounts—that if I had not interfered—Mr. Trelawney who is somewhat warlike in his notions—would have furnished matter on the spot for a fresh action of battery.—Repeating my sense of our obligations to you—I beg you to believe me, dear Sir—with every sentiment of esteem

> your faithful & obliged Sert.
> NOEL BYRON

[TO EDWARD J. DAWKINS] *Pisa. April 18th. 1822*

Dear Sir,—My Servant[1] is I understand exculpated from all suspicion of being art or part of the principal fact.—He is also released from the penalty of having carried arms by the fine being paid, which it was yesterday.——But now they are detaining him under some pretence either because he wears a *beard* or for some other weighty reason—referring to the police only—& not to the Criminal tribunal. —Now—I can find securities for his good conduct if necessary—and I should be glad to know why this man (the best servant I have) is still detained after absolution from the two primary pretexts of his detention. —I hope if it is only a mere affair of *police* and the man is actually absolved that they will not continue to retain him for their own absolute pleasure. Would you have the goodness to avize Collini of this—& if he could do anything before he sets out—but I forget—he will be here —before this letter is at Florence.——A thousand thanks for your letter—I can assure you that there is no expression of regard in it— but what is more than reciprocal.—Do not *bore* yourself to answer my scrawls—which are merely suggestions—& don't require regular answers or answers at all.—Excuse haste & believe me ever & truly with great esteem

> yr. obliged & faithful Sert.
> NOEL BYRON

P.S.—The Man was allowed yesterday to see his friends—to-day they have shut him up again in *"Secret"* as they call it in their jargon— and be d——d to them—excuse the phrase which is neither diplomatic nor decorous—but these fellows make me [lose] all patience with their shuffling—which was to be borne with while the man was *really accused*.——

[TO DOUGLAS KINNAIRD] *Pisa. April 18th. 1822*

My dear Douglas/—The decision is quite satisfactory to me.—It would have been no less so had Sir Francis decided that she was to have

[1] Tita.

all—or nothing at all.—I chose him as an Arbitrator and not as an advocate in the fullest confidence of his ability and integrity—and no result would have altered my opinion of his having decided in the best manner under the circumstances.[1]—I believe I need add nothing except my acknowledgements for his trouble—also the same—to Lord Dacre whose conduct has my full approbation.—You do not mention whether Kirkby [Mallory] is to be tenanted by Lady B. with —or without my option.—If the latter, no more need be said.—If the former—it is probably at her service during Sir R[alph]'s life—and perhaps afterwards.—However I will take your opinion upon this point. About the Child—I merely require that she is *not* to be approached by Mrs. Clermont.—Upon that point my opinion is not to be altered.—I could wish to suggest that the famous picture[2] will be spoilt if it is not occasionally taken out of it's case—and exposed to the air.—Tell Dr. Lushington so.—About "managing the estates" I should like to know *how* I am to manage what I know nothing about— and *how* the *Net* produce is to be ascertained and received?—The fairest way would be for Lady B. & me to appoint a *joint* receiver. I will do any thing they like in reason for the advantage of the property. I am sorry that her health is so precarious *not* on account of the estate only—but for the child's sake and her own.—I wish you would tell Lushington—that now the thing is settled—I hope some more amicable mode of adjusting the *details* of business may be adopted—it would save bickerings and bitterness among rival agents &c. &c.—Lady B's mind—her cold concentration has worked upon her health—while I by saying what comes uppermost am less preyed upon by such considerations.—You will or ought to have received the documents relative to a row here—please to acknowledge them.——I have received & read the defence of "Cain" who is my *Warburton*?[3] he is a clever and a kind man, whoever he be.—

yrs. ever & truly
N B

---

[1] By the terms of the Separation Agreement, on Lady Noel's death (which occurred on January 28) the estate of her brother Lord Wentworth was to be divided by arbitration. Byron's choice of arbiter was Sir Francis Burdett, and Lord Dacre represented Lady Byron.

[2] The portrait of Byron, by what artist is not known, which Lady Noel left in care of the trustees, one of whom was Dr. Lushington, her attorney.

[3] The defender of *Cain* signed himself "Harroviensis". William Warburton was the literary executor and defender of Alexander Pope.

Dear Sir/—I have received the defence of "Cain".—Who is *my* Warburton? for he has done for me what the Bishop did for the poet against Crousaz.[1]——His reply seems to me conclusive—and if you understood your own interest—you would print it together with the poem.——It is very odd that I do not hear from you.—I have forwarded to Mr. [Douglas Kinnaird] the documents on a squabble here, which occurred about a month ago—the affair is still going on—but they made nothing of it hitherto.—I think what with home and abroad —there has been hot water enough for one while.———Mr. Dawkins the English Minister has behaved in the handsomest and most gentlemanly manner throughout the whole business.—

yrs. ever & truly
N B

P.S.—Are you to publish or not? I wish you would let me have a positive answer before the season wears out.——I have directed you how to publish "the Vision of Quevedo &c."—in a small cheap form without your name—also the Pulci with the text of the original.— The Mystery and "Werner" together in what form you please.— Don't dawdle—but let me know.—I have got Lord Glenbervie's book[2] which is very amusing and able upon the topics which he touches upon—& part of the preface pathetic. Write soon.

Dear Sir,—You will regret to hear that I have received intelligence of the death of my daughter Allegra of a fever in the Convent at Bagna Cavallo[1]—where she was placed for the last year to commence her education. It is a heavy blow for many reasons, but must be borne, with time.——It is my present intention to send her remains to England for sepulture in Harrow Church (where I once hoped to have laid my own) and this is my reason for troubling you with this notice ——I wish the funeral to be very private.—The body is embalmed

---

[1] Jean Pierre de Crousaz published his *Examen de l'Essai de Monsieur Pope sur l'homme* in 1737. Warburton replied in *A Vindication of Mr. Pope's Essay on Man from the Misrepresentations of Mr. de Crousaz*, 1738–39.

[2] Murray had just published Lord Glenbervie's *Translation from the Italian of Forteguerri of the First Canto of Ricciardetto. With an Introduction concerning the Romantic, Burlesque and Mock-Heroic Poets.*

[1] Byron's daughter Allegra died on April 20, 1822. She was five years and three months old.

and in lead.——It will be embarked from Leghorn.—Would you have any objection to give the proper directions on it's arrival[?]

I am yours &c.

N B

P.S.—You are aware that protestants are not allowed holy ground in Catholic countries.——

[TO EDWARD J. DAWKINS] *Pisa. April 22d. 1822*

Dear Sir/—An order has come from Florence to exile my Servant.[1]— The Advocate Collini is of opinion that this must be protested against for various reasons which he will state in person.——It is entirely a measure of police and has nothing to do with the tribunals or the process.—It is also a gross injustice to *me*—because sending away the man in the *middle* of the *cause*—leaves always a suspicion.—But I will not plague you with further details as Collini will inform you of all that is necessary.—He is of opinion that the man should pass through Florence to appeal.—The Man is absolutely innocent of every thing relating to this affair and is allowed to be so.—I write in great haste for Collini is just starting and I have only time to repeat how truly I am

yr. obliged & faithful Sert.

NOEL BYRON

[TO PERCY BYSSHE SHELLEY] *April 23d, 1822*

The blow was stunning and unexpected; for I thought the danger over, by the long interval between her stated amelioration and the arrival of the express. But I have borne up against it as I best can, and so far successfully, that I can go about the usual business of life with the same appearance of composure, and even greater. There is nothing to prevent your coming to-morrow; but, perhaps, to-day, and yester-evening, it was better not to have met. I do not know that I have any thing to reproach in my conduct, and certainly nothing in my feelings and intentions toward the dead. But it is a moment when we are apt to think that, if this or that had been done, such event might have been prevented,—though every day and hour shows us that they are

---

[1] Tita, after having faced the indignity of having his beard cut off in prison, was exiled and went temporarily to live with the Shelleys at Casa Magni near Lerici. He later joined Byron again and was with him until the poet's death in Greece.

the most natural and inevitable. I suppose that Time will do his usual work—Death has done his.[1]

Yours ever,
N B

Pisa. April 24th. 1822

Dear Sir,—The answer to the request of Tita (the Barbone) is— fifteen days of delay *granted*—passage through Florence— *granted*— Salvo Condotto—*refused.* I should certainly very much wish to have his exile repealed if possible—as he has not deserved it in any respect.— He is a young—good natured man—& an excellent servant—a little vain of his person—and somewhat *bavard* but far more *harmless* in every respect than the Sbirri who—I understand are his accusers on the plea of their fears.———As I am going to reside for the Summer near Leghorn—perhaps—you might obtain a commutation for a temporary exile from *Pisa* only—if however they persist in driving him from the Tuscan territory—as I mean to retain him in my service nevertheless;—I could wish him to be sent to Lucca or Genoa—in one of which places I can find means to occupy him in some apparent service near one of my ⟨fr⟩ acquaintances.———Believe me to be ever &

very faithfully your obliged St.
NOEL BYRON

P.S.—Excuse anything hurried or abrupt in this—on the night of Collini's departure—I received the intelligence of the death of my daughter Allegra (a natural child) in the Convent of Bagna-Cavallo in Romagna—where she was placed for the commencement of her education.——

P.S.—I open my letter to add that Tita has been in my service four years and that I paid 1200 francs at Venice upon one occasion when he was drawn for the Conscription———I need hardly add that I should not have done so for a man who was a bad subject—or ill-disposed in any way.——

[TO EDWARD J. DAWKINS] *Pisa. April 26th. 1822*

Dear Sir—I wrote to you by Staffetta [express] this morning—but have a few words to add on the subject of Tita—I have applied to the

[1] Byron was partly apologetic in writing about the death of his daughter Allegra to Shelley, who was trying to cushion the shock to Allegra's mother, Claire Clairmont, for she had bitterly condemned Byron for leaving their daughter in the convent. But that Byron felt the loss keenly is apparent.

Auditor for permission to send him to *Spezia* (if exiled) to an English family there—which he has *refused* without an order from *Florence*—which unless obtained by you I know not how to obtain.——For my own part—if I were not embroiled with the houses which I have rented —and some other affairs which detain me here—I would leave their states tomorrow—and if they will permit me to retain the man in his service—I will quit them at any given period they choose to assign;——I wished to have nothing to do with Tuscany beyond it's climate——and as it is, I find myself not allowed even *that* in quiet.——Excuse my adding this much to the letter of this morning & believe me ever & truly yrs.

N B

[TO EDWARD J. DAWKINS]   *Pisa. April 28th. 1822*

Dear Sir.—Notwithstanding your two letters of this morning—for which I beg to add my acknowledgements—an order has arrived to transfer Tita to Florence.——This has rather surprized me because Collini's letter stated that he would be permitted to go to Spezia or elsewhere as he pleased—& yours apprized me that I should hear of any positive decision.——With regard to the rest—I must leave it to the Great Men of this great Nation to settle in their own way—having done my best to save the poor fellow from their persecution—for there has been neither justice nor honour in their proceedings towards him hitherto.——I presume that his *beard* (a whim of his own by the way— which I neither approved nor disapproved of—allowing all about me to wear their faces as they like—so that they don't neglect their business) is as likely to find favour at Florence as in Pisa—where the Auditor &c. actually pleaded the *fear* which he inspired to a City—with twenty thousand thieves for inhabitants—as the reason for his exile!——

My wish was to have got him to Leghorn—or on board of my Schooner—as one of the Crew—or to Spezia for a Season——for they will probably maltreat him in the Austrian territory—because he was in my Service—for there has been some time a sufficient detestation between that tyranny and myself—and I say this without presumption —for there is *no* individual too humble nor too insignificant not to be obnoxious to it's Cowardice or it's Cruelty.—Of this I had sufficient proof both during my residence in Lombardy and in Romagna—so that I do not err in stating what might seem ridiculous if spoken of *any other* Government.—Last year they for a long time refused to permit at Milan the contradiction of a foolish falsehood in their papers with regard to myself—alledging their "hatred of me as the reason"—and it was with difficulty that Mr. Hoppner obtained the counter-statement —although they admitted that they had spoken falsely.—I mention all this nonsense—mainly in proof that I concur with you in my apprehensions of the treatment that this poor devil may meet with in the Austrian states.—especially as he was with me during the threatened trouble in Romagna—which ended when those patriots—the Neapolitans ran away.——I shall be very anxious to hear one word of the result of Tita's presentation to the president of "*Good* Government" the *first* Government of that kind mentioned in history.——Believe me ever & faithfully

yr. obliged & obedt. Sert.
NOEL BYRON

P.S.—"*The party of* the Pisan Professors!"[1] this is the first I have heard of them.——I did not know that there were any professors except Rossini Taaffe's printer—whom I have heard him mention—— What is their profession? I wonder.—Mr. Taaffe is going to Egypt— "*col principe Turco*".—

[TO EDWARD J. DAWKINS]   *Pisa. May 1st. 1822*

Dear Sir,—I by no means intended to "correct you"—& believe that you were perfectly right—I merely asserted my own ignorance of the names of these Professors—and, my consequent innocence of any offence towards them.——With what has been done upon the subject of Tita—I have every reason to be more than satisfied as far as *you* are concerned, and I hope it will be a lesson to him to shave in future;— since the beard of Julian which offended the people of Antioch—I doubt if so much stir has been occasioned by the same quantity of hair, on the same place. However—it shall go hard—but I repay in one way or the other—those Pisan Μισόπογαε [sic].[1]——It is to be feared that I have appeared to you more than enough irritable on this occasion —but I beg you to attribute it to a concurrence of causes—rather than to this one in particular—and to forgive the infirmity which I neither pretend to deny nor excuse.——I have not been insensible to the *generosity* of your conduct throughout which you will call only *justice*— but as the world goes—*Justice is* generosity—and of all others—the

---

[1] Dawkins had written: "A party has been raised against you in Pisa by the professors who flattered them selves with the hope of being admitted to your intimacy and of appearing in appendices to your future works." (Cline, p. 143.)

[1] i.e., beard haters. Byron's Greek is faulty.

generosity least to be met with.——Many thanks for the *book* which Count G[amba] brought safely—I will take all due care of it—till I have a private opportunity of restoring it.——Believe me ever & truly

yr. obliged & sincere St.

NOEL BYRON

[TO JOHN MURRAY] *Pisa. May 1st. 1822*

Dear Sir,—I have received Sir Walter Scott's letter enclosed in yours—which I will answer shortly.—Last week I wrote to apprize you of the death of my natural daughter Allegra.——Of the Pisan affray—the chief documents are in possession of Mr. D[ouglas] K[innair]d—and a further copy was sent to Mr. Hobhouse—both of which I trust have been received. I shall expect the proof of "Werner". —I desired you to obtain "the Mystery" from Mr. K[innair]d also "the Vision"—and as I have already repeated to you my wishes on the subject—I expect that you will publish them as directed.—Can you tell me the author of the defence of "Cain"?[1]—If you understand your own interest—you will get it circulated as much as you can.—I am yours very truly

N B

[TO DOUGLAS KINNAIRD] *Pisa. May 2d. 1822*

My dear Douglas,—It is well that the Insurance is effected.—I wrote to *you* a letter of thanks to Sir Francis and Lord Dacre—which may perhaps render troubling them unnecessary—but if you choose—I will address Sir F. Burdett more directly.—You will regret to hear the death of my natural daughter Allegra a short time ago of a fever.—— You will have received some documents which I sent on the 4th A[pri]l relative to a quarrel here with a Dragoon—in the course of which Mr. Hay was wounded—& dragoon stabbed—both recovered— dragoon some days in danger of life—but now well again.——Mr. Murray does not say whether he has received the Mystery and Vision from you—and I must require an explicit answer from him on the subject.——As I have not limited him to any terms—but leave that discussion till we can ascertain how far the things succeed—I can

---

[1] The defence of *Cain* by "Harroviensis" in reply to "Oxoniensis" [pseudonym for H. J. Todd]. The name of the defender is not now known, but Murray told Byron that he was "a tyro in literature", that is, not well known. See June 6, 1822, to Murray.

151

neither permit nor excuse any evasions on his part.—I have read the defence of "Cain" which is very good—who can be the author?— — As to the "Vision"—Murray has been directed to print it so cheaply as to evade the pirates by the lowness of the price—and (if the row about "Cain" has disturbed him) to put either another name—or no name—as publisher—or to publish it as a foreign edition.—

As to myself—I shall not be deterred by any outcry——they hate me—and I detest them—I mean your present Public—but they shall not interrupt the march of my mind—nor prevent me from telling the tyrants who are attempting to trample upon all thought—that their thrones will yet be rocked to their foundation. It is Madame de Stael who says that "all *Talent* has a propensity to attack the *Strong*"[1]—I have never *flattered* them—I am sure—whether it [be? tal]ent or no. ——But these [words torn off] only strong for the moment—[I] think that they will soon be overthrown.—By the way—I answered you about the mortgage in exchange for the funds—and expect to hear that you have liberated at least a part of my money from that species of security.——Will you remember me to Hobhouse (to whom I sent a duplicate of the documents before alluded to) and also to Sir Francis—believe me

ever & truly yrs.

N B

P.S.—Mr. Rogers passed the other day.—I received and treated him with all attention in my power—in return for which he will probably abuse me—as he does every body—he does not look younger nor better humoured for his Journey.

[TO DOUGLAS KINNAIRD]   *Pisa. May 3d. 1822*

My dear Douglas,—I wrote to you by the last post.—As there appear several confusions & contradictions in the papers—occasioned by their confounding Lady Noel's *personal* property—with the Wentworth Estates—had you not better state the fact?—viz—that the reference and arbitration related to those estates only under the will of the late Lord Wentworth.—It is not pleasant to be the subject of such discussions—when a word of truth can put an end to them.—I have written to you twice—(yesterday and before) to thank Sir F[ranci]s Burdett and Lord Dacre for their decision—and to express

---

[1] *De La Littérature* (1800), Seconde Partie, Chapitre III: "La force de l'esprit ne se développe toute entière qu'en attaquant la puissance."

my contentment with their manner of conducting the reference.——I expected a line of acknowledgement for some documents sent on the 4th. of April—relative to a quarrel with a dragoon—&c.—all of which you have I trust safely received—and will employ—if necessary— to contradict any false statements—for it is now a long time—since a word of truth has been allowed to appear in the journals on *any* subject— literary—or personal—in which I am concerned.——Duplicates of the same were also afterwards forwarded to Mr. Hobhouse.——I need not repeat to you my satisfaction that the Insurance has been effected—I wish you had been as lucky with the funds.—My poor little daughter Allegra—died lately of a fever, and altogether I have had my share of sorrow this winter.——Mr. Murray writes to me— but nothing to the purpose—he does not appear to have obtained from you—(nor to have asked for) the proofs in your hands.—If he continues these tardy evasions—I must recur to my former intention of a separation from him.—I expect him to publish what I require— especially—as I make no *previous* contract—but leave that discussion— till the good or evil success of the publication can be ascertained.— Believe me ever & truly

yr. obliged & aff[ectionat]e
N B

[TO SIR WALTER SCOTT]   *Pisa, May 4th, 1822*

My Dear Sir Walter,—Your account of your family is very pleasing: would that I "could answer this comfort with the like!"[1] but I have just lost my natural daughter, Allegra, by a fever. The only consolation, save time, is the reflection that she is either at rest or happy; for her few years (only five) prevented her from having incurred any sin, except what we inherit from Adam.

"Whom the gods love die young."[2]

I need not say that your letters are particularly welcome, when they do not tax your time and patience; and now that our correspondence is resumed, I trust it will continue.

I have lately had some anxiety, rather than trouble, about an awkward affair here, which you may perhaps have heard of; but our minister has behaved very handsomely, and the Tuscan Government

---

[1] *Macbeth*, Act IV, scene 3.
[2] See *Don Juan*, IV, 12. Byron referred his readers to Herodotus, but the sentiment is to be found in various classical writers, Greek and Latin.

as well as it is possible for such a government to behave, which is not saying much for the latter. Some other English, and Scots, and myself, had a brawl with a dragoon, who insulted one of the party, and whom we mistook for an officer, as he was medalled and well mounted, &c.; but he turned out to be a sergeant-major. He called out the guard at the gates to arrest us (we being unarmed); upon which I and another (an Italian) rode through the said guard; but they succeeded in detaining others of the party. I rode to my house, and sent my secretary to give an account of the attempted and illegal arrest to the authorities, and then, without dismounting, rode back towards the gates, which are near my present mansion. Half way I met my man, vapouring away, and threatening to draw upon me (who had a cane in my hand, and no other arms). I, still believing him an officer, demanded his name and address, and gave him my hand and glove thereupon. A servant of mine thrust in between us (totally without orders), but let him go on my command. He then rode off at full speed; but about forty paces further was stabbed, and very dangerously (so as to be in peril), by some *callum bog*[3] or other of my people (for I have some rough-handed folks about me), I need hardly say without my direction or approval. The said dragoon had been sabring our unarmed country-men, however, at the *gate, after they were in arrest*, and held by the guards, and wounded one, Captain Hay, very severely. However, he got his paiks[4]—having acted like an assassin, and being treated like one. *Who* wounded him, though it was done before thousands of people, they have never been able to ascertain, or prove, nor even the *weapon*; some said a *pistol*, an *air-gun*, a stiletto, a sword, a lance, a pitch-fork, and what not. They have arrested and examined servants and people of all descriptions, but can make out nothing. Mr. Dawkins, our minister, assures me that no suspicion is entertained of the man who wounded him having been instigated by me, or any of the party. I enclose you copies of the depositions of those with us, and Dr. Craufurd, a canny Scot (*not* an acquaintance), who saw the latter part of the affair. They are in Italian.

These are the only literary matters in which I have been engaged since the publication and row about "Cain;—but Mr. Murray has several things of mine in his obstetrical hands. Another Mystery—a Vision—a Drama—and the like. But *you won't* tell me what *you* are doing—however, I shall find you out, write what you will. You say that I should like your son-in-law—it would be very difficult for me to

[3] *Waverly,* Chapter 58.
[4] *Rob Roy,* Chapter 29.

dislike any one connected with you; but I have no doubt that his own qualities are all that you describe.

I am sorry you don't like Lord Orford's new work.[5] My aristocracy, which is very fierce, makes him a favourite of mine. Recollect that those "little factions" comprised Lord Chatham and Fox, the father; and that *we* live in gigantic and exaggerated times, which make all under Gog and Magog appear pigmean. After having seen Napoleon begin like Tamerlane and end like Bajazet[6] in our own time, we have not the same interest in what would otherwise have appeared important history. But I must conclude.

Believe me ever and most truly yours,
NOEL BYRON

[TO JOHN HANSON]   *Pisa. May 4th. 1822*

Dear Sir/—I perceive some confusion and contradiction in the accounts in the papers occasioned by their confounding Lady Noel's personal property with the Wentworth estates.———Had you not better publish a statement that the arbitration referred to the Wentworth estates only—inherited by the will and testament of Lord Wentworth?—This would put an end to all mistakes and misstatements on the subject.—I am anxious to hear what you have done in this—and the Rochdale matters—&c. and will not trespass further on your time at present than by requesting you to believe me—with remembrances to all your family—

yrs. very truly & affectly.
NOEL BYRON

[TO JOHN MURRAY]   *Pisa. May 4th. 1822*

Dear Sir/—I will thank you to be a little more expeditious in our publishing matters—and also a little more explicit—for you do not say whether you have gotten from Mr. D[ougla]s K[innair]d the "Mystery" and "Vision" nor make any reply—about the Pulci— which has now been *two* years in your hands and better.——The Mystery and Werner I mean to print in one volume—with the lines to the "Po"—and the translation of "Francesca" from "Dante".—You by this time will have received "Werner".—I recommend to you

---

[5] *Memoirs of the Last Ten Years of George II* (edited by Lord Holland), 1822.
[6] Ruler of the Ottomans (1389–1402), Bajazet (in Rowe's *Tamerlane*, Act V) was "Closed in a cage, like some destructive beast."

(when you re-publish) to append the defence of "Cain" to that poem.—
Who is the author?—He must be a good-natured fellow as well as a
clever one.—

Believe me yrs. truly
N B

Pisa. May 16th. 1822

Dear Sir.—When I write to you as a friend you will of course take
your own time and leisure to reply, but when I address you—as a
publisher—I expect an answer.——I have written to you repeatedly
to ask whether you have or have not received the compositions of mine
which are (or were) in the hands of Mr. D[ouglas] K[innair]d and
Mr. Moore—and also directing when & how I wished them to be
published.—To all this I have had no satisfactory answer—nor indeed
any answer at all—for the few lines I have received from you are upon
other subjects.——As it was at your own wish that I agreed to continue
our literary connection, this appears a strange mode of renewing it—
but if you have repented of your desire—let me know at once (for you
are not celebrated for knowing your own mind upon such matters as I
hear with regard to others as well as myself) and there is no harm done.
I am told that Moore is in London[1]—if so—make my best remembrances;—tell Sir Walter that I answered his second letter last week.
—Continue to direct to Pisa—though I am going into the Country
near Leghorn in a few days.—Could you send me the *"Lockhart
papers"*[2] a publication upon Scotch affairs of some time since.—Also
Scott's new works and Moore's.——I am quite ignorant of your
English literary matters—and have no great curiosity, having I
believe seen the best of last year—Scott's—Israeli's, Luttrell's—&c.
——Israeli has quoted my remarks frequently in his notes—but I
would have furnished him with better remarks than those of mine—
which he has printed—if I had thought that he reckoned them worth
the copying—or that the book was to fall into his hands.——I gave it
to Capt. Tyler.——I have lately been rather unwell—and out of
spirits as you will suppose—if you have received the letter announcing
the loss of one of my children.——This event has driven me into some
attempts at Composition—to hold off reality—but with no great

---

[1] Moore had left Paris and arrived in London on April 16.

[2] *The Lockhart Papers; containing Memoirs and Commentaries upon the Affairs of
Scotland from 1702 to 1715,* by G. Lockhart. Published from the original manuscripts in the possession of A. Aufrere, 2 vols, 1817.

success.———The busts which you enquire after have been long paid for—but are not even begun—Bartolini is famous for his delays, something like yourself.—

yrs. truly
N B

[TO EDWARD J. DAWKINS]   *Pisa. May 17th. 1822*

Dear Sir,—I return you the paper with many thanks for that and for your letter.—It is the first English Newspaper (except Galignani's *Parisian* English) which I have seen for a long time—and I was lost in admiration of it's size and volume.—The Statement is near enough the truth to prevent any very erroneous impression—and is therefore satisfactory, as far as it goes.———Our friend Collini wrote to me for a hundred sequins—which I shall send him—as soon as I see my banker at Leghorn—where I am going tomorrow.———You are perhaps a little hard on the premature demand of our Man of law—if you had had as much to do with law and lawyers as I have (which I hope you never will) you would perhaps be more inclined to marvel at his modesty—though to be sure—his pecuniary assault is somewhat of the quickest in point of time—as the process is not only not begun at Florence—but perhaps never may—though it *ought*—or else *why* all this bother with Judges &c. both there and at Pisa—on the part of the Tuscan Government?———I am perfectly disposed to do or not to do what you think proper in the affair—and will give you as little further trouble as I can possibly help.———I am very glad that Leoni[1] will undertake Mr. Taaffe's comment———which I think contains valuable matter— & information—and he is so anxious about it that I should be glad to hear of any success for his work—which has been one of time and expence.———My friends in England are a little scandalized at his *own* account of his *own* conduct in the row—and on his trying to swear himself out of it afterwards———but the Man is a goodnatured fellow —and now that any little irritation at his—what shall I call it?—say blunder—it is a decent word—is over—I could wish him & his Commentary to have fair play—& due favour.———I beg leave to repeat myself ever & faithfully

yr. obliged f[rien]d & Se[rvan]t
NOEL BYRON

---

[1] Michele Leone had translated Byron's *Lament of Tasso* and Canto 4 of *Childe Harold* into Italian. (See Vol. 6, p. 42, and Vol. 7, p. 97.)

My dear Douglas,—I have received your letter of ye. third.—As I said before I *approve* of the mortgage—though I am not yet aware—(as it is not for the whole sum) what the exact increase may be upon the income.—Would it not [be] better for the *whole Sum?*—At any rate it is a more satisfactory security.—You will perhaps let me know further.—Hobhouse writes to me and recommends the insurance of Ly. B's life for twenty instead of ten thousand pounds. But I wish to hear what *you* say on that point also—perhaps twelve—or fifteen thousand might be as well—on account of the expence of insurance &c.——You say the Edinburgh has attacked the plays—it is not the first time—as they began on "the Doge" before—but I have no quarrel with them on that account.—I will trust the tragedies to time.—In the *mean* time—if Jeffrey is still in town—make my respects to him—& also to Moore.—I have not seen the Article in question—nor were it as bitter as Gall—would it induce me to forget that Jeffrey has "done the handsome thing" by me for many a long year.——If you come out in Autumn you will probably find me either here or in the Country near Leghorn.——Hobhouse says you are not well—pray take care of yourself & believe me

ever yours
N B

Dear Hay/—I have to acknowledge yours of the 1st. May—The reason of my not writing immediately—was 1stly. that I waited to hear something settled at Florence—and 2dly.—that I have since your departure lost my natural daughter by a fever—an event which drove every thing else from my contemplation for the moment—though I perhaps ought nevertheless to have considered your anxiety.——With regard to the Pisan affair—it remains where it did—nothing done—much said—& little discovered.—They have exiled Tita—*acquitting him entirely* of anything to do with the *fact*—but sent him away because he wore large mustachios &c.—reporting that he and I &c.—carried arms &c. & put Pisa in fear &c. &c. &c.——The other man is still detained—(I mean G[amba]'s servant) and Mr. Dawkins writes that the Tuscan Government do all they can to suppress the business altogether—but that he will urge them through with it—as it is. proper to do so. The accounts in the English papers have been nearer the truth than you would imagine.—Douglas Kinnaird's address is Ransoms & Co. Pall Mall London.—Yesterday I desired Lega to forward to you some directions for a power of Attorney for Collini.—*Your* name has not been mentioned in the newspapers.——I write in haste—and you will observe that I only reply to the part of your letter on *business*—for the reasons which you may suppose prevent me from touching upon the political part of it.—Let me hear from you & believe me

yrs. ever & truly
N B

[TO JOHN MURRAY]   *Pisa. May 17th. 1822*

Dear Sir,—Since I wrote to you yesterday I have received your letter—of the third, or second.——As the Mystery is not in many pages—you had better add it to Werner——and let them take their chance—I do not mean the Pulci—to be published in the same volume with "the Vision"—the latter of course ought to be a separate publication.—As I take the risk upon myself—you will permit me to decide upon the *time* of publication which must be sooner than what you say—for I care nothing about what you call "the Season"—and merely wish to occupy my mind——and the thing is an occupation—at least an Idea.—If I had called upon you for any specific terms—or pretended to any great expectations, you would then have a *right* to decide upon the time &c.—but as I have done nothing of the kind—and will even abide by the loss—if loss there be—you will permit *me* to arrange the publication according to my own will and pleasure.——I hear that the Edinburgh has attacked the three dramas[1]—which is a bad business for *you*; and I don't wonder that it discourages you.—— However, *that* volume may be trusted to *Time*—depend upon it——I read it over with some attention since it was published—and I think the time will come when it will be preferred to my other writings— though not immediately.——I say this without irritation against the Critics—or Criticism—whatever they may be—(for I have not seen them) and nothing that has or may appear in Jeffrey's review—can make me forget that he stood by me for ten good years—without any

---

[1] The *Edinburgh Review* for Feb., 1822 (Vol. 36, pp. 413–452) reviewed *Sardanapalus, The Two Foscari, and Cain.* The review, by Jeffrey, was particularly harsh in discussing *Cain*, and commented on the "pernicious" tendency of *Don Juan*, but granted that "his poems abound with sentiments of great dignity and tenderness, as well as passages of infinite sublimity and beauty".

motive to do so but his own good will.——I hear Moore is in town—remember me to him—& believe me

yrs. truly
N B

P.S.—If you think it necessary you may send me the Edinburgh—should there be any thing that requires an answer—I will reply but *temperately* and *technically*—that is to say—merely with respect to the *principles* of the Criticism—and not personally or offensively—as to it's literary merits.——

[TO THOMAS MOORE]   *Pisa, May 17th, 1822*

I hear you are in London.[1] You will have heard from Douglas Kinnaird (who tells me you have dined with him) as much as you desire to know of my affairs at home and abroad. I have lately lost my little girl Allegra by a fever, which has been a serious blow to me.

I did not write to you lately (except one letter to Murray's), not knowing exactly your "whereabouts." Douglas K. refused to forward my message to Mr. Southey[2]—*why*, he himself can explain.

You will have seen the statement of a squabble, &c. &c. What are you about? Let me hear from you at your leisure, and believe me ever yours,

N B

[TO PERCY BYSSHE SHELLEY]   *Pisa. May 20th. 1822*

Dear Shelley—It is proper that you should prosecute on every account,[1] but you need not apprehend that any punishment will be inflicted on the fellow—or expect any very splendid severity from the Tuscan Government, to their own ragamuffin.—After their obvious injustice in the case of Tita and Antonio—I really see no occasion for any delicacy with regard to the Serjeant—either on account of his own conduct or that of his Government.—As he did *not* assault me—and as I gave him a card (believing him to be an officer) which with us bears a hostile interpretation—*I* cannot prosecute him—but otherwise I

---

[1] When this was written Moore had already returned to Paris, having arrived there on May 8.

[2] Byron's challenge to Southey which he had sent to Kinnaird in February.

[1] Shelley had written on May 16, that he had no desire to prosecute Sergeant Masi for the injury done him (Masi had knocked him from his horse and he remained unconscious for some time).

would I assure you—and shall be very much surprized if you decline to do so.—Indeed it is absolutely necessary on account of Antonio & Tita.———The accounts in England of the Squabble—appear on the whole to have been tolerably fair—& without prejudice as far as I have heard or seen.—

The only literary news that I have heard of the plays—(contrary to your friendly augury) is that the Edinburgh R[eview] has attacked them all three—as well as it could.—I have not seen the article.— Murray writes discouragingly—and says "that nothing published this year has made the least impression" including I presume what he has published on my account also.—You see what it is to throw pearls to Swine——as long as I wrote the exaggerated nonsense which has corrupted the public taste—they applauded to the very echo—and now that I have really composed within these three or four years some things which should "not willingly be let die"[2]—the whole herd snort and grumble and return to wallow in their mire.—However it is fit that I should pay the penalty of spoiling them—as no man has contributed more than me in my earlier compositions to produce that exaggerated & false taste—it is a fit retribution that anything [like a?] classical production should be received as these plays have been treated.——— The American Commodore has invited me on board his Frigate here[3]— and I go to see her and him tomorrow.———I have not yet decided on the subject you mention waiting for letters from England.———Of Hunt I hear nothing—nor you—I suppose that he has embarked then.[4]

yrs. ever & truly
N B

[TO MRS. CATHERINE POTTER STITH]

Villa Dupuis.[1] May 22d. 1822

Madam,—I take the liberty of requesting your acceptance of a memorial less frail than that which you did me the honour of requiring

[2] Milton, *The Reason of Church Government*, Book 2.

[3] Commodore Jacob Jones of the American frigate *Constitution*, then in Leghorn harbour. Jones was commander of the American Squadron in the Mediterranean.

[4] The day this letter was written Shelley received word that Hunt and his family had arrived in Genoa, but they did not reach Leghorn until the first of July.

[1] Byron had moved his household together with Teresa and the Gambas to a villa at Montenero, a few miles from Leghorn. He had rented the villa for the summer months from Francesco Dupuy (as Byron later spelled his name). He was eager to be near the sea and to get the Gambas away from Pisa where their status as exiles was becoming precarious. Cline (p. 164) says that the move was made on May 18, but Byron wrote to Shelley from Pisa on May 20.

yesterday.[2]—The volume which I send contains an outline and some designs from the famous Faust of Goëthe [sic]—which have been much admired both in Germany and England.—I should have preferred to send some publication of my own—but I have none by me at present. —I need hardly add that I feel much flattered and gratified by the interest which you have been pleased to take in my writings.——I have also been ever a Well wisher to your Country and Countrymen— in common with all unprejudiced minds amongst my own.——Will you make my respects acceptable to Major Stith and do me the further honour to believe me

yr. obliged & obedt. Sert
NOEL BYRON

[added note to Major Stith]

Sir,—Of the lines which you did me the honour to request, I have no copy.—Mr. West has—and will of course be glad to send them to you such as they are.—I hope that you are getting well, although you bear sickness much better than most men do health—and diminish our sympathy by increasing our admiration.—With my compliments to Mrs Stith—I have the honour to sign myself your ever obliged & faithful St.

N B

[TO GEORGE H. BRUEN][1]   *May 25th. 1822*

Sir.—If you can make it convenient I am at your commands immediately—or at any hour you choose to fix.—I have the honour to be

yr. obedt. humble Se[rvan]t
N B

[TO DOUGLAS KINNAIRD]   [*Villa Dupuy, Leghorn, May 26th. 1822?*]

P.S.—I was invited by the Americans on board of their Squadron here—and received with the greatest kindness and *rather too much ceremony.*—They have asked me to sit for my picture to an American Artist now in Florence.—As I was taking leave—an American Lady took a *rose* (which I wore) from me—as she said she wished to send

---

[2] Mrs. Stith, wife of an American officer, was on board the *Constitution* when Byron visited it on May 21, 1822. She begged him to give her a rose which he was wearing in his buttonhole as a souvenir to take back to America and also expressed admiration for his poetry. (See *South Atlantic Quarterly*, Vol. 22, Jan 1923.)

[1] Bruen was the American Merchant who commissioned a portrait of Byron by the American painter W. E. West. See also July 4, 1822, to Dawkins.

something which I had about me to America.——They showed me an American edition of my poems &c. &c.—and all kinds of attention & good will.—I also hear that as an author I am in great request in Germany.—All this is some compensation for the brutality of the native English.——Would you write a *German* line to Goethe for me —explaining the omission of the dedication to "Sardanapalus" by the fault of the publisher and asking his permission to prefix it to the following volume of Werner & the Mystery.—Murray must put on his title page "published for the Author" which will throw all upon me of loss or otherwise.——

[TO JOHN MURRAY]   *Montenero. May 26th. 1822*
                                    near Leghorn.——

Dear Sir,—The body is embarked—in what ship—I know not— neither could I enter into the details; but the Countess G[amba] G[uiccioli] has had the goodness to give the necessary orders to Mr. Dunn—who superintends the embarkation[1]—& will write to you. ——I wish it to be buried in Harrow Church—there is a spot in the Churchyard near the footpath on the brow of the hill looking toward Windsor—and a tomb under a large tree (bearing the name of Peachee —or Peachey) where I used to sit for hours & hours when a boy—this was my favourite spot—but as I wish to erect a tablet to her memory —the body had better be deposited in the Church.—Near the door— on the left as you enter—there is a monument with a tablet containing these words—

> "When Sorrow weeps o'er Virtue's sacred dust,
> Our tears become us, and our Grief is just,
> Such were the tears she shed, who grateful pays
> This last sad tribute to her love, and praise."

I recollect them (after seventeen years) not from any thing remarkable in them—but because—from my seat in the Gallery—I had generally my eyes turned towards that monument——as near it as convenient I would wish Allegra to be buried—and on the wall—a marble tablet placed with these words.—

> In memory of
> Allegra—
> daughter of G. G. Lord Byron—

[1] Henry Dunn, a merchant at Leghorn, superintended the embarkation of Allegra's body when it was shipped to England.

who died at Bagnacavallo
in Italy April 20th. 1822.
aged five years and three months.—
"I shall go to her, but she shall not return to me.—"[2]

2d. Samuel 12.—23.—

The funeral I wish to be as private as is consistent with decency—and I could hope that Henry Drury will perhaps read the service over her. —If he should decline it—it can be done by the usual Minister for the time being.—I do not know that I need add more just now.——I will now turn to other subjects.—

Since I came here I have been invited by the Americans on board of their Squadron where I was received with all the kindness which I could wish, and with *more ceremony* than I am fond of.—I found them finer ships than your own of the same class—well manned & officered. —A number of American gentlemen also were on board at the time & some ladies.—As I was taking leave—an American lady asked for a *rose* which I wore—for the purpose she said of sending to America something which I had about me as a memorial.—I need not add that I felt the compliment properly.—Captain Chauncey showed me an American and very pretty edition of my poems, and offered me a passage to the United States—if I would go there.——Commodore Jones was also not less kind and attentive.—I have since received the enclosed letter desiring me to sit for my picture for some Americans.[3]—It is a singular that in the same year that Lady Noel leaves by will an interdiction for my daughter to see her father's portrait for many years— the individuals of a nation not remarkable for their liking to the English in particular—nor for flattering men in general, request me to sit for my "portraicture"—as Baron Bradwardine[4] calls it.——I am also told of considerable literary honours in Germany.——Goëthe I am told is my professed patron and protector.—At Leipsic this year—the highest prize was proposed for a translation of two Cantos of Childe Harold.— —I am not sure that this was at *Leipsic*—but Mr. Bancroft[5] was my

[2] Because of the objection of J. W. Cunningham, Vicar of Harrow, and some of his influential parishioners, no memorial inscription to Allegra was placed in the church, though the body was buried near the entrance. (See *LJ*, VI, 70–72.)

[3] The request came from George H. Bruen of New York, then in Leghorn, for Byron to sit for his portrait to William Edward West (1788–1857) of Philadelphia, who had come to Italy to study painting in 1819. He later painted in London from 1825 to 1839.

[4] *Waverley*, Chap. 13.

[5] George Bancroft, the American historian, then a young man on his travels, who had just returned from studying in Germany, visited Byron at Montenero on May 22, 1822.

authority—a good German Scholar (a young American) and an acquaintance of Goëthe's.——Goëthe and the Germans are particularly
fond of Don Juan—which they judge of as a work of Art.—I had heard
something like this before through Baron Lutzerode.[6]—The translations have been very frequent of several of the works—and Goëthe
made a comparison between Faust and Manfred.——All this is some
compensation for your English native brutality so fully displayed this
year—(I mean *not your* individually) to it's brightest extent.—I forgot
to mention a little anecdote of a different kind—I went over the Constitution (the Commodore's flag ship) and saw among other things
worthy of remark a little boy *born* on board of her by a sailor's wife.—
They had christened him "Constitution Jones"—I of course approved
the name—and the woman added—"Ah Sir—if he turns out but half as
good as his name!"

yrs. ever & truly
N B

[TO DOUGLAS KINNAIRD]   *Montenero. Leghorn. May 27th. 1822*

My dear Douglas,—My above address as at Pisa may probably be
the same in Sept. and I need not add that you will be welcome there or
any where else—that may happen to [be] my residence.——I have
received the enclosed letter from Mr. Hanson Jr.—when I constituted
you my *Power of* Attorney—I meant it to be also *Power over* my
Attorney—and so deal with the Attorno according to your despotism.
——Does he mean that the *whole* balance—or *his separate* balance is
£600?——for if I recollect rightly they set up a sort of *separate* claim
—and a double claim besides.——I see no use in their appealing to me
—because if I empowered you to act during my absence—it was with
the wish that you should do so—else *why* make you my Potestas at all?
—You see they are getting on but slowly with that eternal Mortgage
—if the funds fall—(& war seems imminent) I shall lose all owing to
the cursed dilatoriness of trustees and Solicitors—& yet he seems eager
enough for his bill.——Hanson is always too sanguine about Rochdale
matters—however the sum obtained for the tolls—is better than nothing.—I wonder when that blessed Appeal on the minerals will be heard
& decided——I suppose my politics will prevent it's success—"Well
Heaven's above all!"[1]

As to the temporary & precarious tenure of the Noel affair—manage

---

[6] Baron Lutzerode had translated *Cain* and was a Byron enthusiast.

[1] *Othello*, Act II, scene 3. The phrase was such in editions of Shakespeare available
in Byron's time. Most modern editions give it: "God's above all".

it as you please—with those two fellows for trustees—I expect little profit—& less comfort——Hobhouse proposed to ensure *her* life for *twenty* instead of *ten* thousand pounds—what think you?——*When* & *how* & where are the *rents* paid—or to be paid—when are they due—or are they ever due?——what sum do you think I should set aside for liquidations &c.?—on all these points I desiderate illumination.—— What *is* Lady N.B.'s *complaint?*—for of this even I know nothing.— There is another thing I wish to say—as Mr. Murray should not run risks unnecessarily while I am going down hill in the world of scribbling I will be at the *whole* expence of the publication of the things in hand— & any little profit—which may accrue—I can take—or at any rate undergo the probable loss.——I care nothing about the Edinburgh Review (which I have not seen)—though it will do much harm.—I have no hesitation in saying that the late volume contains by far the best of my writings—& the time will come when it will be thought so.— You must also advance for me to Murray the expence of poor little Allegra's funeral. I have directed that she may be buried at Harrow on the Hill,—and committed the care of the funeral (which I wish to be as private as is consistent with decency) to Mr. M[urray] not wishing to trouble *you.*—

yrs. ever
N B

[TO JOHN MURRAY]   *Montenero. near Leghorn. May 29th. 1822*

Dear Sir,—I return you the proofs revised.—Your printer has made one odd mistake "poor as a *Mouse*" instead of "poor as a *Miser*"[1] the expression may seem strange—but it is only a translation of "Semper avarus eget".[2]——You will add the *Mystery*—and publish as soon as you can.—I care nothing for your "Season" nor the *blue* approbations nor disapprobations.—All that is to be considered by you on the subject —is as a matter of *business*—and if I square that to your notions— (even to the running the risk entirely myself) you may permit me to choose my own time & mode of publication.——With regard to the late volume—The present run against *it* or *me*—may impede it for a time—but it has the vital principle of permanency within it—as you may perhaps one day discover.——I wrote to you on another subject a few days ago.

yrs.
N B

[1] *Werner*, Act I, scene 2.
[2] Horace, *Epistles*, I, ii, 56: "The covetous is ever in want."

P.S.—Please to send me the dedication of Sardanapalus to Goëthe—which you took upon you to omit—which omission I assure you I take very ill.—I shall prefix it to Werner—unless you prefer my putting another stating that the former had been omitted by the publisher.——On the title page of the present volume—put "published for the Author by J. M."

[TO THE EARL OF CLARE]   *Villa Dupuy. June 5th. 1822*

My dear Clare—I expected your return at *two*—so my fools of Servants said—& that is the reason I did not write or come to you immediately.—As I should probably find you out of doors at Leghorn I send this to apprize you that at two tomorrow I will go to Leghorn or you shall come here—as you please.——I will send my carriage for you—or saddle horses—if you prefer them.——I did not answer your letters expecting to see you here—or to hear you were in England.[1]—I have had plenty of vexations lately—but the pleasure of seeing you again will compensate for them all—though accompanied with the regret that it is for so transient a glimpse.—

ever yrs. most truly
NOEL BYRON

[TO JOHN MURRAY]   *Montenero. June 6th. 1822*

Dear Sir,—I return you the revise of Werner and expect the rest.—With regard to the lines to the "Po"—perhaps you had better put them quietly in a second edition (if you reach one—that is to say) than in the first—because though they have been reckoned fine—and I wish them to be preserved—I do not wish them to attract IMMEDIATE observation—on account of the relationship of the Lady to whom they are addrest with the first families in Romagna and the Marches.———The defender of "Cain"—may or may not be as you term him—"a tyro in literature"; however I think both you and I are under great obligation to him—but I suppose *you* won't think so unless his defence serve as an advertisement.—I have read the Edinburgh R[eview] in Galignani's magazine—and have not yet decided whether to answer

[1] Byron had met Lord Clare on the road between Imola and Bologna in October, 1821, but they had only a few minutes together. Byron was on his way to Pisa and Clare was going to Rome, but promised to stop by to see him on his return. This letter gives evidence that they did meet again. It is addressed to Clare at the Globe Hotel, Livorno. See also letter to Moore of June 8.

them or not—for if I do—it will be difficult for me not to make sport for the Philistines by pulling down a house or two—since when I once take pen in hand—I *must* say what comes uppermost—or fling it away———I have not the hypocrisy to pretend impartiality—nor the temper (as it is called) to keep always from saying—what may not be pleasing to the hearer—or reader.—What do they mean by "elaborate"—why *you* know that they were written as fast as I could put pen to paper—and printed from the *original* M.S.S. & never revised but in the proofs—*look* at the *dates* and the M.S.S. themselves—whatever faults they have must spring from carelessness and not from labour—they said the same of "Lara"—which I wrote while undressing after coming home from balls and masquerades in the year of revelry *1814*.

yrs. ever
N B

June 8th. 1822

P.S.—Since the last was written I have sent you by my earliest and dearest friend—Lord Clare—a common-place book[1]—about half filled—which may serve *partly* hereafter—in aid of the Memoirs purchased by you from Mr. Moore. There are parts which have no reference to nor will answer your purpose, but some others may do perhaps.—You give me no explanation of your intention as to the "Vision—by Quevedo redivivus" one of my best things.—Indeed you are altogether so abstruse and undecided lately—that I suppose you mean me to write—"John Murray Esqre. a *Mystery*" a composition which would not displease the Clergy nor the trade.———I by no means wish you to do what you don't like but merely to say what you will do. The Vision *must* be published by some one.—As to *Clamours*—the die is cast—and "come one come all"—we will fight it out—at least one of us.———The difference between you and me is—that you are of *every man's* opinion (especially the last man who talks to you) and I of *no* man's.—Both extremes are bad—but we can't establish a medium.——

[TO EDWARD J. DAWKINS]   *Monte Nero. Livorno. June 7th. 1822*

My dear Sir,—For my sins (I presume) & for your troubles I must intrude upon you again about this business of the Pisans &c.———We are waiting here in a most unpleasant state of suspense———they refuse to give any answer or decision—and the family of the Gambas

---

[1] The "Detached Thoughts" begun on October 15, 1821.

are without any renewed papers or security of any kind[1]—and all for *what?* what on earth had *they* to do with the matter?—Is it because they are exiles and weak that they are to be persecuted or because they are friends of mine?——I know that *you* can do little for them—as they are not English subjects—but you may perhaps be able to obtain some information.—Of course their fate—must be mine—where they go—I accompany them.——Madame Guiccioli who is ill was ordered here by Vacca for the benefit of Sea-bathing and we know not whether she will be permitted to remain.—Such conduct is indeed infamous—and can have but one object—viz.—the persecuting *me* through *them*— that when they have driven us from their States—they may tell the Story in their own way.—*This* will I trust at least be prevented—and that you will obtain a *publication* of the conduct of the whole business.—— Whatever personal vexation or inconvenience it may be to give up my house &c.—& remove my furniture before the expiration of the period assigned for their occupation——I care ⟨nothing⟩ little for leaving such a country—but I *do* care for the constructions to which (at this time) my departure may give rise.——The Courier (they may exile him if they like) is in danger from his blow[2]—as the enclosed note will certify.—All that I could wish to know is a *decision* of some kind—that I may know where to go—of course—what they decree about the Gambas is decisive with regard to myself.—Collini has had his 100 Sequins—and I hear no more of him.——I have taken the liberty with *you*—to request the elder Count Gamba to present this note—which has swelled into a letter—as he can explain anything you may think worth asking.——Believe me in all cases and in all places—with much esteem and obligation

ever yrs. faithfully

N B

P.S.—With regard to the fellow who has (I am *now* sorry to say) survived the consequences of his cowardly outrage—the other Gentlemen may prosecute—but it would be difficult for *me* to do so—as I was not one of his victims, except in the bad language which he has sufficiently paid for.——When I say that I am *sorry* that he has recovered—it is because I see many innocent persons suffering on account of such a miscreant.—

[1] Because of Pietro Gamba's involvement in the Masi affair, the Pisan Governor, who along with the Tuscan Government wanted to get rid of the Gambas and also of Byron, gave only a ten day renewal of the visitors' cards of Pietro and his father.

[2] Byron's courier, Guiseppe Strauss, was struck by Masi in the affray at the city gate and was still under doctor's treatment.

Montenero, Villa Dupuy, near Leghorn, June 8th, 1822

I have written to you twice through the medium of Murray, and on one subject, *trite* enough,—the loss of poor little Allegra by a fever: on which topic I shall say no more—there is nothing but time.

A few days ago, my earliest and dearest friend, Lord Clare, came over from Geneva [Genoa?] on purpose to see me before he returned to England. As I have always loved him (since I was thirteen, at Harrow) better than any (*male*) thing in the world, I need hardly say what a melancholy pleasure it was to see him for a *day* only; for he was obliged to resume his journey immediately.

* * * * * * * * * * * * * * *

I have heard, also, many other things of our acquaintances which I did not know; amongst others that

* * * * * * * * * * * * * * *

Do you recollect, in the year of revelry 1814, the pleasantest parties and balls all over London? and not least so at * *'s. Do you recollect your singing duets with Lady * *, and my flirtation with Lady * *, and all the other fooleries of the time? while * * was sighing, and Lady * * ogling him with her clear hazel eyes. *But* eight years have passed and, since that time, * * has * * * * * *; —— has run away with * * * * *; and *mysen* (as my Nottinghamshire friends call themselves) might as well have thrown myself out of the window while you were singing, as intermarried where I did. You and * * * have come off the best of us. I speak merely of my marriage, and its consequences, distresses, and calumnies; for I have been much more happy, on the whole, *since*, than I ever could have been with * * * * * * * * * *

* * * * * * * * * * * * * * *

I have read the recent article of Jeffrey in a faithful transcription of the impartial Galignani. I suppose the long and short of it is, that he wishes to provoke me to reply. But I won't, for I owe him a good turn still for his kindness by-gone. Indeed, I presume that the present opportunity of attacking me again was irresistible; and I can't blame him, knowing what human nature is. I shall make but one remark:— what does he mean by elaborate? The whole volume was written with the greatest rapidity, in the midst of evolutions, and revolutions, and persecutions, and proscriptions of all who interested me in Italy. They said the same of *Lara*, which *you* know, was written amidst balls and fooleries, and after coming home from masquerades and routs, in the summer of the sovereigns.[1] Of all I have ever written, they are perhaps the most carelessly composed; and their faults, whatever they may be, are those of negligence, and not of labour. I do not think this a merit, but it is a fact.

Yours ever and truly,
N B

P.S.—You see the great advantage of my new signature;—it may either stand for "Nota Bene" or "Noel Byron," and, as such, will save much repetition, in writing either books or letters.[2] Since I came here, I have been invited on board of the American squadron, and treated with all possible honour and ceremony. They have asked me to sit for my picture; and, as I was going away, an American lady took a rose from me (which had been given to me by a very pretty Italian lady that very morning), because, she said, "She was determined to send or take something which I had about me to America." *There* is a kind of Lalla Rookh incident for you! However, all these American honours arise, perhaps, not so much from their enthusiasm for my "Poeshie," as their belief in my dislike to the English,—in which I have the satisfaction to coincide with them. I would rather, however, have a nod from an American, than a snuff-box from an emperor.

[TO ISAAC D'ISRAELI]
Montenero, Villa Dupuy, nr. Leghorn, June 10th, 1822
(to ye care of John Murray, Esqre.)

Dear Sir,—If you will permit me to call you so. I had some time ago taken up my pen at Pisa to thank you for the present of your new Edition of the *Literary Character*, which has often been to me a consolation, and always a pleasure. I was interrupted, however, partly by business, and partly by vexations of different kinds, for I have not very long ago lost a child by a fever, and I have had a good deal of petty trouble with the laws of this lawless country, on account of the prosecution of a servant for an attack upon a cowardly Scoundrel of a dragoon, who drew his Sword upon some unarmed Englishmen;

---

[1] The year 1814 when sovereigns, statesmen and generals were in London to celebrate the allied victories.

[2] Leigh Hunt said that Byron "delighted, when he took the additional name of Noel . . . to sign himself N.B.; 'because,' said he, 'Bonaparte and I are the only public persons whose initials are the same.'" (*Lord Byron and Some of His Contemporaries*, I, 125.)

and whom I had done the honour to mistake for an officer, and to treat like a Gentleman. He turned out to be neither—like many others with medals and in uniform; but he paid for his brutality with a severe and dangerous wound inflicted by nobody knows whom:[1] for of three suspected and two arrested they have been able to identify neither, which is strange, since he was wounded in the presence of thousands in a public Street during a feast day and full promenade.

But to return to things more analogous to the *Literary Character*. I wish to say that had I known that the book was to fall into your hands, or that the M.S.S. notes you have thought worthy of publication[2] would have attracted your attention, I would have made them more copious and perhaps not so careless.

I really cannot know whether I am or am not the Genius you are pleased to call me, but I am very willing to put up with the mistake, if it be one. It is a title dearly enough bought by most men, to render it endurable, even when not quite clearly made out, which it never *can* be till the Posterity, whose decisions are merely dreams to ourselves, has sanctioned or denied it, while it can touch us no further.

Mr. Murray is in possession of an M.S.S. Memoir of mine (not to be published till I am in my grave) which, strange as it may seem, I never read over since it was written and have no desire to read over again. In it I have told what, as far as I know, is the *truth—not* the *whole* truth—for if I had done so I must have involved much private and some dissipated history; but, nevertheless, nothing but the truth, as far as regard for others permitted it to appear.

I do not know whether you have seen those M.S.S.; but as you are curious in such things as relate to the human mind, I should feel gratified if you had.

I also sent him (Murray) a few days since, a common-place book, by my friend Lord Clare, containing a few things which may perhaps aid his publication in case of his surviving me.

If there are any questions which you would like to ask me as connected with your Philosophy of the literary Mind (*if* mine be a literary mind), I will answer them fairly or give a reason for *not*—good, bad,

[1] Byron himself knew that his coachman Vincenzo Papi was the one who wounded Sergeant Masi, but since the authorities dismissed him without discovering his guilt, Byron, always protective of his servants, kept his knowledge to himself, since he thought Masi the more culpable of the two.

[2] In the 3rd. edition of *The Literary Character* (1822), D'Israeli included the manuscript notes which Byron had written in a copy of an earlier edition. That copy is now in the Meyer Davis Collection in the University of Pennsylvania Library.

or indifferent. At present I am paying the penalty of having helped to spoil the public taste, for, as long as I wrote in the false exaggerated style of youth and the times in which we live, they applauded me to the very echo; and within these few years, when I have endeavoured at better things and written what I suspect to have the principle of duration in it, the Church, the Chancellor, and all men—even to my grand patron Francis Jeffrey Esqre. of the E[dinburgh] R[eview]—have risen up against me and my later publications. Such is Truth! Men dare not look her in the face, except by degrees: they mistake her for a Gorgon, instead of knowing her to be a Minerva.

I do not mean to apply this mythological simile to my own endeavours. I have only to turn over a few pages of your volumes to find innumerable and far more illustrious instances.

It is lucky that I am of a temper not to be easily turned aside though by no means difficult to irritate. But I am making a dissertation instead of writing a letter. I write to you from the Villa Dupuy, near Leghorn, with the islands of Elba and Corsica visible from my balcony, and my old friend the Mediterranean rolling blue at my feet. As long as I retain my feeling and my passion for Nature, I can partly soften or subdue my other passions and resist or endure those of others.

I have the honour to be, truly, your obliged

and faithful Sert.

NOEL BYRON

[TO EDWARD ELLICE][1]   *Montenero, Leghorn. June 12th. 1822*

My dear Ellice,—It is a very long time since I have written to you but I have not forgotten your kindness—and I am now going to tax it—I hope not too highly.—But *don't* be alarmed—it is *not* a loan—but *information* which I am about to solicit.—By your extensive connections —no one can have better opportunities of hearing the real state of *South* America—I mean Bolivar's Country——I have many years had transatlantic projects of Settlement—and what I could wish from you—would be some information now of the best course to pursue, and some letters of recommendation in case I should sail for Angustura.[2] ——I am told that land is very cheap there—but though I have no great disposable funds to vest in such purchases—yet my Income such

1 See Oct. 3, 1819, to Hobhouse, note 2. (Vol. 6, p. 225.)
2 Angostura or Ciudad Bolivar was a port on the Orinoco River in Venezuela. Byron's interest in South American emigration began in 1819 and continued in the back of his mind until he resolved to return to Greece.

as it is—would be sufficient in any country (except England) for all the comforts of life, and for most of it's luxuries.——The War there is now over—and as I do not go there to *speculate*—but to settle—without any views but those of independence—and the enjoyment of the common civil rights—I should presume such an arrival would not be unwelcome.——All I request of you is not to *dis*courage nor *en*courage—but to give me such a statement as you think prudent & proper.——I do not address any other friends upon this subject—who would only throw obstacles in my way, and bore me to return to England—which I never will do—unless compelled by some insuperable cause——I have a quantity of furniture—books &c. &c. &c. which I could easily ship from Leghorn—but I wish "to look before I leap" over the Atlantic.——Is it true that for a few thousand dollars a considerable tract of land may be obtained? I speak of *South* America—recollect—I have read some publications on the subject—but they seemed violent and vulgar party productions. Please to address your answer to me at this place—and believe me

ever and truly yrs.
NOEL BYRON

[TO GEORGE W. BRUEN]   *June 15, 1822*

. . . [Byron says he is "more than occupied with some visitors" and therefore cannot lodge Mr. Nast (West?)] Could you help me through any of your American friends to a loan of the life of Patrick Henry—I have since I saw you met with a slight outline of his life—by which he appears worthy to complete a triumvirate with Franklin and Washington . . . .

[TO EDWARD J. DAWKINS]   *Villa Dupuy. June 16th. 1822*

Dear Sir,—I have received your letter, & I fear that I have not made myself quite understood. Believe me I never did nor could intend to throw the slightest shadow of blame upon you, for the evasions and apparent uncertainties of the T[uscan] Government in this affair.—Were I now or in future to do so—I should not only be *ungrateful* but *insolent.*—If I express myself strongly—on *their* apparent conduct—it is because I *feel* so—& because I never could—and I fear never *shall* be able to measure my words and phrases as a wiser man would in similar circumstances.—But I am not quite Child enough to beat my

Nurse—nor to confound for an instant your kindness—with their conduct.—I shall be very glad to find it as you state—and that the Gamba family at least will have fair play, for myself it is a matter of much less importance—and I must bear it—as I have borne greater injuries.———My friend Lord Clare—who came over the other day from Genoa to see me—states to me in a letter since his return (I had requested him to ask Mr. H[*ill*]¹ some question[s] as to the probability of their permitting the Gambas to remain in the Sardinian States²— with me—in case of our quitting Tuscany) that Mr. H[ill] agreed with Clare and myself in thinking that *I* (and not *they*) was the obnoxious object.—I am very glad to hear it—so that it secures *them.*——

It is very presumptuous in me perhaps to conceive myself of importance enough to be obnoxious at all—but you know what human Nature is—and especially in Italy at present—where few persons who can read or write are sufficiently insignificant to be beyond the dislike or Suspicion of the existing Governments, whether they be native or foreign.—As to Collini when he has drunk out—or otherwise expended his Sequins—I presume that he will proceed to earn them.— You seem almost to blame me for sending them—but what could I do? I never knew a lawyer that would move without them.—You say he is "profligate"—it is a great consolation to think that a Gentleman can continue so to so respectable a period of longevity.—I conceive that our friend must be between fifty and sixty—and he has a servant constantly by him at nights to change his linen—having apparently the same malady with the Canon Sedillo in Gil Blas.—It would not be unpleasant to know of what peculiar species his *present* profligacy may consist, that one might be aware of what may be reckoned upon in reserve at threescore.——Will you do me the honour to believe me ever and truly

yr. obliged & faithful St.

N B

June 18th. 1822

P.S.³—The Elder Count Gamba is here—and will convey this letter.—Collini was at Pisa & was conversed with by Count Pietro— but of course nothing decisive could be ascertained from that "Light of the Council".—I enclose you an extract from an Austrian journal, in which you will perceive how they have sunk all that made against

¹ William Noel Hill was British Minister at Genoa.
² Genoa was then part of the Kingdom of Sardinia.
³ This manuscript is detached, but the postscript was probably sent with the letter of June 16 to Dawkins.

the Serjeant—and added circumstances untrue.—The fellow had no blow from me—for I took him for an Officer—and expected of course a more satisfactory atonement.———I hear that Masi goes about Florence telling a story *different* even from his *own* deposition!—Let him make the best of it[;] he acted like a bully in the beginning, & with no great valour in the end—for when he was wounded—why did he not face about? he had strength enough to ride off at full gallop for a quarter of a mile—*after* he was hit—calling for help—in very distinct terms—with the same effort he might have cut down a dozen.—But he seems to have expended his force in drawing on the unarmed and arrested party at the Gates.———I have every wish that the Investigation should be as full & fair as possible—without any favour to me.———

[TO DOUGLAS KINNAIRD]   *Villa Dupuy. Livorno. June 20th. 1822*

My dear Douglas/—I have received the enclosed letter from Mr. Hanson, and as I perfectly agree with him upon the subject—I appoint Mr. Charles Hanson to act on my behalf in these matters—subject to you as trustee. I know no right which Dr. Lushington has—& will go to law with them on that score—if necessary—Burdett and Brand *positively* left the estates to my controul—(unless they choose to break their word *now*) nor will I go to the expence of a Surveyor—in these times—when we shall be but too lucky to obtain any rent at all.—This is my fixed opinion & determination, be the consequences what they may.———With regard to the insurance—I do not quite understand you —you say that for ten thousand pounds—it is *138* pounds [;] in a former letter you said that it would be *270* for ten thousand pounds—how am I to reconcile this?—I should be willing to go as far as *300* pounds in insurances—but even that is almost more than I can afford—for you remember that I have debts still to liquidate—and I reckon we shall have more trouble than profit from the new acquisitions.—Mr. Davidson (I know him) is a Yorkshire Man and may be a good fellow when drunk—and honest when *sober* (which is not often) but he is as fit to be Steward to an estate as *I* am to manage your bank—and I think I have said enough.——

I see the matter must go to a Court of law—& so be it—I never looked to anything but dishonour and discomfort from the house of Atreus into which I married.———You may insure for me as far as three hundred pounds will go——but *out* of the *Noel* rents—when we receive [any?][I] look to have my *own* fee entire.—I have read Jeffrey's attack—and shall probably answer it—but *temperately*—if possible.—

176

I wrote to ask you whether Hanson's bill—which he states at 600 pounds—is his Son's or his *own* account—or *one* or both—and what is his remaining balance against me?—When the Rochdale toll-men pay their five hundred pounds—you may advance them something—or the whole of it—but this I leave to your discretion.——I am just now far from well—from the excessive heat and a disordered state of Stomach. I rejoice to hear you are getting well—A Mr. Fuller called on me the other day by "*desire* of Mr. Hobhouse" I refused to see him (but *civilly* of course) for I will see no Englishmen but those I knew before or have business with. Tell Hobhouse that it was painful to refuse a friend of *his* —but that it is a rule—& I hope that he will introduce nobody else.—

ever yrs. most &c.
NOEL BYRON

[TO JOHN HANSON] *Leghorn. June 20th. 1822*

Dear Sir,—As I fully agree with you in your view of the question— I hereby appoint and direct *Charles Hanson Esqre.* to act in my behalf in the management of the Noel Estates—and I further wish to have *my rights* ascertained—even if we go into a Court of law for that purpose. —The Arbitrators are men of honour and I understood from them *distinctly* that the Estates were under *my* controul—and I will not be dictated to by Dr. Lushington—or any one else.—I expect neither comfort—nor honour—nor *fair* dealing—from Lady Byron nor any of her Agents never having met with it hitherto from *any* of them—as to Mr. Davidson he may be an *honest* man—but he is *not* (to my knowledge) *a sober* one—and I do not approve of his nomination.—I see that we must go to law with them at once—there appears little else left for it.——You may show this letter to Mr. Kinnaird or Dr. Lushington— —I will stand by what I say as to *Lushington's* & the Noel people's conduct—and give him satisfaction with the greatest pleasure—though I suspect *his* weapons are only *libels—in* and out of Doctor's Commons. ——As to going to the expence of surveying an estate—from which we shall be but too lucky to obtain any *rent at all*—It seems to me—at *present*—a kind of insanity—and even a *shame* to distress the farmers further at such a moment.——I do not know that I need to add anything further at present except [several lines cut out with the signature].

P.S.—Have you anything to add on the Rochdale Coal Suits?—when will they be decided? one way or the other?—If you are *sure* that the *Noel trustees* are assuming an *undue right*—let us go to law with them at once.——

177

Dear Sir,—As a further specimen of the kindness and civility of the Tuscan authorities towards me—I am obliged to inform you that they refuse at Leghorn to accord permission to cruize in sight of the port in my little yacht—which arrived from Genoa last week.—They also refused to let me have a boat from the port (off the Sea-baths which are in *shallow* water—) to undress in when I go out to swim—which I prefer of course in deep water.——My Yacht which was allowed to cruize at Genoa without molestation & which cost me a considerable sum in building &c.—is thus rendered perfectly useless to me—& the expence entirely thrown away.——She is a little thing of about 22 tons —but a model to look at—& sails very fast.—She has nothing obnoxious about her that I know—unless her name ("the Bolivar")[1] should be so—and all her papers are in regular order—& admitted to be so—& no one on board but the Crew.—Tita is still at Spezia.[2] ——Thus matters stand with me at present—I only wait for a decision in the affair of the Serjeant to take steps for quitting a country from whose authorities I have experienced every petty vexation and insult —which they could devise—and without cause that I know of. I neither write nor speak [of] them—nor *to* them.——I merely state this to you—(for I have long given up any idea of obtaining [any] species of redress from the Government) to show you the kind of disposition which their authorities uniformly evince in all which regards me.— Believe me

> very truly & faithfully yr. obliged Sert.
> NOEL BYRON

[TO JOHN MURRAY?] *June 26th. 1822*

. . . I return you the revise—with an addition to the preface, you need not add the "lines to the Po" & the translation from Dante . . . .

[TO THE GOVERNOR OF LEGHORN] *[July 2, 1822?]*

Sir—I write to you in English since I know you do us the honour of understanding our language. There has been issued by you an order of

---

[1] The correspondence of the Tuscan authorities indicates that they were suspicious of Byron and were eager to get him out of the territory. Byron's desire to defy them and to bait them, as well as his interest in South America, prompted him to name his boat after the revolutionary hero.

[2] Tita was with the Shelleys at Casa Magni near Lerici.

arrest and of exile for my courier and an intimation to the family of Count Gamba to leave Tuscany at the end of three days.[1] I am preparing to depart with them as I do not wish to stay any longer in a country where my friends are persecuted and where asylum is denied to the unfortunate. Since I have some affairs to arrange, I beg you to grant them a delay in order that I may depart with them.

[NOEL BYRON]

[TO JOHN MURRAY]   *Pisa, July 3d, 1822*

Dear Sir,—I sent you the revise of *Werner* last week. As you thought proper to omit the dedication of *Sardanapalus* to Goethe, you will please to append it to *Werner*, making only the necessary alteration in the title of the work dedicated.

You will please also to deliver to the bearer, Mr. John Hunt, the *Vision of Judgement* by Quevedo Redivivus, with the preface—I mean the corrected copy of the proofs which you had from the Hon[oura]ble Douglas Kinnaird.

Yours ever and truly,
NOEL BYRON

[TO EDWARD J. DAWKINS]   *Pisa July 4th. 1822*

Dear Sir—I regret to say that my anticipations were well founded.—The Gamba family received on Tuesday—an order to quit the Tuscan States in four days.—Of course this is virtually my own exile—for where they go—I am no less bound by honour than by feeling to follow.—I believe we shall try to obtain leave to remain at Lucca—if that fails—Genoa—and failing that—probably America—for—both Captain Chauncey of the American Squadron—(which returns in Septr.) and Mr. Bruen an American Merchant now at Leghorn offered me a passage in the handsomest manner—the latter sent to me to say that he would even send his vessel round to Genoa for us—if we chose to accept his offer.—With regard to the interpretations which will be put upon my departure at this time—I hope that you will do me the favour of letting the truth be known—as my own absence will deprive me of the power of doing so for myself—and I have little doubt

[1] Following a quarrel between the servants of Byron and those of the Gambas at Montenero on July 1, Pietro Gamba and his father were summoned to Leghorn and told that they must leave Tuscany in four days. Byron wanted to leave with them, but Leigh Hunt had just arrived from England and he had to get him settled in the Casa Lanfranchi in Pisa.

that advantage will be taken of that circumstance.——This letter will be presented to you by Mr. Taaffe—who is in considerable confusion at a measure to which his own heedlessness has a good deal contributed.—But—poor fellow—I suppose that he meant no harm.— He wanted the Countess Guiccioli to go to Florence and fling herself at the feet of the Grand Duchess—

> "a supplicant to wait
> While Ladies interpose, and Slaves debate"[1]

I can only say—that if she did any thing of the kind—I would never fling myself at *her* feet again.——Collini's office has now become a Sinecure—and I wish him joy of it.—The inconvenience—and expence to me will be very considerable—as I have two houses, furniture— Wines, Dinner Services—linen,—books, my Schooner—and in short— a whole establishment for a family—to leave at a moment's warning— and this without knowing where the Gambas will be permitted to rest— and of course where I can rest also.——The whole thing—the manner in which it was announced—by the Commissary—&c. was done in the most insulting manner.—The Courier treated as if he were a delinquent—& sent away with Soldiers to take charge of him and lodged in the prison of Pisa—by way of Hostel.——I trust that this just Government is now content, my countrymen have been insulted and wounded by a rascal—and my Servants treated like Criminals though guiltless—while a noble and respectable family including a sick lady are ordered away like so many felons—without a shadow of justice, or a *pretence* of *proof*.——With regard to yourself—I can only add that my obligations and feelings towards you, are the same as if your exertions had been attended with Success.—I certainly did at one time think—that whether they considered the person who applied in our behalf—or the persons in whose behalf the application was made—we should at least have had a *fair* trial—as I afforded every facility for the investigation—as it is—I will *not* express my sentiments — at least for the present I cannot—as no words could be at all adequate to describe my Sense of the manner in which the whole has been conducted by these people who call themselves a Government.——

[TO EDWARD J. DAWKINS]   *Pisa. July 6th. 1822*

Dear Sir,—Certainly—if any thing will be of use at Lucca it is probable that a letter from you may have that effect.—I should be

---

[1] Adapted from Johnson's *Vanity of Human Wishes*, lines 213–214.

sorry to give you the personal trouble of a journey—on any account.—
—With regard to the Gambas I beg leave to observe that the Countess Guiccioli is *not* an exile, and her passport is or was given in the usual manner.—When She was separated from her husband in 1820—by the Pope's decree—it was enjoined by his Holiness that she was to reside with her father—or—otherwise to forfeit the Alimony or *any* money (or whatever the word may be in the Roman or Romagnolo Doctors' Commons) allotted to her from her husband's estates by the Papal order.— When her father and brother were exiled for political reasons —Count Guiccioli as was natural and conjugal applied to have her shut up in a Convent—on the plea that she was no longer residing with her family.——A minister of the Legation[1] gave me notice of this application and it's probable result in time for her to rejoin her relations in Tuscany—*I* could not then accompany her in person—as it would have [been] construed into an Elopement, but I joined her afterwards at Pisa. If you can obtain permission for *them* or for *her* at least to reside within the Lucchese territory—it would be a great service—till I can make arrangements for the removal of my establishment—I shall go with them—but could then return here to settle my business.—I do not even know upon what pretext She was ordered to quit Tuscany or even if she really was so—since her name is not in the letter—nor is she an exile—and is besides in very delicate health as Sr. Vacca testified & can testify.——

Believe me yrs. very truly & obliged
Noel Byron

P.S.—Would you like to take a cruise in my little Schooner? It would console me for not being allowed to use it myself—if it could be of any pleasure to you while at Leghorn.——

[TO JOHN MURRAY]   *Pisa. July 6th. 1822*

Dear Sir,—I return you the revise—I have softened the part to which Gifford objected—and changed the name of Michael to Raphael who was an Angel of gentler sympathies.—By the way recollect to alter—Michael to *Raphael* in the *Scene* itself throughout—for I have only had time to do so in the list of the Dramatis Personae—and *Scratch out all the pencil marks* to avoid puzzling the printers.—I have given the *"Vision of Quevedo Redivivus"* to John Hunt—which will relieve you from a dilemma.—He must publish it at his *own* risk—as

[1] Count Alborghetti.

it is at his own desire.—Give him the *corrected* copy which Mr. K[innair]d had—as it is mitigated partly—and also the preface.—

yrs. ever

N B

[TO JOHN MURRAY]   *Pisa. July 8th. 1822*

Dear Sir,—Last week I returned you the packet of proofs.—You had perhaps better not publish in the same volume—the *Po*—and *Rimini* translation.—I have consigned a letter to Mr. John Hunt for the "Vision of Judgement"—which you will hand over to him.—Also the Pulci—original and Italian—and any *prose* tracts of mine—for Mr. Leigh Hunt is arrived here & thinks of commencing a periodical work —to which I shall contribute——I do not propose to you to be the publisher—because I know that you are unfriends——but all things in your care except the volume now in the press—and the M.S.S. purchased of Mr. Moore—can be given for this purpose—according as they are wanted—and I expect that you will show fair play—although with no very good will on your part.——With regard to what you say about your "want of memory"—I can only remark that you inserted the note to "Marino Faliero"—against my positive revocation and that you omitted the dedication of "Sardanapalus" to Goëthe (place it before the volume now in the press) both of which were things not very agreeable to me & which I could wish to be avoided in future as they might be with a very little care—or a simple Memorandum in your pocket book.—It is not impossible that I may have three or four cantos of D[on] Juan ready by autumn or a little later—as I obtained a permission from my Dictatress to continue it—*provided always* it was to be more guarded and decorous and sentimental in the continuation than in the commencement.—How far these Conditions have been fulfilled may be seen perhaps by and bye. But the Embargo was only taken off [upon these] stipulations.——You can answer at yr. leisure.

yrs. ever

N B

[TO THOMAS MOORE]   *Pisa, July 12th, 1822*

I have written to you lately, but not in answer to your last letter of about a fortnight ago. I wish to know (and request an answer to *that* point) what became of the stanzas to Wellington (intended to open a canto of Don Juan with)[1] which I sent you several months ago. If they have fallen into Murray's hands, he and the Tories will suppress them, as those lines rate that hero at his real value. Pray be explicit on this, as I have no other copy, having sent you the original; and if you have them, let me have *that* again, or a *copy* correct. * * * * * * * * *

* * * * * * * * * * * * * * *

I subscribed at Leghorn two hundred Tuscan crowns to your Irishism committee:[2] it is about a thousand francs, more or less. As Sir C[harles] S[tuart], who receives thirteen thousand a year of the public money, could not afford more than a thousand livres out of his enormous salary, it would have appeared ostentatious in a private individual to pretend to surpass him; and therefore I have sent but the above sum, as you will see by the enclosed receipt.

Leigh Hunt is here, after a voyage of eight months, during which he has, I presume, made the Periplus of Hanno the Carthaginian, and with much the same speed. He is setting up a Journal, to which I have promised to contribute; and in the first number the "Vision of Judgement, by Quevedo Redivivus," will probably appear, with other articles.

Can you give us any thing? He seems sanguine about the matter, but (entre nous) I am not. I do not, however, like to put him out of spirits by saying so; for he is bilious and unwell. Do, pray, answer *this* letter immediately.

Do send Hunt any thing in prose or verse of yours, to start him handsomely—any lyrical, *iri*cal, or what you please.

Has not your Potatoe Committee been blundering? Your advertisement says, that Mr. L. Callaghan (a queer name for a banker) hath been disposing of money in Ireland "sans authority of the Committee". I suppose it will end in Callaghan's calling out the Committee, the chairman of which carries pistols in his pocket, of course.

When you can spare time from *duetting, coquetting*, and claretting with your Hibernians of both sexes, let me have a line from you. I doubt whether Paris is a good place for the composition of your new poesy.

---

[1] The opening stanzas of Canto IX of *Don Juan* attacking Wellington were written July 10, 1819, and intended for Canto III, but Byron suppressed them and they were appended to Canto IX when it was published by John Hunt in 1823. In fact they had more relevance there following the devastating picture of meaningless slaughter in the battle scenes of Cantos VII and VIII.

[2] On June 10, 1822, a committee was formed in Paris, with Sir Charles Stuart as chairman, to raise money for the distressed Irish peasantry.

Pisa. July 14th. 1822

My dear Sir,—Your opinion has taken from me the slender hope to which I still clung.[1]—I need hardly say that the Bolivar is quite at your disposition as she would have been on a less melancholy occasion—and that I am always

yr. obliged & faithful friend & Servant
NOEL BYRON

[TO EDWARD J. DAWKINS] *July 15th. 1822*

Dear Sir—Up to this moment I had clung to a slender hope that Mr. Shelley had still survived the late Gale of Wind.—I sent orders yesterday to the Bolivar to cruize along the coast in search of intelligence—but it seems all over.——I have not waited on you in person being unshaven—unshorn—and uncloathed at this present writing after bathing.——I hope you may do something at Lucca[1]—which has induced me to delay proceeding to Genoa—or addressing Mr. Hill again till this day.—Many thanks.

yrs. ever
N B

[TO EDWARD J. DAWKINS] *July 16th. 1822*

Dear Sir,—Excuse the wet condition of your Marchese's letter—I received it in a bath—and have scrambled out of the water to acknowledge your note.—I shall feel greatly obliged if you will do what you can for the Gambas—or rather us all—at Lucca. Did you receive a letter I sent you by Mr. Trelawny of Count Pietro's—stating that they were afraid of *me* and my turbulence!!—& not of the Gambas at Lucca; I enclose you a letter received from Mr. Hill yesterday—which I will thank you to return—excuse haste—I am dripping like a Triton—& believe me

ever & faith[fu]lly yrs.
N B

[1] Shelley and Williams had left Leghorn in their boat the *Don Juan* on July 8 to return to Lerici. They were caught in a storm on the Bay of Spezia and drowned. When Roberts learned of their not arriving at their destination, he sent a note asking for the use of the *Bolivar* to explore the coast. It was several days before their bodies were washed ashore near Viareggio.

[1] The Gambas, father and son, had found temporary asylum in Lucca, while Teresa remained in the Casa Lanfranchi in Pisa with Byron, who was exploring the possibility of moving them all to Genoa.

Dear Sir,—Your letter would be as satisfactory as it is kind—if the Lucchese Government had given papers of Security even for a few months to the Gambas.—In the present state of uncertainty—it would be useless for me to take a villa out of which we might be all turned tomorrow as we have been here—and have the whole contract to pay nevertheless.—As it is we are exactly where we were—in a continual state of doubt and indecision,—but I am not the less obliged to you for having done all that could be done in the circumstances.—Believe me

ever & truly yrs.
NOEL BYRON

P.S.—I had no intention of residing in the City—nor indeed *would* do so if they would make me a present of it.—I wished to have obtained a quiet Country residence if possible not *very* far from the Sea.——

[TO DOUGLAS KINNAIRD]   *Pisa. July 19th. 1822*

My dear Douglas/—Your letter is dated the 5th. but makes no allusion to the dividend from the funds which I expected and expect still about this time. I regret that you have given up your journey, though I could not have received you very cheerfully, for since the beginning of the year one displeasure has followed another in regular succession. Shelley and Capt. Williams were drowned last week going to Spezia in their boat from Leghorn—supposed to have been swamped in a Squall.—A Boatman was also lost with them.—Shelley's body has been found and identified (though with difficulty) two days ago—chiefly by a book in his Jacket pocket[1]—the body itself being totally disfigured & in a state of putrefaction.—Another body supposed Capt. Williams's also found—with various articles belonging to the boat.—You may imagine the state of their wives and children—& also Leigh Hunt's—who was but just arrived from England.——Yesterday and the day before I made two journeys to the mouth of the Arno and another river (the Serchio) for the purpose of ascertaining the circumstances—and identifications of the bodies—but they were already interred for the present by order of the Sanità or Health Office.

yrs. ever
N B

[1] Keats's *Lamia* volume had been in Shelley's pocket, but nothing remained except the leather binding to identify it.

Dear Sir,—I have just received your letter.—The account seems to tally with all that We had heard before.—Trelawny is expected in Pisa this evening with the ladies—who are not aware of the extent of their calamity—and still cling to some slight hopes.—Shelley's body has been completely identified by a book in his pocket—which was found by the Health-Officers upon him—in his Jacket.—That of Williams is supposed to be the one found near the Serchio—(where we went in search on Thursday. [)]—You have done well to heave down "the Bolivar".—Do you know where Mr. Wentworth is? or could you find out? and do me the favour to write him a line to say that I should not be indisposed to treat with him?[1] Believe me

ever & truly yrs.
N B

. . . You may be sure that all that family and all it's connections by their own side will act unfairly and dishonourably—and Lushington like a Scoundrel, if he can.——

P.S.—I hope that you have not sold out of the funds—before *dividend* time—I shall be [fairly?] helped up if you have—for the plagues and removals of all kinds which I have had this year in consequence of politics and the war with that blackguard who was stabbed lately have caused great inconvenience and expences—what with journeys—lawyers to pay—and a foolish expence about a small Schooner which I built at Genoa.—A friend of mine late from England told me that Ld. Le Despenser[1] is dreadfully dipped—& that Kent is *not* a *register* County—so I hope you will look twice before you risk my cash on security no better than the funds—& without even an advance of Income.———I know you are a friend to the family—but that is no reason to act too hastily.——As for the Noel property—I expect nothing but unpleasantness from the House of Atreus.

---

[1] Possibly for the sale of the *Bolivar* since the authorities would not permit him to cruise along the coast.

[1] Lord Le Despencer succeeded in 1781 as the 16th Baron on the death of his father, who as Sir Francis Dashwood had spent a riotous life on the Continent in his youth and who founded the famous "Hell-fire Club, or Society of the Monks of Medmenham Abbey".

My dear Douglas—I wrote to you last week to mention the death of poor Shelley and another (Capt. Williams) who perished at Sea in a Squall a fortnight ago—in his passage to Spezia from Leghorn.——I now write to remind you that some time has past since the payment of the dividends—and that mine have not been remitted.—I trust that you have not sold out of the funds previous to the day—as this would be a dead loss of half a year's income without any advantage that I foresee.—I am the more particular upon this point—as all we can expect from the Noel acquisition—is—defamation—litigation—any thing but profit—the lawyers and arbitrators together having completely neutralized any control of mine over the property.—Add to this—that I can calculate no further upon any literary speculation—which used once to be an occasional addition convenient enough—so that I am naturally more anxious to realize my own income—& to have it paid to the day.—As to the Noels they are inherently a bad race—and by no means honourable in business—Lushington is also hostile to me—and *cannot* be an honest man from his profession.—You will find this true perhaps shortly.——I have a great wish to see the Mortgage secured—but I hear that the Le Despencers are deeply involved—and not likely to be regular paymasters.—Now *this* is a first point to ponder on—as you yourself say that the increase of income will be trifling—if any.——I thought it would not be much—but I did think that it would be a little.—You never answered my Query—of what becomes of the interest of Lady N[oel] B[yron]'s *fortune* (I mean the inherited twenty thousand pounds) in the event of Survivorship on my part.——Does the *part* which she possesses—revert to her family—to the child, or to me—I mean—the interest only?——I write to you of disagreeable things and in disagreeable circumstances—but could not well help it or them.

yrs ever & truly
N B

P.S.—To occupy my mind—(which had need of it—& in such a way as to distract it from present things) I have nearly completed three more Cantos of D[on] Juan—which will perhaps be ready by Novr. or sooner.—If Murray publishes them he ought to print at the same time very small & cheap editions of the same price & size as the pirates' to anticipate & neutralize them.—Pray tell him so—and let me know what he thinks.—I have obtained permission to continue the poem—if I will make it more sober—that is—dull.[1]—How I have kept that part of the compact—I do not know—we shall see by & bye.—

P.S.—I ge*ts* at Leghorn from my bankers there 4 per cent for my monies—while that lies in their hands.—Egad—I think you ought at least to send the notes out particularly since you don't pay me not no interest at all,—and so Lushington & the trustees are to bank with you —that's the reason those fellows meet with so much civilization from you—while I am diddled by those d——d arbitrators.—a pretty fellow *Shadwell* to refer to—he *is* their counsel—& even their *referee* firstly named—but I'll have it out in Chancery—how goes the R[ochdale] Appeal?—do they put it off—Eldon will never give any thing like fair play to me.——Ask Murray if Lord Clare did not bring him a M.S.S. Journal or Notebook of mine[2]—the Albemarle St. Scribe never writes.——

[TO DOUGLAS KINNAIRD]   *Pisa. July 25th. 1822*

My dear Douglas/—Since I wrote the enclosed I have received yr. letter of the 9th. which is satisfactory as announcing the approach of *fee*.—I certainly wish Mr. Hanson's accounts to be investigated by another Solicitor.—It would be not at all against my wish to appoint Sir F[rancis] B[urdett]'s Steward to manage the L[an]c[aster] property.— I like his name—*Crabtree*—presuming him to be [the] same Cadwallader Crabtree mentioned in Peregrine Pickle.[1]—With regard to the insurance—I think we can lay out another *hundred* pounds on it now—& perhaps more by and bye—as we have any incomings or assetts.—As my natural child is gone—in case of the insurance being valid—and I the survivor—I might probably lay out the produce in life annuities—merely to secure a better income.——The additional *hundred* would make the whole about twelve or fourteen thousand pounds would it not?—You know best.——As to the Arbitration—I do not see how Sir Francis can revoke his former decision that the property was to be under my controul.—There is another thing I wished to mention.—The Rochdale appeal—is before the House of Lords.—I wish it to be postponed if possible till the present Chancellor goes out

[1] In the summer of 1821, Byron had promised Teresa Guiccioli not to continue *Don Juan* after he had finished the fifth Canto. Although he did not get her permission to resume the poem until the following year, he had begun the sixth canto before she relented, with a further promise from him that it be made more "decent".
[2] The "Detached Thoughts".
[1] Smollett, *Peregrine Pickle*, Chaps. 76, 77.

(which they talk of) as he has shown himself so decidedly hostile to me
—that I doubt of his giving me fair play in this cause more than in the
others.—What think you?

yrs. ever
N B

[TO DOUGLAS KINNAIRD] *Pisa. July 31st. 1822*

My dear Douglas/—It is fit that I should again apprize you—that
notwithstanding the assurance in yr. letter received a fortnight ago—
that the dividend would be sent [in] a *day* or *two*—and notwithstanding
the time elapsed since it's payment at the bank—[I] have received no
remittance up to this [time]. I presume of course that the letter must
have miscarried——As I wrote to you lately on the same and other
Subjects—I will not trouble you further now—Pray has "Glory" yet
settled the Arbitration?—

yrs. ever
N B

P.S.—If I do not receive the remittances by next post I shall write—
and would recommend you to take the numbers of the *notes* and *not*
pay them without my advice—Somebody may have intercepted them &
perhaps got them changed in my name.———At any rate your house
should be more punctual.

[TO JOHN MURRAY] *Pisa. ⟨July⟩ August 3d. 1822*

Dear Sir/—I have received your scrap—with H[enry] D[rury]'s
letter enclosed.—It is just like him—always kind and ready to oblige
his old friends.—Will you have the goodness to *send immediately* to
Mr. Douglas Kinnaird—and inform him that I have *not* received the
remittances due to me from the funds a month & more ago—& *promised
by him to be sent by every post*—which omission is of great inconvenience
to me——and indeed inexcusable—as well as unintelligible.—As I
have written to *him* repeatedly I suppose that *his* or *my* letters have
miscarried.—I presume you have heard that Mr. Shelley & Capt.
Williams were lost on the 7th Ulto. [actually the 8th.] in their passage
from Leghorn to Spezia in their own open boat. You may imagine the
state of their families—I never saw such a scene—nor wish to see such
another.—You are all brutally mistaken about Shelley who was without

189

exception—the *best* and least selfish man I ever knew.—I never knew one who was not a beast in comparison.—

yrs. ever

N B

[TO THOMAS MOORE]   *Pisa, August 8th, 1822*

You will have heard by this time that Shelley and another gentleman (Captain Williams) were drowned about a month ago (a *month* yesterday), in a squall off the Gulf of Spezia. There is thus another man gone, about whom the world was ill-naturedly, and ignorantly, and brutally mistaken. It will, perhaps, do him justice *now*, when he can be no better for it.

I have not seen the thing you mention,[1] and only heard of it casually, nor have I any desire. The price is, as I saw in some advertisement, fourteen shillings, which is too much to pay for a libel on oneself. Some one said in a letter, that it was a Dr. Watkins, who deals in the life and libel line. It must have diminished your natural pleasure, as a friend (vide Rochefoucault), to see yourself in it.[2]

With regard to the Blackwood fellows, I never published any thing against them;[3] nor, indeed, have seen their magazine (except in Galignani's extracts) for these three years past. I once wrote, a good while ago, some remarks on their review of Don Juan, but saying very little about themselves, and these were *not* published.[4] If you think that I ought to follow your example (and I like to be in your company when I can) in contradicting their impudence, you may shape this declaration of mine into a similar paragraph for me. It is possible that you may have seen the little I *did* write (and never published) at Murray's:—it contained much more about Southey than about the Blacks.

If you think that I ought to do any thing about Watkins's book, I

[1] Moore had mentioned a new book, *Memoirs of the Life and Writings of the Right Honourable Lord Byron.* . . . It was anonymous, but the author was known to be John Watkins, author of a biographical dictionary and of biographies of Sheridan and Queen Charlotte.

[2] Watkins had mentioned the fact that Byron had attacked Moore in *English Bards and Scotch Reviewers* and then had written a profusely complimentary preface addressed to him for *The Corsair.*

[3] The preface to Vol. XI of *Blackwood's Edinburgh Magazine* (Jan.–June, 1822) said that Byron "has written something about us—but whether a satire or an eulogy seems doubtful".

[4] This was Byron's "Some Observations upon an Article in Blackwood's Magazine", which was not published during his lifetime.

should not care much about publishing *my Memoir now*, should it be necessary to counteract the fellow. But, in *that* case, I should like to look over the *press* myself. Let me know what you think, or whether I had better *not*:—at least, not the second part, which touches on the actual confines of still existing matters.

I have written three more cantos of Don Juan, and am hovering on the brink of another (the ninth). The reason I want the stanzas again which I sent you is, that as these cantos contain a full detail (like the storm in Canto Second) of the siege and assault of Ismael, with much of sarcasm on those butchers in large business, your mercenary soldiery, it is a good opportunity of gracing the poem with * * *. With these things and these fellows, it is necessary, in the present clash of philosophy and tyranny, to throw away the scabbard. I know it is against fearful odds; but the battle must be fought; and it will be eventually for the good of mankind, whatever it may be for the individual who risks himself.

What do you think of your Irish bishop?[5] Do you remember Swift's line, "Let me have a *barrack*—a fig for the *clergy*?"[6] This seems to have been his reverence's motto * * * * * * * * *

* * * * * * * * * * * * * * *

Yours, etc.

[TO JOHN HANSON]   *Pisa August 10th. 1822*

My dear Sir/—Will you have the goodness to apprize Mr. Kinnaird that I have not yet received any remittance from the funds now due several weeks—& which he promised punctually in his letters.—I suspect that his letter of Credit has either been lost—or intercepted which makes me very uneasy.——Please to do this immediately.—My respects to Charles and the family[.]

yrs. ever
N B

P.S.—You have not written for some time.

P.S.—You had better keep back the Rochdale Appeal till this Chancellor goes out.—*He* will never be fair in any cause in which *I* am interested.—

[5] The Hon. Percy Jocelyn, Bishop of Clogher, was deposed because of "a scandalous crime" involving a soldier named Moverly.
[6] The last line of Swift's "The Grand Question Debated".

Pisa. August 10th. 1822

Dear Sir/—Will you have the goodness to advise Mr. Kinnaird that from the non-arrival of the remittance due to me since the first of July —I very much suspect some unfair play to his letters or to mine—and that I beg to apprize him accordingly.—If he has not [sent it] duly—I can only add that it has occasioned & still occasions to [me] great anxiety & trouble.—

yrs.
N B

[TO EDWARD JOHN TRELAWNY] *Pisa. August 10th. 1822*

Dear T.—I always foresaw and told you that they would take every opportunity of annoying me in every respect.[1] If you *can* get American papers and permission I shall be very glad and should much prefer it but I doubt that it will be very difficult.—

yrs.
N B

[TO DOUGLAS KINNAIRD] *Pisa. August 10th. 1822*

My dear Douglas/—Still no letter! and no remittance!—the omission seems so very strange and protracted—that I cannot help suspecting that either your letters or mine have not had fair play—since I have written so repeatedly to request you to set [my] mind easy on this point.———I shall continue to write however uselessly—you do not know the extreme annoyance and trouble—the delay has occasioned & continues to occasion.—

yrs. ever
N B

[TO EDWARD JOHN TRELAWNY] *Pisa. August 14th. 1822*

Dear T.—Hunt and I propose being with you tomorrow by about noon[1]—I do not know the distance between the two places of V[iareg-

---

[1] In an effort to get rid of Byron and his friends, the Tuscan authorities had refused to give him a permit to sail along the coast and discharge passengers as he chose.

[1] Trelawny had been making preparations for the cremation on the beach of the bodies of Williams and Shelley. Byron took Hunt in his carriage to the mouth of the Serchio on the 15th, when the body of Williams was cremated. And the next day the gruesome ceremony was repeated with Shelley's remains on the beach at Viareggio.

gio] & S[erchio] & therefore you had better let a man be at the former where we shall stop first.——I delayed to-day on account of the post which however brought me no news.

yrs. ever
N B

[TO THE REV. THOMAS HALL]¹   *Pisa, Aug. 14, 1822*

Sir,—I am much obliged by your information, and will thank you to direct Mr. Dunn to bring with him on Saturday next (if convenient) the necessary stamped papers, and a Notary, when I will do my best to follow your directions.²

I have observed in Galignani's paper lists of the Subscribers and Subscriptions for the Irish Poor from *Florence*, but *not* from *Leghorn*. I should be glad to know the cause of this omission, which is not very fair on the part of the Committee to the other English residents in Tuscany.

I have the honour to be your very obedient, humble servant,

NOEL BYRON

P.S.—Have the goodness also to send me a copy of the *usual form* of a Will made in Tuscany by an English resident.

N B

[TO DOUGLAS KINNAIRD]   *Pisa. August 16th. 1822*

My dear Douglas/—I have just received a long letter from you— which however does not mention nor even allude to what I have written to you upon *twenty times* at least—viz—my half years' remittance from the funds which has never arrived *here* nor at *Leghorn.*——I need hardly repeat the extreme anxiety—as well as inconvenience this un-accountable delay has occasioned—now still increased by your *silence* upon the subject.—Do pray—let me know what I am to think of this— has the money been sent? has it miscarried—or what has occurred?—— With regard to the arbitration—I shall only observe that Mr. Shadwell was a most improper person to refer to—as he was *their referee* named in the first instance.—*I* will not consent to Mr. *Davidson's nomination*—he has *no claim* to a pension from the Noel property—having served there

¹ The English chaplain at Leghorn.
² Byron apparently intended to make a new will following the death of Allegra, leaving the money he had intended for her to the Countess Guiccioli, who was offended at the idea and positively refused to accept it. In the end Byron made no new will.

only *seven* years—he was previously in that of Halnaby—let Halnaby pension him.———But they may all go to the devil together in their own way.—I merely wish to know and reiterate my request that you will cause to be remitted my *own money* from the funds—and am

ever & truly yrs.

N B

[TO DOUGLAS KINNAIRD]   *Pisa. August 20th. 1822*

My dear Douglas/—I must still continue as in duty bound to bore you by every post till my remittance from the funds arrives—*which it has not yet done.*——I have been very unwell and all my skin *peeled off in blisters* —besides some fever—owing to swimming three hours in the sea at Viareggio—in the heat of the Sun.—But all this has been increased by the vexation of this unaccountable delay.—I receive at length a long letter from you about business—but not *one* word of my money!—so that I do not know whether it has been sent or not!—This is really most irritating and hardly excusable.——Every thing seems to go wrong— and instead of gaining by this pretended accession of property—you actually withhold my *own*—so that I am anything but a winner.—Now as to the Noel Affair—*Shadwell* was *their first referee*—& yet to *him* the Arbitrators *refer* for an *impartial law* opinion!—I never heard of such a thing.—2dly.—I will have the question settled in Chancery.—3dly. Mr. Davidson has no pretensions to a *pension* from the *Noel* estates—he served twenty years on the *Halnaby* but only seven on the *Noel*—besides he is a most improper person—from drunkenness & incapacity—ask Barrett—or Hobhouse—or even Lady B[yron] herself whom I have heard laugh at him a thousand times. 4thly. You say what *"has Surveying* the estate to do with raising the rents"* now—in the devil's name did ever any one hear of surveying an estate to *lower them?*—& would you at such a time have me throw away hundreds of pounds on a survey? for *what?* since *you say it is not to raise the rents?*—I really do not quite under- stand you—all that I know is—first you *agree* with me—& then with the next *person* who talks differently on the subject.—The Affair must go into Chancery—I will not allow *their Counsel* Mr. Shadwell to decide for me—and I wonder how Sir Francis could consent to such a reference.— but anything I suppose because Dr. Lushington is a pretended reformer. I can tell you *Gentlemen* reformers—that whatever happens—or when- ever it does happen. the *people* will never have confidence in any lawyer or similar scum of the worst earth, nor will *I*—and I suspect that some of these days if I live and come to England—I will startle some of your politicians.—

yrs. ever & truly
N B

P.S.—I do reiterate once for all—send me my fee—you have no idea of the inconvenience & anxiety I have undergone from this omission.

[TO DOUGLAS KINNAIRD] *Pisa. August 24th. 1822*

My dear Douglas/—I am ⟨puzzled⟩ pacified & soothed by the arrival of *"fee"* though tardy—but do not send your notes on the tour of Europe another time—it is making them too *Circular*—by nature as well as by name.—By the way—you "have stinted me in my sizings"[1] —the sum ought to have been more—the whole interest—is 2525 £ S.D.—for fee besides 190 £ S. D. from Sir Jacob annually—Now —you only sent me in January *twelve* hundred of regular fee & ditto now—making but 2400 £ S. D. & besides kept back 81 at the beginning of the year to meet any sundries——what have you done with those parings?—paid the insurance—or what?—if so I wonder at your *ass*urance—let the Noel Assetts pay for their insurance[.] I will have my own fee entire—and then the Rochdale Swop of 500—have you been liquidating Spooney or others therewith?——And now *when* will be the first Noel incoming? at Michaelmas eh?—& how much do you have the modesty to propose that I should give up to liquidation?— please to recollect no *"Davidson"*—he has no claim to a pension except from *Halnaby*—having only mismanaged Kirkby for seven years— surely it is not *honest* to wish to quarter a drunken supernumerary upon me—it is base—& you should think & say so.—And the 4000 £ which you say Sir Jacob means to pay—where will it be invested?—not in the funds I hope at their present price—but on some other security. ——You did not answer my *real* question [;] I asked in the event of my surviving Lady B[yron] & her daughter (and I have no wish to do either) but I asked in *that* case what becomes of her original portion— does it go back to the N[oe]l family or remain in mine?—Reply— please your honour—on these financial matters.——

I have also *quite three* nearly *four* Cantos of D[on] J[uan] ready—now I wish to consult you—supposing them at *par* as compositions—what ought they to produce us in the present state of publicating?—I will be guided by you—Murray has had the late things cheap enough—and I don't expect much for them—but for the D[on] J[uan]s I conceive

[1] See Vol. 8, p. 250, note 4.

that we ought to have a previous stipulation.—The argument consists of *more* love—and a good deal of War—a technical description of a modern siege (in the style of the Storm in the 2d. C[ant]o which is or was reckoned Good) with much philosophy—and satire upon heroes and despots and the present false state of politics and society.—Now—about *fee* from *Mortgage*—don't contrive to sell out so as that I may lose—a half year's income—or I shall be somewhat salvage—as you may presume.—If you would only let me know what you think I shall have in the earliest payment from the Noel Estate—& *when*—& how much we ought to have for the new D[on] J[uan]s &c. I will then arrange with you what I ought to set apart for liquidation & insurances —& what to receive for privy purse expenditure.—

ever yrs.
N B

P.S.—If we have upon the whole a *good* year—I should be inclined to encrease the insurance even to £25000—but that will depend on so many contingencies.——Have you sold out of the funds—I wish you would? *now* is about [the] right time—and I don't think that they will hold up much longer.—With regard to the literary paction with Ridgeway—or others—for those M.S.S.—I do not mean to be hard upon them—indeed my expectations on that score are moderate enough.—Shall I finish the 12th. C[ant]o—and send it—it would make the whole *two* volumes of the former size—of course it is by no means expected—that an encrease in the Number of Cantos—is to bring an exactly proportional encrease of price—but *that* matter will be easily settled—for I leave it to you—and will not have any discussion about it.—With regard to "omissions"—recollect that the *Cant* of the Day has already taken it's tone—and that if the whole were reduced to an actual homily—they would *cant* the same. We are not to yield to such things.—Let me have the proofs to revise—and I will do what I can however.——

[TO THOMAS MOORE]   *Pisa, August 27th, 1822*

It is boring to trouble you with "such small gear;"[1] but it must be owned that I should be glad if you would inquire whether my Irish subscription ever reached the committee in Paris from Leghorn. My reasons, like Vellum's,[2] "are threefold:"—First, I doubt the accuracy of all almoners, or remitters of benevolent cash; second, I do suspect

[1] Probably an echo of *King Lear*, Act. III, scene 4: "such small deer."
[2] Vellum, steward to Sir Thomas Truman in Addison's *Drummer*, always enumerated his reasons.

that the said Committee, having in part served its time to time-serving, may have kept back the acknowledgment of an obnoxious politician's name in their lists; and third, I feel pretty sure that I shall one day be twitted by the government scribes for having been a professor of love for Ireland, and not coming forward with the others in her distresses.

It is not, as you may opine, that I am ambitious of having my name in the papers, as I can have that any day in the week gratis. All I want is to know if the Reverend Thomas Hall did or did not remit my subscription (200 scudi of Tuscany, or about a thousand francs, more of less,) to the Committee at Paris.

The other day at Viareggio, I thought proper to swim off to my schooner (the Bolivar) in the offing, and thence to shore again—about three miles, or better, in all. As it was at mid-day, under a broiling sun, the consequence has been a feverish attack, and my whole skin's coming off,[3] after going through the process of one large continuous blister, raised by the sun and sea together. I have suffered much pain; not being able to lie on my back, or even side; for my shoulders and arms were equally St. Bartholomewed. But it is over,—and I have got a new skin, and am as glossy as a snake in its new suit.

We have been burning the bodies of Shelley and Williams on the sea-shore, to render them fit for removal and regular interment. You can have no idea what an extraordinary effect such a funeral pile has, on a desolate shore, with mountains in the back-ground and the sea before, and the singular appearance the salt and frankincense gave to the flame. All of Shelley was consumed, except his *heart*, which would not take the flame, and is now preserved in spirits of wine.

Your old acquaintance Londonderry has quietly died at North Cray![4] and the virtuous De Witt [5] was torn in pieces by the populace! What a lucky * * the Irishman has been in his life and end. In him your Irish Franklin est mort!

Leigh Hunt is sweating articles for his new Journal; and both he and I think it somewhat shabby in *you* not to contribute. Will you become one of the *properrioters*? "Do, and we go snacks."[6] I recommend you to think twice before you respond in the negative.

[3] While Shelley's body was being cremated Byron swam out to the *Bolivar* and in consequence suffered a severe sunburn which caused him to shed his skin. Teresa Guiccioli had a piece of blistered skin among her Byron relics after his death.

[4] Byron had heard of Castlereagh's (Londonderry's) death, but did not yet know that he had committed suicide.

[5] John De Witt (1625–1672), the great Dutch statesman who did much for his country but opposed the monarchy, was finally torn to pieces by a mob angered by his opposition to William III.

[6] Pope, "Epistle to Dr. Arbuthnot", line 66.

I have nearly (*quite three*) four new cantos of *Don Juan* ready. I obtained permission from the female Censor Morum of *my* morals to continue it, provided it were immaculate; so I have been as decent as need be. There is a deal of war—a siege, and all that, in the style, graphical and technical, of the shipwreck in Canto Second, which "took" as they say in the Row.

Yours, etc.

P.S.—That * * * Galignani has about ten lies in one paragraph. It was not a Bible that was found in Shelley's pocket, but John Keats's poems. However, it would not have been strange, for he was a great admirer of Scripture as a composition. *I* did not send my bust to the academy of New York; but I sat for my picture to young West, an American artist, at the request of some members of that Academy to *him* that he would take my portrait,—for the Academy, I believe.

I had, and still have, thought of South America, but am fluctuating between it and Greece. I should have gone, long ago, to one of them, but for my liaison with the Countess G[uicciol]i; for love, in these days, is little compatible with glory. *She* would be delighted to go too; but I do not choose to expose her to a long voyage, and a residence in an unsettled country, where I shall probably take a part of some sort.

[TO DOUGLAS KINNAIRD] *Pisa. August 31st. 1822*

My dear Douglas/—Your Circular or rather Circuitous notes— arrived & were acknowledged last week after their long tour.——I do not understand how Lady Noel who died in *January*—can be entitled to rents beyond *Lady Day*——and I never heard of payments of rents except at Lady-day & Michaelmas.—Do you mean to tell me that *I* should be entitled to the *next* half year's rent if Lady B[yron] was to be translated at present?——And a Mortgage too!—will you please to explain to me at once these mysteries——you are a man of honour—& I shall take your word—but my own opinion is that it is a base [haggle?] of the trustees—I look upon Lushington as a mere legal Swindler who will pick a pocket either *for* or *of* a Client—the *former* that he may effect the latter.—I shall attack him publicly the very first opportunity—and in the terms he deserves.—What do you talk of "proceeds" for when there are none—but 300 pounds?—It is the duty of these fellows to explain in a detailed manner what these posthumous rights of the last Woman are or were? and I should have thought as my friend that you would have required as much—I have already sent you my opinion of the reference to *Shadwell their Counsel* by

198

the impartial Arbitrators? When *are* the rents paid?—at what period—
& when am I to derive any proprietorship from the property? They
are as rank a gang of sharpers as ever cheated.——With regard to
the money in the funds—I suppose the transfer will be made so that by
selling out at this period—I shall lose my *own* next half year's income—
as I have the last of the Noel property by those rascally trustees.——
What *possible* right could the woman have beyond *Lady Day*—the next
rent day following her decease.—Curse them altogether[;] I neither
have nor ever shall have [word torn off with seal] except cheating——
& the basest & meanest injustice from the whole crew.——But I'll
be even with them—

"I have a weapon".[1]—

Has Noel paid the 4000 balance of his bastard's fortune (for she is
as much *his* daughter as *you* are *his* Son) and how is it to be vested—let
me know—as to appropriating "proceeds"—how can I appropriate—
what is not in existence either to pay Creditors or any one else? Has
he paid the half year's interest of the 190 £—I mean Sir Jacob because
your two last payments of income have been 2400 in all—whereas the
whole is 2525—besides Sir Jacob's 190. i.e. 2715.—You enquire after
the 5th. Canto. the 5th. of D[on] J[uan] was published last year—but
I have the 6th. 7th. 8th. 9th. ready or nearly—but I presume Murray
will be like the rest.—I am in d——d ill humour.

yrs. ever
N B

What do you think we should ask for the 4 new C[ant]os supposing
them at par as compositions—they are upwards of 420 octave stanzas.

[TO DOUGLAS KINNAIRD]   [*Sept., 1822?*]

[First sheet missing]

My balance after those investments and the payment of the fifteen
hundred—(i.e. the three five hundreds from Rochdale toll—surplus of
Kirkby M[allor]y and—surplus of the fee—and 1200—now remitted)
will be for actual cash—at present—the fourteen hundred pounds in
last year's circulars.——When Murray accounts for Werner—I
should be glad to know what he is to give for the Copyright.—He will
of course between pique and avidity—do his best or worst.—Are you
quite sure—that Davison[1] is not his *Sub-agent* or Middleman—in

---

1 *Othello*, Act V, scene 2.
1 Thomas Davison, Murray's printer.

199

secret—to negociate for the D[on] J[uan]'s—and yet keep behind the Curtain.—It is no matter—if he is.—I must tell you to recollect one thing—whatever you may hear.—It *is this fact*—which I have in Murray's own hand-writing—after *all* the *piracy*—&c. &c. &c. he offered to me a thousand pounds a Canto—for as many cantos as I chose to write;—which I *refused* as *too much*,—so much for his boasted consistency—and affected morality—this will be enough to teach you to go a little cautious with Davison—*not* in *dealing*—but in believing his statements—for either he acts for Murray—or he does *not*—if he *does* he will do the best for him—if in the latter for himself—and in neither case is he likely to overstate former profits—which might raise the immediate demand upon himself or employer.——

If you will let me know—when monies are received from any quarter —I shall know how to dispose of them—but my intention is—always to lay out a thousand pounds at interest—(if the Sum arrives at this) and any hundred pounds over till it reaches at two thousand—may be applied to liquidating the claims—which I much wish to see neutralized. —Should any emergency require me to draw *more*—I will let you know —in time—to re-convert the Exchequer bills into cash again;—pray— how—and in whose name are they invested?—in case of accidents, (as you are now able to break more collar bones—do take care—will you?) and are all the receipts of the yet paid creditors to be gotten at—for I should ill like to have the Scoundrels to pay twice over.——I have no remorse about postage—as all letters are business—and packets will go to my account.—You have no occasion to answer except by a word of assent or dissent—or acknowledgement—especially of any packets— such as the present—or even others less valuable—such as poeshie.—

yrs. ever

N B

P.S.—If you will turn to the Quarterly review no. *53* (for July 1822) you will see in Article sixth—that Murray's own Critics [say] that the piracy is not likely to stop the *eventual* profit—but merely to make the publisher print *cheaper* editions in a greater number—these are their words *"It is probable that his aggregate profit may be as great or greater— though it will be obtained with more trouble."* Again *"The publication is profitable to the pirate or he would not undertake it—it must be more so to the* original publisher as he has the advantage of preoccupying the market." —If the Bridge Street fellows are now....

[TO DOUGLAS KINNAIRD]   *Septr. 1st. 1822*

Dear Douglas/—I wrote the enclosed in very bad humour—but as
it contains matter of business it must go—for I have not time to re-
write it.—But you must own that the whole of this Noel affair has been
but a series of vexations from beginning till now.——You tell me of
a paltry sum [paid] in—& *then* ask me to assign the proceeds to Creditors!—*whole* proceeds—& *when?* am I in possession or no? and when or
ever will the rents or any part of the rent be ever paid by that gang of
Swindlers—that bitch and her lawyers?—When any thing is *really* paid
—it will then be time enough to talk of liquidating the bonds—have I
not been paying lawyers bill[s]—& the devil knows what for these four
years past?—Has not the whole of the Rochdale money—& Claughton's
—and I know not what besides been swallowed up in this *very year*—
beside the insurance of the life of the fiend who (as far as I am concerned)
had better never have existed.—Recollect the accompt you sent me at
the beginning of the year—how much of the whole was kept back—as
also of Sir Jacob's Money—to pay Murray's bill for books—& all sorts
of bills.——I really do not [know] who is paid or *not* paid unless you
send me a memorandum.

                                                        yrs. ever
                                                          N B

All the pretended accession of property has hitherto occasioned but
expence on my part——& chicane on theirs—Damn them all.——

[TO JOHN CAM HOBHOUSE]   *Pisa. Septr. 2d. 1822*

Dear Hobhouse/—I wrote to you as you requested to Geneva but—
you have not apparently received the letter.——I am in all the agonies
of hiring feluccas—& packing furniture—&c. &c. for *Genoa*—where I
have taken a house for a year—and mean to remove shortly—as I told
you in my Swiss epistle—and I have not a chair or table—and hardly a
stool to sit on—besides the usual confusion attending such operations.
——If you come on to Florence—we must contrive a meeting (should
I be still here on your arrival) or perhaps you will take Genoa on your
way back.—These transient glimpses of old friends are very painful—
as I found out the other day after Lord Clare was gone again—however
agreeable they make the moment.—They are like a dose of Laudanum
—and it's subsequent langour.—It is a *lustre* since we met—and I am
afraid it is the only *lustre* added to one of us—but you I trust are more
resplendent in health & heart.—I have been lately ill—(*all* my Skin

peeled off) from swimming three hours in a hot Sun at Via Reggio—
but my new Skin is come again—though it is plaguy tender still. Could
you not contrive to voyage to Genoa with me—Madame Guiccioli is
with me but she will travel with her father—& we could confabulate in
the old *imperial* Carriage as heretofore—and squabble away as usual.—
I don't know whether your temper is improved—I hear that the
hustings have made you somewhat haughty—but that is natural—a
man who addresses Senates and Constituents has some right to be so—
my own temper is about the same—which is not saying much for it.
—However I am always

yrs. truly
N B

[TO W. WEBB][1]   *Pisa Septr. 2d. 1822*

Dear Sir,—Your present of the raspberries was very agreeable—
they are the first of the kind I have seen in Tuscany, and I thank you
for the regale.—I shall send over the Circulars for the Cash (duly
received a day or two ago—) in a cover which will be conveyed by
Mr. Dunn[2] in a day or two—as he is coming over on some business
shortly.—I greatly doubt if Mr. Shelley has left any effects;—or at
least the debts will probably exceed the assetts—the extreme liberality
of his disposition generally left him in arrear & the day before he was
lost he borrowed of me fifty pounds, which were on board in cash when
the boat went down.———He had I believe the right to dispose of his
father's estate—after the demise of the latter—who is very old and
infirm from a paralytic stroke—but of the exact tendency of his will
in 1817—I am ignorant and even if there may not be a subsequent one
with alterations.—In the event of my being his Executor[3]—you may
rely on my using my best endeavours that the Creditors should be
duly paid—and of course that your claim should not be overlooked—or
neglected.—In the meantime there can be no harm in addressing Sir
Timothy [Shelley] upon the subject—although from what I have
heard of him—it is not very likely that he will be disposed to liquidate

[1] A partner in the banking firm of Webb & Co., Leghorn, Byron's banker and
friend.
[2] Henry Dunn, a merchant who had a general store in Leghorn. Byron used him
as a business agent.
[3] Shelley had appointed Byron joint executor with Thomas Love Peacock, but
after a quarrel with Leigh Hunt and Mrs. Shelley, Byron declined to act in that
capacity and refused to accept a legacy of £2,000 left him in the will. See June 28,
1823, to Hunt.

his Son's debts—as they were not upon good terms—and I have observed that even the tenderest parents are somewhat tenacious on the score of similar disbursements.—The moment I know anything certain of the present and future state of his affairs—you shall be duly advised—and I will try (as Executor, if I am so) to put your business in a train for settlement—as early as possible.—Believe me to be with compliments to Mrs. and Miss Webb and the Messrs. Mayer—

yr. obliged & very obedt Sert.
Noel Byron

[TO EDWARD JOHN TRELAWNY]   *Septr. 2d. 1822*

Dear Trelawny—You must send off for the Bolivar to be *here* immediately[1]—it is absolutely necessary—as the other sails to-morrow evening

yrs.
N B

[TO DOUGLAS KINNAIRD]   *Pisa. Septr. 6th. 1822*

Dear Douglas/—Thank you kindly but now the Circuitous Circulars have described their Orbit—I have no immediate occasion for a further credit—having (besides two hundred pounds in Cash—) Circulars (including the late remittance) to the tune of three thousand five hundred p[oun]ds—and about [between?] (3000 Drs.) six or seven hundred pounds in the bank [of] Messrs. Webb & Co. of Leghorn —for which they allow me *four* per cent.—To be sure I *did* expect something better from the Kirkby property—than has yet turned out and I think we ought to have something for the four new Cantos of D[on] J[uan] which I shall forward to you soon.—The enclosed is a letter to Murray which you may present if you do not deem it too harsh.—At any rate it contains my opinions—& I wish you to act upon them in dealing with the absolute John.———I hear that Murray goes about telling every body that *he* loses by the works—&c. &c. &c. indeed I heard that he said so several years ago—if he does he is a— but never mind.—I am sorry to have given you so much plague lately— but as I am about to remove in a short period to Genoa—I am anxious to have my Circulars in all their circumference.—You may however

---

[1] Byron was already packing for the move to Genoa and expected to use the *Bolivar*. As it turned out, he went by land to Lerici and then by felucca to Sestri, while Trelawny brought the *Bolivar* to Genoa.

address to Pisa as usual till I write to you that I am removed or removing.—You will excuse all this & believe me

yrs. ever
N B

Pisa. September 7th. 1822

Dear Douglas,—Enclosed are the 6th. and 7th. cantos of D[on]
J[uan]. In a post or two I will send you the 8th. and 9th. Also at the
time a letter to you, written yesterday, containing one for J. Murray,
Esq. (it is open that you may read it), with instructions or *hints* to
you; the two following cantos (8th. and 9th.) are longer than the
enclosed. You will let me know what you think.

Yours ever
N B

Septr. 10th. 1822

My dear T.—I received an account from Dunn which has a good
deal surprized me—I perceive 60 crowns a month—for the expences
of the boat—which I thought could not exceed *forty*—and besides
these a bill for all kinds of expences—[and] additions &c.—when I
thought that she had [alrea]dy cost more than enough.—In all 227
Scudi—I have paid it however but I trust that it will be the last of the
kind—for I really cannot afford it—& would rather lay her up at
once.—I have been obliged in consequence to decline the purchase
of Williams' pistols—which I have re-consigned to Dunn at Leghorn.
I hope you had a good voyage—

yrs. ever
N B

Septr. 10th. 1822

Dear Douglas/—On the 7th. I sent you the 6 & 7th. Cantos of
D[on] J[uan]—I now transmit you the 8 & 9th.—and request a line
of acknowledgement—and also your opinion—I have no objection to
listen to any suggestion of omissions *here* & *there*—but I *wont* be
dictated to by *John Murray Esqre*—remember—let me hear from you.
——Address to me—*Genoa—Villa Saluzzi*—where I mean to pass
the winter—and don't forget to let me hear from you.

yrs. ever
N B

September 10, 1822

Dear Mary S.—Enclosed is Murray's letter, which partly confirms Mrs. Godwin's. With regard to the will, if it is valid, as presumed, why should you make a traffic of your Boy's prospects for a temporary convenience? You best know if Mr Shelley took any steps to render it nugatory, or made any alteration.

Upon the subject of your journey,[1] I do not like to give any positive opinion; but I cannot see the immediate advantage, or even future, from such a step, *just now*. The will is known to exist; it cannot be altered, or made away with; but you can consult Mrs. Mason, and regulate yourself by the mechanism of "Clare's Minerva".[2] As to sharing Mrs. Godwin's small estate, I rather suspect that 'tis your own which she means. At any rate, write to Godwin to take a copy of the will to my solicitors, John and Charles Hanson, Esquires, Chancery Lane, and the Stamp Office, or Bloomsbury Square, for they reside or have offices in all three.

Yours ever,
BYRON

To Mrs. Shelley, Pisa.

[TO DOUGLAS KINNAIRD] *Pisa. Septr. 11th. 1822*

Dear Douglas/—I write a few lines to advise you that I have sent you lately in *two* packets by different posts (the 7th. & 10th. of this Month) the 6th. 7th. 8th. & 9th. Cantos of D[on] J[uan]—with preface & so forth and all for your decision.—As I could wish to know exactly or nearly—the probable state—or rather statement of my budget in the ensuing [year?] I wish you would let me know what I am likely to have to trust to—for hitherto your Kirkby addition has proved a complete bubble—and I presume that that Scoundrel Lushington will contrive to make it continue so.—Why am *I* to be loaded on a sudden with this mortgage which never was levied till now—on the Kirkby estate?—You must not allow yourself to be talked over by that villain whom I mean to attack publicly as soon as possible—I will make him

---

[1] Mary was thinking of returning to England to see what could be done to get a settlement with Shelley's father. But partly on Byron's advice she postponed her journey and moved to Genoa where she lived with the Hunts until after Byron left for Greece.

[2] Mrs. Mason (Lady Mountcashell) was a friend and adviser of Claire Clairmont and Mary Shelley.

repent his tricks before I have done with him.—My Income *ought* to be
—(supposing the woman to live) for 1823 thus——

Kirkby M[allor]y	3168—(half of *6336*)
My own	2715
	5883

Say—from Murray for the 4 new Cantos and the volume already in
press—two thousand Guineas—at the lowest—or three thousand at
the highest.—

K[irkb]y	3168
M[y] own	2715
From Murray	2100
	7983

I have in your bank or in that of Messrs. Webb [,] Leghorn (630
pounds in Messrs Webbs) better than four thousand pounds still—of
which Supposing that I spend two thousand before January—there
ought still to remain two thousand.

Total for 1823	
Kirkby	3168
My own	2715
From Murray	2100
Surplus of this year	2000
	9983

If Lady B[yron] goes out of this world—the remaining five hundred
per annum comes to me don't it? also ten thousand insurance or for
how much have you insured?—say 12000 or 15000 £ S.D. What has
become of the Rochdale appeal? I wish I could sell that Gulph of
Litigation & have done with it.—You may well doubt if the Chancellor
will give fair play in any cause of mine.——

[TO JOHN MURRAY]   *Pisa. Septr. 11th. 1822*

Dear Sir,—I write a line to advise you that by the two last posts—
I sent off to Mr. D[ouglas] K[innaird] the four new Cantos of D[on]
J[uan]. I hear by the way—that Rogue Southey says that he does not
know what I meant by hinting that I had been kind to one of his connections.——All I know is—that in 1815 Mr. *Sotheby* wrote to me
saying that Coleridge was in great distress—& that the literary fund
had given him 20—or more pounds [and] wishing me to help him—&

that I immediately sent him one hundred pounds—being at a time—
when I could not command 150—in the world—having (as you know)
dunns [sic] & executions in my house daily & weekly.—I also recommended him to you as a publisher.—I have no wish to trumpet this
—but if Rogue Southey denies it—I shall prove it to his face.—I hear
that he says his wife was not a milliner at Bath.[1]—Ask Luttrell—I
have heard Nugent his friend say twenty times—that he knew both
his & Coleridge's Sara at Bath—before they were married & that they
were Milliners—or Dress-maker's apprentices.—There is no harm
if they were that I know—nor did I mean it as any.—

yrs. &c. &c.
N B

Address to *Genoa*—ferma in posta.

Pisa. Septr. 12th. 1822

My dear Douglas/—Enclosed, you will find a curious budget of
mine for the ensuing year at which the *banker* will laugh—and the
friend will sigh—the *trustee* however ought to blush for allowing his
trust*ing* or trust*er*—to be overreached by two such scoundrels as
Lushington & Colbourne.[1]—As to what regards Murray—that great
man ought to be narrowly watched—don't you be talked over by the
fellow.—He will prate of piracy—but recollect that he might neutralize
this in a great measure by publishing *very cheap* small editions of the
same type with former piracies—at the same time—reserve his *smooth*
octavos—for former publishers [purchasers?]—of the same more
expensive Calibre.——Now—do not allow yourself to be carried
away by first impressions—which is your grand propensity—so as to
make your letters to me a series of contradictions the moment you
get off business—though upon *that*—you are very oracular & sensible
and of this world.—In short—Doug.—the longer I live—the more I
perceive that Money (honestly come by) is the Philosopher's Stone—
and therefore do thou be my Man of trust & fidelity—and look after
this same—my avarice—or cupidity—is *not* selfish—for my *table*
don't cost four shillings a day—and except horses and helping all
kinds of patriots—(I have long given up *costly* harlotry) I have no
violent expences—but I want to get a sum together to go amongst the

---

[1] See *Don Juan*, Canto III, Stanza 93. The Fricker sisters, whom Coleridge
and Southey married, were of humble origin, but they were not milliners, a profession that in the 19th century was associated with women of loose morals.

[1] Lady Byron's trustees. Ridley Colbourne was a family friend. See Elwin,
Lord Byron's Wife, p. 460.

Greeks or Americans—and do some good—my great expence this year has been a Schooner which cost me a thousand pounds or better—

yrs. ever

N B

Address to *Genoa*. either—poste restante or Villa Saluzzo.

P.S.—The four new Cantos will (or *ought* to succeed) for they contain (with poesy intermingled plentifully)—some good sensible practical truths that you don't hear every day in the week;—or at least put so pithily and prudently.

[TO DOUGLAS KINNAIRD]   *Pisa, Sept. 13th. 1822*

By the last two posts I sent off to you the four new Cantos of Don Juan. So rogue Southey says that he does not know what I meant by hinting that I had shown some kindness to one of his relations. I tell you what it is. In 1815 Mr. Sotheby wrote to me saying that Coleridge was in great distress—that the Literary Fund had granted him only £20, and wishing me to come to his assistance. I immediately sent him one hundred pounds—more than two thirds of what I could command in the world. This happened at a time when (as you know) I had duns and executions in my house daily. I have no desire to trumpet this, but thus much for rogue Southey's "information".

[TO LEIGH HUNT]   *Septr. 15th. 1823* [*1822*]

My dear Hunt,—Of course.——But never mind—and besides you will have two days more of it—for I have just discovered a plan of charging two hundred Crowns for *your* voyage to Genoa—which is rather *more* than mine will be with three carriages per *post*—and not by vettura.—On this discovery—I have decided to "shame the rogues" and stay a day longer—"and bully—and bounce" which as Johnson says "sticks to our last sand".[1]—For whatever money you want apply to Lega—I never have any about me—in pocket for I love it in a *casket*, but not in a purse.——Pray do not deem this out of the way—for when I have occasion for a sixpence—I send after it to him——and he is [a] damned rascal.—

Believe me yrs. ever

N B

[1] The last part of the quotation is in Pope, *Moral Essays*, I, 225.

My dear Douglas/—My letters were I grant you very impatient—but I regret very much that they should have "worked you"—the haste arose because I am going to Genoa—& could not account for the non-arrival of the Circuitous notes—and if I had gone there without them—I might have waited so much the longer without knowing what had become of them.—I sent you on the 7th. & 10th. *two* packets—containing *four* new C[ant]os of D[on] J[uan]—the arrival of which please to acknowledge—addressing to *Genoa* Villa Saluzzo.—I do not rely on Shadwell's opinion—consult Mr. *Bell*—I will abide by his opinion—as to Chancery—*they* will suffer as much as I shall—and with that consideration it is not to be shrunk from.—But first let us have Bell's counsel—*he* is the *first* at the Chancery *Bar* as they very properly call that barrier between people and their property.——I positively object to drunken Davi[d]son—what to sit down and be saddled with *two* hundred a year for an old superannuated toss-pot of Sir Ralph's [;] let him go back to Halnaby—as he has got drunk in Sir Ralph's service—let him provide for his liquid necessities.—

Why the deuce did you lodge the 4000 in the *funds now*—when they are at 80? could not one have got exchequer bills or some other security pro tempore—as it will not only be like the loss of Trinculo's bottle—"disgrace and dishonour but an infinite loss"[1] having to sell out when they are low again.—I wish the eternal Mortgage could be settled once for all—it is now eight months—we have had of shilly shally.—It would be difficult for me to judge whether anything can be extracted from Albemarle Street for the new Cantos &c.—you will be the best judge of that.—Take an edition of *Humphrey Clinker*—and read to John Murray the *bookseller's* letter to the Welch Clergyman in the *introduction*—it will be a good lesson to him.—As to piracies—he ought to print very cheap editions and *undersell* them—and reserve his *octavos* for former purchasers.—You will perpend and pronounce.—The present C[ant]o's will perhaps sell—as they are full of politics—and some poesy.——Hobhouse has been here this week—and I will leave a place for him to add a line to you

yrs. ever
N B

P.S.—I sent you a week or two ago—a sort of *budget* for the ensuing year—which I dare say you will laugh [at] as part of it may be as visionary as a Minister of State's—Here is an epitaph for the Examiner.—

---

[1] *The Tempest*, Act IV, scene 1.

Oh Castlereagh! thou art a patriot now!
Cato died for his Country—so dos't thou.—
He perished rather than see Rome enslaved,
Thou cuts't thy throat that Britain may be saved.

[In Hobhouse's hand]

My dear Kinnaird—Byron calls this leaving a place for me.—This small space would have been better filled by Lord B's prose or verse— but I must occupy it by just asking you to write to me—and let me hear how you are—& how going on & what doing or going to do— direct to Rome—no more room but to tell you how truly I am yours—

J. C. HOBHOUSE

[*Sept. 18, 1822?*] *p.m. Oct. 3. 1822*

[TO DOUGLAS KINNAIRD]
[In Byron's hand]

Another
So Castlereagh has cut his throat; the worst
Of this is—that his own was not the first,

Another
So *He* has cut his throat at last—*He? Who?*
The Man who cut his Country's long ago.—

[In Hobhouse's hand]

I found another bit of paper here and for fear of its being filled with more libels in verse subjoin to my other note that finding myself at the Devil's bridge at the bottom of the St. Gothard I thought of carry- ing our party merely that less into Italy—I did so on horseback—& sent my servant around for the carriage which he brought over the Semplon—we went to Como & he went by the Lago Maggiore—we arrived after two days' separation at Milan within an hour & a half of each other—and I think since the junction of Hannibal & his brother nothing more grand has been concerted or executed—I went to Genoa & drove here & shall go on to Florence & Rome—vexatious your brother is not there—Byron is very well indeed. I shall leave him & Pisa the day after tomorrow—I shall not stay long in Italy but return after showing the common sights to my sisters.

[Last line cut off in copy except for signature: H]

[TO W. E. WEST] *Pisa. Septr. 19th. 1822*

Dear Sir,—I am anxious to have an engraving from your picture
for the Academy of N.Y. by Morghen.[1] Would you have the goodness to propose this to the Engraver Morghen—at his *own* price—
and at *my* expence.—I wish also to know what I am in your debt for
Madame G[uiccioli]'s picture—as I am about to set off for Genoa.—
You will oblige me by an answer addressed to me at Pisa as usual.—
Believe me ever and truly

yr. obliged & obedt. Sert.
NOEL BYRON

[TO DOUGLAS KINNAIRD (a)] *Pisa. Septr. 21st. 1822*

My Dear Douglas,—Hobhouse went this morning—these glimpses
of old friends for a moment are sad remembrancers.——You have sent
a credit on Balatreri for two thousand pounds—but I don't want [it]—
thank you the same—having cash enough for the present.——Write
to me at Genoa—where I am going directly. It is a pity to invest Sir
Jacob's 4000—in the funds while they are so *high*—why not rather in
exchequer bills?—Manage the mortgage so as that I may not lose half
a year's interest by selling out at a wrong time.—By the post of the
7th. and 10th. I sent you the four new Cantos of D[on] J[uan]—and will
take your advice as to disposing of them. Murray should *print* very
cheap editions to undersell the pirates—and keep his gay Octavos of 7
shillings for the purchasers of higher priced former editions.—Have we
nearly liquidated Hanson's bill?—pray keep a look out upon him and his
progeny.—I wish that Rochdale appeal could be settled before a new
Chancellor—I doubt this one won't give us fair play.—Lady B's life
should be ensured for £15000 instead of 10000 £. As much *Crabtree*
as you please—but no *Davidson*[;] it is a *job*—a glaring—flaring—
staring job of Lushington's to saddle me with a drunken blackguard.—
Don't you be cajoled by the bitch's banking with you—but remember

yrs. ever
N B

[TO DOUGLAS KINNAIRD (b)] *Pisa. Septr. 21st. 1822*

Dear Douglas,—Since I wrote this morning, I have received a
letter of credit from you—and the enclosed from Charles Hanson—

[1] Raphael Morghen, a famous engraver, had settled in Florence. Since he wanted
4,000 dollars for making the engraving and would not promise it in less than three
years, the idea was abandoned.

which you must allow to be handsome on his part.———I have but one word to say—*Davi*[*d*]*son* shall *not* be steward at Kirkby—am *I* or am *I* not to have a voice in such matters? if not:—the Estate shall go into Chancery at once—the appointment of Davi[d]son is an infamous *plot* to settle him there at my expence.

yrs. ever
N B

Address to Genoa.—

The thing must go to Chancery—I foresee that—so lose no time—it will at least make *them* feel also—damn them.———I have written to Messrs Hanson to take Bell's opinion—and file the Bill.——

[TO CHARLES HANSON]   *Pisa. Septr. 21st. 1822*

Dear Charles/—I have but a moment to answer your letter.—The Arbitrators say that it is Shadwell's opinion that the house is vested in the trustees.—Consult Mr. Bell or other sound lawyers—and if their opinion is contrary to Shadwell's—throw the thing [in]to Chancery.— We shall there at least know the truth.—I will not consent [to] Davi[d]son's appointment—and I have written to protest against it— and beg you will repeat what I here say to all whom it may concern.— It is merely an attempt on the part of Sir Ralph at a job in favour of a drunken Steward who served *him* at *Halnaby* and *now*—he wishes to saddle me with the maintenance of an incapable Servant of his own.— The shortest way is at once to wait on Sir Francis our Arbitrator and state that I must have the question of the right decided before the Chancellor—so take the necessary steps—first—advising Mr. Kinnaird of this intention.

yrs. truly
NOEL BYRON

P.S.—Address your answer to me at Genoa—where I go next week I believe. Mr. Kin[nair]d will suggest a mode of sending the deeds safely.

[TO JOHN MURRAY]   *Pisa. Septr. 23rd. 1822*

Dear Sir/—I have been in daily—but as usual idle expectation of hearing from you before I went to Genoa.—In the mean time I have seen your brother.[1]—who—I must say—by no means loses in the

---

[1] Archibald Murray, the publisher's half-brother, of the *H.M.S. Rochfort*, then in Leghorn harbour, paid two visits to Byron at Pisa, on Aug. 30 and about Sept. 15. He was as much taken with Byron as the poet was with him. (See Smiles, I, 429, 430.)

comparison —I like him very much. The bust does not turn out a very good one—though it may be like for aught I know—as it exactly resembles a superannuated Jesuit.———I shall therefore not send it as I intended—but I will send you *hers*—which is much better—and you can get a copy from Thorwaldsen's.—I assure you Bartolini's is dreadful—though my mind misgives me that it is hideously like. If it is—I can not be long for this world—for it overlooks seventy.——
If you can't be civil to Mr. John Hunt—it means that you have ceased to be so to me—or mean to do so. I have thought as much for some time past—but you will find in the long run (though I hear that you go about talking of yourself like Dogberry "as a fellow that hath had losses")[2] that you will not change for the better.———I am worth any "forty on fair ground"[3] of the wretched stilted pretenders and parsons of your advertisements.—By the way send me a copy of the M.S.S. lines on *Samiel*[4]—which were sent some years ago.—I hear from Mr. Hobhouse that he hath said something which is like him—it is time to teach him—and if I take him in hand—I'll show him what he has been these sixty years. Send me a copy of the lines.—

yrs.
N B

[TO DOUGLAS KINNAIRD]   *Pisa. Septr. 23d. 1822*

My dear Douglas/—You will have had good store of letters and packets from me lately—I want Chancery Bell's opinion—for I doubt that the matter will have to end there—Lushington and his Client encroach knowing my reluctance to a lawsuit—but they are *out* for once—and "they must law and claw before they get it."——
Davi[d]son's *Job* is worthy of a minister or of a d——d bitch—and an old rogue—which I take to be *their* present compound——but you will see if I don't make Master Lushington wince before I have done with him.—He had better raise the devil than set me to work with the truth about him.—I will show the reformers what a prize they have in him.——I thank you for your additional credit for £2000—but I have no immediate occasion for it—but as I have some flying notions of emigration—it is as well to have such a thing by me—in case of accidents.—What do you think of the *budget* for the year 1823 which I sent you—I suppose you laugh at part of the proposed supplies.—You

2 *Much Ado about Nothing*, Act IV, scene 2.
3 *Coriolanus*, Act III, scene 1.
4 The lines on Samuel Rogers.

must do what you can in the literary tax for me—I think that much of the four new Cantos will turn to account if Murray gives fair play to them.—You should insure Lady B——'s (fill in the blanks as you please) life for at least *15000*—if practicable.—Could you obtain any information about *Rochdale* for me—I would it were over, one way or the other—owing to the expence and anxiety.—How much do we *cwe* now?

yrs. ever
N B

Minute of supposed possibilities.—

Calculate to have an unspent surplus of the present year in J[anuar]y 1823—at about 3000

            3000 of Noel Accession
    Say about 2700 of my own
        2625—Produce of M.S.S. more or less
        ——————
        11325

Will there not also be a half *year* of this year 1822, from Kir[k]by Mallory?—I presume that the deceased does not take a whole year and she died in J[anuar]y 1822 was it not so? if so—Say suppose

        1500   )   11325
        add   )   1500
        —————   —————
        11325   )   12825

Address to me at Genoa—Villa Saluzzo.

[TO W. E. WEST]   *Pisa. September 23rd. 1822*

Dear Sir—Three years!—Of course it is out of the question. However I shall not think of any other engraver—he is the only one. Will you just look at the thing which he has done from Bartolini's bust. I do not mean as a *work* of art, for the incision is excellent, but for the *effect*. It is like a superannuated Jesuit. Had he 4000 dollars for that too? You will see it at Bardi's the print-seller. I wonder who ordered it. I would have given any thing to have suppressed it altogether.—I am going to Genoa.—

yours ever
N B

P.S.—Address your answer to Pisa for the present.

Caro Giuliani—Vi Prego prevenire quel' perfido *Fidia* Bartolini, che essendo per partire dal' indegno paese—voglio avere ⟨il⟩ i due busti—terminati o non terminati.—Avete veduto l'incisione del' detto busto?—pare un vecchio Jesuita quasi rimbambito.——Pregate il Sr. Bartolini—di campare il gesso—e credetemi

divot[issi]mo Ser[vitor]e &c. &c. &c.

N B

[TRANSLATION]   *Pisa September 23. 1822*

Dear Giuliani[1]—I beg you to inform that perfidious *Phidias*, Bartolini, that being about to depart from this worthless region—I want to have the two busts—finished or unfinished.—Have you seen the etching of the aforesaid bust?—it looks like an old Jesuit almost in his dotage.——Ask Sr. Bartolini—to throw the plaster cast into relief—and believe me

[Your] most devoted Servant &c. &c. &c.

N B[2]

[TO DOUGLAS KINNAIRD]   *Septr. 24th. 1822*

Dear Douglas/—Enclosed is another epistle of mine—full of questions and calculations—which I imagine will raise the smiles of such an expert financier as your worship—who bank for "late Queens"—and ladies with separate establishments.—The reason why I am so anxious to settle my affairs—and learn [what] I may have to trust to is, that I have long had a notion of emigration from your worn out Europe— but am undecided as to the *where*—South America——The United States—or even van Dieman's land—of which I hear much as a good place to settle in—you will perhaps let me know what you think I may realize (the Gods willing) in 1823—by the probablilties or possibilities within stated.—Do what you can for me & let me hear

yrs. ever

N B

---

[1] Byron elsewhere identifies him as "Intendant of the Russian Count Tattailin at Florence". See Feb. 20, 1823, to Messrs. Webb & Co.

[2] Translated by Ricki B. Herzfeld.

[Added to letter of Leigh Hunt to John Hunt]
[In Leigh Hunt's hand]

My dear John,—It has struck me, that you would feel more at ease
& *sure*, if I were to send you such an introduction to our [Junction?] as
Lord B. is known to you to approve, as well as myself. I have therefore
written the enclosed.—Since my last letter, I have received another
from you. I hope our new plan will not hurt you with your new office in
Regent Street. Perhaps it would be advisable to publish the Examiner
there, considering it's new modification, especially if you print many
[now Byron's hand] of the things over again.—But upon this as upon
a variety of other matters—connected with a variety of *other* matters—
of which you will be the best Judge as being on the spot—you can
determine—as we have full confidence in your "discretion"—as well as
"emphasis" when requisite.—As Galignani has rectified the mistake
about Ld. B's Irish subscription you need not insert what I last stated
on that subject (in my late letter) in the Examiner.—Omit or retain
the preface as you please.—

[Leigh Hunt's hand again] Ld. B. took the pen from me & wrote, as it
was after dinner & the blood got into his head.

yrs affectionately
L H

Lord B. as well as myself will be glad to have [Hazlitt?] write in any
work in which we are engaged,—so much so, that he mentioned it to
me himself before your letter arrived. Remember me to him, and
kindly, though tell him that I have often had bitter feelings upon a
certain work when thinking of my lost friend.[1]

[TO JOHN CAM HOBHOUSE] *Pisa. Septr. 26th. 1822*

My dear Hobhouse,—I am glad that the letters have been of any use
—but such as they are—they are owing to the Guiccioli and her family
& not to me.—I have had a little conflict with the rheumatics—but by
dint of Opodeldoc and a warm bath—have fought off the flannels for
this time.—You may do as you like about Bartolini—it don't much

---

[1] Hazlitt's essay "On Paradox and Commonplace" in *Table Talk* (No. 15)
attacked Shelley rather savagely for his extremist views which did the liberal
cause no good, calling him a "philosophic fanatic". And Hunt saw his own portrait
in Hazlitt's "On People with One Idea". He wrote a letter of protest to Hazlitt,
April 20, [1821] (William Carew Hazlitt, *Memoirs of William Hazlitt*, I, 305–308.)

matter how a man is sculped after 30 years of age.—My best respects to the Miss H[obhouse]'s—to whom I desiderate all the amusements possible at Florence.———Do you go on to Rome? we sent you a letter to the Mda. Sagrati—through Giuliani the other day.—Salute Collini—and Giuliani for me.—The Guiccioli is pleased that you like her letter—and her bust—I hope Bartolini as he has a better subject in her—will have more luck in the effect.—We are all a packaging—to set off at *day break* tomorrow morning—a preliminary which by no means agrees with my dormitory habitudes—The very idea makes me yawn to that degree that my pen—[a paragraph in Italian in Countess Guiccioli's hand follows.] [Byron resumes] I need only add my signature to this [word torn off] epistle—believe me ever & truly yrs.

N B

did you pay—or deliver the monies to Giuliani—8 Scudi—I forget whether it was consigned to you?—

[TO DOUGLAS KINNAIRD]   *Pisa. Septr. 26th. 1822*

My dear Douglas/—I have received yrs. of ye. 7th. with the banking account of assetts and disbursements. But I am still ignorant of the sum total of my remaining bond debts—by the three years Int[erest] paid up in the beginning of ye. current year—360—the principal should be two thousand four hundred pounds—but I suspect that there are more —and especially a bond to Claughton—which Charles Hanson bought from him at a considerable profit.—There may be yet others for aught I know.———Now to meet these—let me see.———Besides your late Credit of 2000 in *advance* (which I do not mean to touch unless in some emergency) I have still £1700 in your former circulars—and 1200 in ditto lately received in all 2900 £—also in the hands of Messrs. Webb of Leghorn 630 £ Sterling—(3580 in all between you) and about three or four hundred pounds cash in the house—total about £4000— more or less.—Now supposing me to spend a thousand pounds between this and J[anuar]y 1823—in moving to Genoa—which is expensive as comprising furniture and a complete establishment—there would still be a surplus of 3000 remaining to begin the year withal.—This would have been still greater but I was foolish enough to build a slight Schooner—which *was* to have cost £300—but which eventually cost nearly £800—her expences since amount monthly to about 60 *dollars*—i.e. 720 dollars per annum—say about 180 £ sterling per annum including men's wages and sundries.——

217

I have however sold *three* horses and keep of course that number less in my stable—having still six—three carriage and three saddle. —Then I lent Leigh Hunt 250—last winter—bought him 50 pounds worth of furniture—have advanced him about 50 more—and lent Shelley fifty besides buying his furniture since his decease—in all about —say—about five hundred pounds more or less.—This—with one or two unexpected expences of about one hundred more—make in all about fourteen or fifteen hundred pounds—which *would* have been added to the 3000 of present surplus at the end of this year—had I not been imprudent.—I could not help assisting Hunt—who is a good man—and is left taken all aback by Shelley's demise.—You see I am explicit with you—in my finance matters,—Now say—

3000—of Surplus of 1822.
3168—moiety of Kirkby Rental stated at 6336—for 1823.
2625—for the new J[uan]'s at 2500 guineas but *more* or *less* of course according to circumstances including the things already in M[urray]'s hands.
2700 Of my own for 1823
———
11403.

and perhaps something more *this* year from Kirkby Mallory as you say that there will be a payment at Michaelmas.—Now with regard to the new C[ant]os—I think you will see that they are likely to take—at least as likely as the others.—Be as cautious as you can with Murray— who will strain every nerve to make the best of you.—His protest about piracy—amounts to this—that he *ought* to print *cheap* editions to undersell the pirates—while he reserves his polished Octavos for former purchasers of the same.—I hope you will not think my estimate too much for the four new cantos—indeed in other times it ought to have been more;—and I have the 10th. Canto also nearly concluded. —You will see what you can do.—There is I doubt something wrong about M[urray].—I suspect that he has lost by speculations in books of travels &c. and would willingly throw it on us—because of course he calculates his *gains* in the total of his publications—and like tradesmen —would make one good customer pay for twenty bad ones.—He told me months ago—that he had lost *fifteen* thousand pounds by a *brother*. —I saw his brother not long ago (purser of the Rochefort) who said he never owed him a farthing. So you [see] there is something queer in all this.—Now if I knew pretty nearly what I was likely to have in all —for the year 1823—I could then settle with you how much debt we can afford to liquidate.——I shall not send the 10*th.* Canto—

which would make 5 new ones—till I know what advantage it would be—or otherwise.—I sent you the four i.e. 6. 7. 8. 9. on the 7— & 10th. Insts. in two packets.—Address to me at Genoa *Villa Saluzzo*. Hobhouse is at Florence.————Excuse this long letter from

yrs. ever
N B

P.S.—I am furious about Davi[d]son's job—for a job it is.—Do pray get Hanson's Bill—and tax them—I must really break with him if he don't send them in.—See if his Son has Claughton's bond—i.e. mine to Claughton.—I see no account of ye. money lately paid by Claughton—nor the Rochdale 500—Discover *who* has had it—the lawyers I take it.—Are you aware that writers get 16 guineas a sheet in the Magazines for *prose* and not very good prose either?—So you see that literary property is still something in the market—keep this in mind.——

LIST OF LETTERS AND SOURCES

Date	Recipient	Source of Text	Page
		1821	
Oct. 15, 1821– May 18, 1822	"Detached Thoughts"	MS. Murray	11
[Nov. ?]	John Murray	MS. Murray	53
Nov. 3	John Murray	MS. Murray	53
Nov. 4	Douglas Kinnaird	MS. Pierpont Morgan Library	55
Nov. 4	Augusta Leigh	MS. The Earl of Lytton	56
Nov. 9	John Murray	Text: Moore, II, 557	57
Nov. 10	Lorenzo Bartolini	MS. John S. Mayfield Library, Syracuse University	57
Nov. 12	John Murray	MS. Murray	58
Nov. 14	John Murray	MS. Murray	58
[Nov. 15–16?]	John Murray	MS. Murray	59
Nov. 15	Douglas Kinnaird (*a*)	MS. Murray	60
Nov. 15	Douglas Kinnaird (*b*)	MS. Murray	61
Nov. 16	Douglas Kinnaird	MS. Murray	61
Nov. 16	Thomas Moore	Text: Moore, II, 558–559	63
Nov. 17	Lady Byron	MS. Carl H. Pforzheimer Library	64
Nov. 20	Lord Kinnaird	MS. Murray	66
Nov. 23	John Cam Hobhouse	MS. Murray	67
Nov. 24	John Cam Hobhouse	MS. Murray	69
Nov. 24	John Murray	MS. Murray	69
Nov. 28	Douglas Kinnaird	MS. Murray	71
Nov. 29	Douglas Kinnaird	MS. Murray	72
[Dec.?]	[Douglas Kinnaird?]	Text: Hobhouse Proof	73
Dec. 4	John Murray	MS. Murray	74

Date	Recipient	Source of Text	Page
		1821 (continued)	
Dec. 8	[Henry Dunn?]	MS. Harrow School Library	75
Dec. 8	John Sheppard	MS. Roe-Byron Collection, Newstead Abbey	75
Dec. 10	John Murray	MS. Murray	77
Dec. 12	John Taaffe	MS. Stark Library, University of Texas	78
Dec. 12	Percy Bysshe Shelley	MS. Österreichische Nationalbibliothek, Vienna	78
Dec. 12	Frederick North, Earl of Guilford	MS. Carl H. Pforzheimer Library	79
Dec. 12	Thomas Moore	Text: Moore, II, 565–567	79
[Dec. 13?]	Thomas Moore	MS. Stark Library, University of Texas	81
Dec. 14	Douglas Kinnaird	MS. Murray	81
Dec. 16	John Cam Hobhouse	MS. Murray	81
Dec. 18	Douglas Kinnaird	MS. Murray	82
		1822	
[1822?]	Rev. Dr. Bryce	Text: Myers, Cat. 360, Winter, 1949	83
[1822?]	Bryan Waller Procter	Text: Procter, *An Autobiographical Fragment*, 245–247	83
[Jan?]	Douglas Kinnaird	MS. Murray	84
Jan. 12	Sir Walter Scott	MS. National Library of Scotland	85
Jan. 18	John Cam Hobhouse	MS. Murray	88
Jan. 18	Douglas Kinnaird	MS. Murray	89
Jan. 22	John Murray (*a*)	MS. Murray	90
Jan. 22	John Murray (*b*)	MS. Murray	90
Jan. 22	Douglas Kinnaird	MS. Lord Kinnaird	91
Jan. 23	John Murray	MS. Murray	91
Jan. 23	Douglas Kinnaird	MS. Murray	92
Jan. 26	Douglas Kinnaird	MS. Lord Kinnaird	93
Jan. 29	Douglas Kinnaird	MS. Murray	94

Date	Recipient	Source of Text	Page
		1822 (continued)	
[Feb, 1822?]	[?]	MS. British Library (Ashley B351)	95
[Feb.?]	Bryan Waller Procter	MS. Houghton Library, Harvard University	95
Feb. 3	Thomas Medwin	Text: Copy, Keats–Shelley Memorial, Rome	95
Feb. 5	Editor of *The Courier*	MS. Pierpont Morgan Library	95
Feb. 6	Douglas Kinnaird	MS. Murray	100
Feb. 6	Captain John Hay	MS. Harrow School Library	102
Feb. 7	Robert Southey	MS. Lord Kinnaird	102
Feb. 8	John Murray	MS. Murray	103
Feb. 9	[Henry Dunn]	MS. Robert H. Taylor Coll., Princeton University Library	105
Feb. 17	Douglas Kinnaird	MS. Murray	105
Feb. 17	John Hanson	MS. Murray	106
[After Feb. 17]	Teresa Guiccioli	MS. Biblioteca Classense, Ravenna	107
Feb. 19	Douglas Kinnaird	MS. Murray	107
Feb. 19	Thomas Moore	Text: Moore, II, 575	109
Feb. 20	Thomas Moore	Text: Moore, II, 576	110
Feb. 20	Douglas Kinnaird	MS. Murray	111
Feb. 20	John Hanson	MS. Carl H. Pforzheimer Library	112
Feb. 23	Douglas Kinnaird (*a*)	MS. Murray	113
[Feb. 23?]	Douglas Kinnaird (*b*)	MS. Lord Kinnaird	114
Feb. 27	John Hanson	MS. Carl H. Pforzheimer Library	115
Feb. 28	Thomas Moore	Text: Moore, II, 577	115
[Feb. 29?]	[?]	MS. Pierpont Morgan Library	116
[March?]	F. C. Armstrong	MS. British Library (Add. 22130)	116
March 1	Thomas Moore	Text: Moore, II, 577–578	116
March 4	Thomas Moore	Text: Moore, II, 579–580	118
March 4	Augusta Leigh	MS. The Earl of Lytton	120

Date	Recipient	Source of Text	Page
		1822 (continued)	
March 6	Thomas Moore	Text: Moore II, 581–583	120
March 6	John Murray	MS. Murray	121
March 8	Thomas Moore	Text: Moore, II, 587–588	122
March 9	John Cam Hobhouse	MS. Murray	123
March 15	John Murray	MS. Murray	125
March 20	W. H. [Reingamun?]	MS. Milton S. Eisenhower Library, The Johns Hopkins University	126
March 22	John Hanson	MS. Murray	126
March 22	Douglas Kinnaird	MS. Murray	127
March 25	John Hay	MS. Harrow School Library	128
March 26	John Taaffe	MS. Stark Library, University of Texas	129
March 27	Edward Dawkins (a)	Text: LJ, VI, 43–44	129
March 27	Edward Dawkins (b)	MS. Stark Library, University of Texas	130
March 28	Douglas Kinnaird	MS. Murray	130
March 28	[Sir Walter Scott]	MS. Rosenbach Foundation, Philadelphia	131
March 28	John Taaffe (a)	Text: Cline, p. 115	131
March 28	John Taaffe (b)	MS. Stark Library, University of Texas	131
[March 29]	John Taaffe	Text: Cline, p. 120	131
March 31	John Murray	MS. University of Leeds Library	132
March 31	Edward Dawkins	MS. Stark Library, University of Texas	132
[April?]	John Taaffe	MS. Stark Library, University of Texas	133
April 2	Douglas Kinnaird	MS. Murray	134
April 4	Edward Dawkins	MS. Stark Library, University of Texas	135
April 6	John Hay	MS. Robert H. Taylor Coll., Princeton University Library	135
April 8	John Hanson	MS. Murray	136
April 9	John Murray	MS. Murray	136

Date	Recipient	Source of Text	Page
		1822 (continued)	
April 9	Douglas Kinnaird	MS. Murray	137
April 9	Trelawny to Capt. Roberts (P.S. by Byron)	MS. Carl H. Pforzheimer Library	137
April 11	John Cam Hobhouse	MS. Murray	138
April 12	Edward Dawkins	MS. Stark Library, University of Texas	139
April 12	John Hay (*a*)	MS. Harrow College Library	139
April 12	John Hay (*b*)	MS. Stark Library, University of Texas	140
April 13	Douglas Kinnaird	MS. Murray	141
April 13	John Murray	MS. Murray	141
April 16	Edward Dawkins	MS. Stark Library, University of Texas	142
April 18	Edward Dawkins	MS. Stark Library, University of Texas	144
April 18	Douglas Kinnaird	MS. Murray	144
April 18	John Murray	MS. Murray	146
April 22	John Murray	MS. Murray	146
April 22	Edward Dawkins	MS. Stark Library, University of Texas	147
April 23	Percy Bysshe Shelley	Text: Moore, 591–592	147
April 24	Edward Dawkins	MS. Stark Library, University of Texas	148
April 26	Edward Dawkins	MS. Stark Library, University of Texas	148
April 28	Edward Dawkins	MS. Stark Library, University of Texas	149
May 1	Edward Dawkins	MS. Stark Library, University of Texas	150
May 1	John Murray	MS. Murray	151
May 2	Douglas Kinnaird	MS. Murray	151
May 3	Douglas Kinnaird	MS. Murray	152
May 4	Sir Walter Scott	Text: Moore, II, 592–594	153
May 4	John Hanson	MS. Murray	155
May 4	John Murray	MS. Murray	155
May 16	John Murray	MS. Murray	156

Date	Recipient	Source of Text	Page
		1822 (continued)	
May 17	Edward Dawkins	MS. Stark Library, University of Texas	157
May 17	Douglas Kinnaird	MS. Murray	158
May 17	John Hay	MS. Stark Library, University of Texas	158
May 17	John Murray	MS. Murray	159
May 17	Thomas Moore	Text: Moore, II, 594–595	160
May 20	Percy Bysshe Shelley	MS. Carl H. Pforzheimer Library	160
May 22	[Mrs. Catherine Potter Stith]	MS. Goethe Coll., Yale University Library	161
May 25	George H. Bruen	MS. Fales Coll., New York University Library	162
[May 26?]	Douglas Kinnaird	MS. Murray	162
May 26	John Murray	MS. Murray	163
May 27	Douglas Kinnaird	MS. Lord Kinnaird	165
May 29	John Murray	MS. Murray	166
June 5	Earl of Clare	MS. Ludwig Walter Trinast	167
June 6	John Murray	MS. Murray	167
June 7	Edward Dawkins	MS. Stark Library, University of Texas	168
June 8	Thomas Moore	Text: Moore, II, 599–601	170
June 10	Isaac D'Israeli	Text: LJ, VI, 83	171
June 12	Edward Ellice	MS. National Library of Scotland	173
June 15	George H. Bruen	Text: Sotheby Cat., Nov. 12, 1963	174
June 16–18	Edward Dawkins	MS. Stark Library, University of Texas	174
June 20	Douglas Kinnaird	MS. Murray	176
June 20	John Hanson	MS. Murray	177
June 26	Edward Dawkins	MS. Stark Library, University of Texas	178
June 26	[John Murray?]	Text: Myers, Cat. 377, Autumn 1953	178
[July 2?]	Governor of Leghorn	Text: Cline, 175	178
July 3	John Murray	Text: LJ, VI, 92	179

Date	Recipient	Source of Text	Page
		1822 (continued)	
July 4	Edward Dawkins	MS. Stark Library, University of Texas	179
July 6	Edward Dawkins	MS. Stark Library, University of Texas	180
July 6	John Murray	MS. Murray	181
July 8	John Murray	MS. Murray	182
July 12	Thomas Moore	Text: Moore, II, 605–606	182
July 14	Capt. Daniel Roberts	MS. Stark Library, University of Texas	184
July 15	Edward Dawkins	MS. Carl H. Pforzheimer Library	184
July 16	Edward Dawkins	MS. Stark Library, University of Texas	184
July 19	Edward Dawkins	MS. Stark Library, University of Texas	185
July 19	Douglas Kinnaird	MS. Lord Kinnaird	185
July 21	Capt. Daniel Roberts	MS. Stark Library, University of Texas	186
[July 23?]	Douglas Kinnaird	MS. Murray	186
July 24	Douglas Kinnaird	MS. Lord Kinnaird	187
July 25	Douglas Kinnaird	MS. Murray	188
July 31	Douglas Kinnaird	MS. Murray	189
Aug. 3	John Murray	MS. Murray	189
Aug. 8	Thomas Moore	Text: Moore, II, 607–608	190
Aug. 10	John Hanson	MS. Murray	191
Aug. 10	John Murray	MS. Murray	192
Aug. 10	Edward John Trelawny	MS. Henry E. Huntington Library	192
Aug. 10	Douglas Kinnaird	MS. Murray	192
Aug. 14	Edward John Trelawny	MS. Berg Coll., New York Public Library	192
Aug. 14	Thomas Hall	Text: *LJ*, VI, 106	193
Aug. 16	Douglas Kinnaird	MS. Murray	193
Aug. 20	Douglas Kinnaird	MS. Murray	194
Aug. 24	Douglas Kinnaird	MS. Murray	195
Aug. 27	Thomas Moore	Text: Moore, II, 608–610	196
Aug. 31	Douglas Kinnaird	MS. Murray	198
[Sept?]	[Douglas Kinnaird]	Text: MS. Murray	199
Sept. 1	Douglas Kinnaird	MS. Murray	201

Date	Recipient	Source of Text	Page
		1822 (continued)	
Sept. 2	John Cam Hobhouse	MS. Murray	201
Sept. 2	W. Webb	MS. Biblioteca Labronica, Leghorn	202
Sept. 2	Edward John Trelawny	MS. Carl H. Pforzheimer Library	203
Sept. 6	Douglas Kinnaird	MS. Murray	203
Sept. 7	Douglas Kinnaird	MS. Murray	204
Sept 10	Edward John Trelawny	MS. Henry E. Huntington Library	204
Sept. 10	Douglas Kinnaird	MS. Murray	204
Sept. 10	Mary Shelley	Text: Lady Jane Shelley, *Shelley and Mary*, 4 vols., privately printed, 1882, Vol. III, pp. 869–870.	205
Sept. 11	Douglas Kinnaird	MS. Murray	205
Sept. 11	John Murray	MS. Murray	206
Sept. 12	Douglas Kinnaird	MS. Murray	207
Sept. 13	Douglas Kinnaird	Text: Sotheby Cat., June 10, 1909	208
Sept. 15	Leigh Hunt	MS. Berg Coll., New York Public Library	208
[Sept. 18?]	Douglas Kinnaird	MS. Murray	209
Sept. 19	W. E. West	MS. Facsimile, *Literary Souvenir* (1827) Preface, x	211
Sept. 21	Douglas Kinnaird (*a*)	MS. Murray	211
Sept. 21	Douglas Kinnaird (*b*)	MS. Murray	211
Sept. 21	Charles Hanson	MS. Murray	212
Sept. 23	John Murray	MS. Murray	212
Sept. 23	Douglas Kinnaird	MS. Murray	213
Sept. 23	W. E. West	Text: *New Monthly Magazine*, March 1826, Vol. XVI, 244	214
Sept. 23	Giuliani	MS. Facsimile, *Literaturnoe Nasledstvo* [*Literary Heritage*] Academy of Sciences of the U.S.S.R., Moscow, 1952	215

FORGERIES OF BYRON'S LETTERS

Nov. 18, 1821: To Capt. Hay. Schultess-Young, XXXVII, 217–19.

[1822?]: To [Mac?]. MS Rosenbach Foundation Library.

Feb. 9, 1822: To Sir James Mackintosh. Schultess-Young, IX, 167–9.

March 1822: To Douglas Kinnaird. MS. Facsimile, Wise, *Byron Bibliography*, I, p. xx.

March 4, 1822?: To Douglas Kinnaird. Text: Isographie des Hommes Célèbres, Vol. 1.

March 15, 1822: To Douglas Kinnaird. MS. Dartmouth College Library.

March 20, 1822: To Major P. Gordon. Text: Schultess-Young, XXXIX, 220–22.

April 11, 1822: To Percy Bysshe Shelley. Text: Schultess-Young, ILI, 224–5.

April 12, 1822: To Sir Godfrey Webster. Text: B-SP, II 690–91.

April 14, 1822: To Douglas Kinnaird. Text: Schultess-Young, XXII, 190–2.

April 22, 1822: To [?]. Text: *LJ*, VI, 50n.

April 24, 1822: To Percy Bysshe Shelley. Text: Schultess-Young, XLII, 225–26.

April 24, 1822: To Percy Bysshe Shelley. Text: Hodges Cat., 1848, p. 10.

May 11, 1822: To Lord Holland. MS. Historical Society of Pennsylvania.

May 18, 1822: To Douglas Kinnaird. Text: Schultess-Young, XXIII, 192–93.

May 19, 1822: To Percy Bysshe Shelley. MS. Gardner Museum, Boston.

May 23, 1822: To Percy Bysshe Shelley. Text: H. Sotheran, Cat. 6, 1895.

May 25, 1822: To T. Curtis. Text: Schultess-Young, XLV, 229–30,

May 27, 1822: To Percy Bysshe Shelley. Text: Schultess-Young. XLIV, 228–29.

May 27, 1822: To Percy Bysshe Shelley. Text: Schultess-Young, XLIII, 226–27.

Aug. 1822: To Douglas Kinnaird. Text: Maggs Cat., 449, 1924.

Aug. 1822: John Hay. Text: Murray Coll.

Aug. 5, 1822: To T. Curtis. MS. Morgan Library.

Aug. 27, 1822: To Douglas Kinnaird. Text: Schultess-Young XXIV, 193–95.

Aug. 27, 1822: To W. J. Bankes. Text: Schultess-Young, XXXIII, 210–11.

Aug. 28, 1822: To Sir Godfrey Webster. MS. Stark Library, University of Texas.

Sept. 1, 1822: To John Hay. MS. Carl H. Pforzheimer Library.

BIBLIOGRAPHY FOR VOLUME 9

(Principal short title or abbreviated references)

Astarte—Lovelace. Ralph Milbanke, Earl of: *Astarte; A Fragment of Truth, Concerning George Gordon Byron, Sixth Lord Byron.* Recorded by his grandson. New Edition by Mary Countess of Lovelace. London, 1921.

Boswell, *The Life of Johnson*, Oxford edition.

Broughton, Lord [John Cam Hobhouse]: *Recollections of a Long Life*, ed. by his daughter, Lady Dorchester. 6 vols. London, 1909–11.

Cline, C. L.: *Byron, Shelley and their Pisan Circle.* London, 1952.

Dictionary of National Biography.

D'Israeli, Isaac: *The Literary Character.* London, 3d. ed., 1822.

Hunt, Leigh: *Lord Byron and Some of his Contemporaries*, 2 vols. 2nd ed. London, 1828.

Keats-Shelley Journal, Vol. II (1953); Vol. III (1954).

LBC—Lord Byron's Correspondence, ed. John Murray, 2 vols. London, 1922.

LJ—The Works of Lord Byron. A New, Revised and Enlarged Edition. Letters and Journals, ed. Rowland E. Prothero, 6 vols., London, 1898–1901.

Marchand, Leslie A.: *Byron: A Biography*, 3 vols. New York, 1957; London, 1958.

Medwin, Thomas: *Medwin's "Conversations of Lord Byron"*, ed. Ernest J. Lovell, Jr. Princeton, 1966.

Moore, Doris Langley: *The Late Lord Byron.* London, 1961.

Moore, Thomas: *Letters and Journals of Lord Byron, with Notices of his Life*, 2 vols. London, 1830.

——*The Letters of Thomas Moore*, ed. by Wilfred S. Dowden, 2 vols. Oxford, 1964.

Origo, Iris: *The Last Attachment.* London, 1949.

Poetry—The Works of Lord Byron. A New, Revised and Enlarged Edition. Poetry, ed. Ernest Hartley Coleridge, 7 vols. London, 1898–1904.

Procter, Bryan Waller: *Autobiographical Fragment and Biographical Notes.* Boston, 1877.

Shelley, Mary W.: *The Letters of Mary W. Shelley*, ed. Frederick L. Jones, 2 vols. Norman, Okla., 1944.

Shelley, Percy Bysshe: *The Letters of Percy Bysshe Shelley*, ed. Frederick L. Jones. London, 1964.

Smiles, Samuel: *A Publisher and his Friends: Memoir and Correspondence of the Late John Murray*, 2 vols. London, 1891.

St. Clair, William: *Trelawny, The Incurable Romancer*. London, 1977.

Trelawny, Edward John: *The Letters of Edward John Trelawny*, ed. H. Buxton Forman. London, 1910.

——*Recollections of the Last Days of Shelley and Byron*. London, 1858.

White, Newman Ivey: *Shelley*, 2 vols. London, 1947.

Williams—Maria Gisborne and Edward E. Williams, Shelley's Friends: Their Journals and Letters, ed. Frederick L. Jones. Norman, Okla., 1951.

BIOGRAPHICAL SKETCHES

OF PRINCIPAL CORRESPONDENTS AND PERSONS FREQUENTLY MENTIONED

(*See also sketches in earlier volumes*)

JOHN HUNT (1775–1848)

Leigh Hunt's brother John had a joint partnership with him in *The Examiner* when Leigh came to Italy in 1822 to edit with Byron and Shelley the new periodical called *The Liberal*, of which John was to be the publisher. Before leaving, Leigh had drained his brother's finances to the point that he had no capital and was dependent on Byron's gift of manuscripts for the journal. Byron gave for the first number, *The Vision of Judgment*, which caused the publisher to be prosecuted for libel. Byron instructed Kinnaird to get the best counsel possible to defend him, and offered to come to England himself and take his place in the trial, but was assured that it would do no good and would not be permitted.

Although he soon saw that *The Liberal* would not succeed and wanted to withdraw from it, he continued to give Hunt manuscripts for each of the four numbers before it expired. Byron never met John Hunt, but he respected him and had confidence in his integrity. He wrote to Murray: "Mr. J. Hunt is most likely the publisher of the new cantos [of *Don Juan*]; with what prospects of success I know not, nor does it very much matter, as far as I am concerned; but I hope it may be of use to him, for he is a stiff, sturdy, conscientious man, and I like him; he is such a one as Prynne or Pym might be." Actually Hunt did publish the last eleven cantos of *Don Juan* in a profit-sharing venture, as well as all Byron's subsequent work, for he had no money to buy copyrights. He accepted a very modest proportion of the net proceeds (by his own wish) and rendered faithful accounts of the sales which ran into the hundreds rather than the thousands of pounds such as Byron had received from Murray for the earlier cantos. But Byron was satisfied with him as a publisher and admired his straightforward and business-like conduct more than that of his brother Leigh.

THOMAS MEDWIN (1788–1869)

Shelley's second cousin Thomas Medwin was born in Horsham, the town nearest to Shelley's home at Field Place. He had known Shelley as a boy, and though four years older, they had been at the same school and spent holidays together at Horsham. Thomas was intended by his father for a career in the law, but when after some reckless spending, an imprudent attachment, and a dislike for his profession caused a quarrel with his father, he joined a regiment of dragoons and left for India in 1812. After his return in 1819, he retired on half-pay and spent some time in Geneva before joining his cousin Shelley in Pisa in October, 1820. He was responsible for drawing others into Shelley's circle, including Edward Williams, who had been with him in India, and later Trelawny, whom he had met in Geneva. Although there is no evidence that he rose beyond the rank of lieutenant, he later took the title of Captain Medwin. Like others of the Shelley circle, he had literary ambitions. He had already published at Geneva *Oswald and Edwin: an Oriental Sketch*. After he had been some time at Pisa the Shelleys found him a little boring. Medwin departed, travelling to Florence, Rome, and Venice. He was in Geneva again when a letter from Shelley announcing the imminent arrival of Byron brought him back to Pisa. He arrived on November 14, 1821, and was soon riding and dining with Byron. He was duly impressed with Byron's agreeable company and with his stature as a poet. Very early he conceived the idea of becoming his Boswell. He drew Byron out on many subjects, both literary and personal, but apparently he took no notes and depended upon his not too accurate memory later when he composed his *Journal of Conversations with Lord Byron*, published soon after the poet's death. But Medwin was able to capture the tone and spirit of Byron's conversation, though his critics found abundant factual errors and attacked him bitterly for revealing Byron's indiscretions. For he recorded some of Byron's franknesses that other contemporaries either failed to note or preferred to remain silent about. It is possible that Byron knew he was being Boswellized, but that only encouraged him to be more frank and sometimes indiscreet. This made Medwin's *Conversations* the more intriguing and possibly more valuable as revealing the flavour of Byron's uninhibited discourse. Medwin's subsequent career was hectic and colourful. He married a rich Countess in Switzerland, spent all her money in extravagant living in Florence, and imprudent speculation in Italian paintings, many of which turned out not to be genuine. He left his wife to struggle as best she could and returned to England where he supported himself by writing for periodicals. He turned his attention more to Shelley than to Byron. His "Shelley Papers" grew into a Shelley Memoir and a *Life of Shelley*. But despite the abuse he had encountered for his *Conversations* of

Byron, he continued to think him the greater poet. "It is as a poet, and a great one, that we are to consider him," he wrote in 1834. "Poetry died with Byron, and is not likely to have a second resuscitation."

JOHN TAAFFE, JR. (1787?–1862)

Soon after arriving in Pisa on November 1, 1821, Byron had drawn into his circle an Irish expatriate and friend of Shelley, John Taaffe, Jr. Eldest son of a prominent Catholic family in Louth, Taaffe had gone into exile in 1812 following an unfortunate affair with a woman in Edinburgh, and had been living in Italy since 1815. There his friendship with Madame Regny brought him into contact with the best families in Pisa, Lucca, and Florence. Byron called on Taaffe to use his acquaintanceship and influence to stop a supposed *Auto da Fé* in Lucca in December, 1821. Taaffe was driven by literary ambitions and soon after he made the acquaintance of Byron, the latter was writing to Murray urging him to publish or find a publisher for Taaffe's *Comment on the Divine Comedy of Dante*. After a time he became a little tiresome. Mary Shelley was inclined to ridicule his literary pretensions, and Shelley found his formal calls and small talk boring. Most of the circle turned against him after his conduct in the affair of the dragoon in March, 1822, and his contradictory account of his part in the affray. Byron too was annoyed. Yet after it was all over and tempers had cooled, he still spoke kindly of Taaffe and was willing to befriend him.

EDWARD JOHN TRELAWNY (1792–1881)

A picturesque Cornishman, an adventurer and teller of tall tales, Trelawny entered the Pisan circle in January, 1822, having been drawn to the company of Byron and Shelley by Edward Williams, whom he had met in Geneva. He was already an admirer of Byron's oriental tales. Byron was a little embarrassed at first by his emulation. He told Teresa: "I have met today the personification of my Corsair. He sleeps with the poem under his pillow, and all his past adventures and present manners aim at this personification". Although he sometimes made sport of Trelawny, Byron grew to like him as a practical man. Trelawny arranged for Captain Roberts to build a boat (the *Bolivar*) for Byron and later took command of it for him. After Shelley's death, Trelawny carried out the cremation of the remains of Williams and Shelley on the beach at Viareggio, which Byron witnessed in admiration. When the time came to go to Greece Trelawny aided in the preparation and Byron took him along and launched him on a new career of adventure. Trelawny was glad to profit from his association with Byron whose prestige he traded on to build up his own heroic posture. With this boost he soon detached himself and joined forces with the wily Greek leader Odysseus in Athens.

After Byron's death Trelawny was divided between his desire to capitalize on his close association with the poet and jealousy of his fame. A few months later, having boasted that he was now a "Greek Chieftain", a companion of Odysseus, he fancied that he would fill Byron's shoes in Greece. He wrote to Mary Shelley: "I now feel my face burn with shame that so weak and ignoble a soul could so long have influenced me. It is a degrading reflection, and ever will be. I wish he had lived a little longer, that he might have witnessed how I would have soared above him here, how I would have triumphed over his mean spirit." When, toward the end of his long life he wrote his recollections of Byron and Shelley, something of this mingling of pride and jealousy is reflected in the stories he told of their intimacy.

EDWARD WILLIAMS (1793–1822)

Four days after Byron arrived in Pisa, Shelley brought his friend Edward Williams, a half-pay lieutenant with literary leanings and ambitions and liberal sympathies, to call on him. Williams, who had served with Thomas Medwin, Shelley's cousin, in India, had run off with a brother officer's wife and they lived together in Italy as Edward and Jane Williams. They had already cemented a close friendship with the Shelleys and lived in the same house with them across the Arno and a short distance from Byron's Casa Lanfranchi. Williams was immediately won over by Byron's cordiality. He wrote in his journal on November 5, 1821: "So far from his having a haughtiness of manner, they are those of the most unaffected and gentlemanly ease—and so far from his being (as is generally imagined) wrapt in a melancholy gloom he is all sunshine, and good humour with which the elegance of his language and the brilliancy of his wit cannot fail to inspire those who are near him." From this time on Williams became one of Byron's constant visitors and companions, along with others of Shelley's Pisan circle, on his daily rides into the country and weekly dinners at the Casa Lanfranchi. And the journal which he kept records his many intimate insights into Byron's character and habits, as well as his attitudes and interests. While there are no extant letters from Byron to Williams, there is mention of him in some of Byron's letters and evidence of his esteem and respect in his comments after Williams was drowned with Shelley the following year.

INDEX OF PROPER NAMES

Page numbers in italics indicate main references and Biographical Sketches in the Appendix. Such main biographical references in earlier volumes are included in this index and are in square brackets.

Davies, Scrope Berdmore—*contd.*
duellist, 25; gamester, 38–9;
stabbed by Hobhouse, 39
Davidson, Mr, and Lady Noel's
estate, 176, 177, 193–4, 209,
211–12, 213
Davidson, Thomas, Murray's printer,
199 and n
Davy, Sir Humphry, 16, 34
Dawkins, E. J., British *chargé d'affaires*,
and Masi affray, 129–47 *passim*,
154, 158, 168–9, 179–80; writes
of a party raised against B. in Pisa,
150 and n
Dawson, Capron and Rowley, attor-
neys, 73
De Witt, John, torn in pieces, 197 and n
Dearden, and Rochdale, 127, 128
Dibdin, Thomas, 36
D'Israeli, Isaac, 156; *The Literary
Character*, 136 and n, 171, 172;
inclusion of B.'s MS notes, 172n
D'Ivernois, Sir François, 22 *and n*
Demosthenes, 14
Diogenes, 11
Dodd, Rev. William, executed for
forgery, Johnson on, 99, and n
Drury, Henry Joseph, [*Vol. 1, 144n*],
16, 43, 189
Dryden, John, 11
Duff, Mary, 102n
Dunn, Henry, B.'s agent, 75, 105, 135n,
202 and n, 204; shipment of
Allegra's body to England, 163
and n, 193
Dupuy, Francesco, rents B. a villa, 161
and n

Edgeworth, Maria, 33–4; *Tales of
Fashionable Life*, 34 and n
Edgeworth, Richard Lovell, and fourth
wife, 33–4
Eldon, John Scott, first Earl of, 45, 97;
antagonistic towards B., 188–9,
191, 206
Ellice, Edward, [*Vol. 6, 225n*], and B.'s
interest in S. America, 173 and n,
174
Elliot, Sir Gilbert, first Earl of Minto, *15n*
Epaminondas, 48
Epictetus, 45
Erskine, Thomas Erskine, first Baron,
[*Vol. 3, 247n*], 15, 96; B. on, 44
Euripides, 11

Falcieri, Giovanni Battista ('Tita'), and
Masi affray, 139 and n, 142, 144,
150, 151, 160–1; in exile with the
Shelleys, 147 and n, 148–9, 178
and n; with B. till his death, 147n
Farebrother, Newstead auctioneer, 82
Fielding, Henry, 50–1; *Amelia*, 124
and n; *Jonathan Wild*, 50; *Joseph
Andrews*, 50 and n, 124 and n;
Tom Thumb, 28
Fletcher, William, 74 and n, 140
Flood, Henry, *13n*, 27; silenced by
Courtney, 12–13
Foote, Mrs, actress, 83n
Foscolo, Ugo, 90
Fox, Charles James, 14; East India
Bill, 13n; names best speech, 13
Fox, Henry, first Baron Holland, 155
Frederick Augustus, Duke of York, 18
Frederick the Great, 121 and n
Fricker sisters, wives of Coleridge and
Southey, 207 and n
Fry, Mrs Elizabeth, 74 *and n*

Galignani, Jean Antoine, 117, 126, 216;
requests a Memoir of B., 79 and n;
French copyrights, 84, 92, 93;
suggested publisher of *Heaven and
Earth*, 100; and *Edinburgh* review
of B., 167–8; *Messenger*, 74;
Parisian, 157
Gamba Ghiselli, Count Pietro, [*Vol. 7,
272*], 42, 56; and Masi affray, 135,
139 and n, 168–9, 169n; ordered
to leave Tuscany, 179 and n;
asylum in Lucca, 184 and n
Gamba Ghiselli, Count Ruggero, [*Vol.
7, 272*], and Masi affray, 168–9,
169n; ordered to leave Tuscany,
169n, 179 and n; asylum in Lucca,
184 and n
Genoa, B.'s proposed move, 201, 202,
203n, 209, 211, 214, 217; Villa
Saluzzo, 214, 219
Geramb, François Ferdinand, Baron de,
96 and n
Gibbon, Edward, 76, 100, 103, 116;
on his *History*, 117
Gifford, William, 53, 60–1; and *Cain*,
103, 104; *Baviad*, 70
Giordani, Pietro, 30 and n
Giuliani, identification, 215 and n, 217
Glenbervie, Lord, trns. *First Canto of
Ricciardello*, 146 and n
Glover, Mrs Julia, 35

Jeffrey, Francis—contd.
reviews B. in the *Edinburgh*, 170, 173, 176
Jersey, George Childe-Villiers, fifth Earl of, [*Vol. 2, 173n*], 44, 45
Jocelyn, Hon, Percy, Bishop of Clogher, 191 and n
Johnson, Samuel, 68, 86; Boswell and, 86, 89 and n; on Dr Dodd, 99 and n; Life of Edmund Smith, 69 and n; 'The Vanity of Human Wishes', 32 and n, 180 and n
Johnston, James, attributes poems to B., 44; defended by Leach, 44
Jones, Jacob, Commodore of frigate *Constitution*, invites B. on board, 161 and n, 162n, 164, 165, 171
Julius Caesar, 48, 77, 89 and n

Kames, Henry Home, Lord, 47
Kean, Edmund, 11, 31, 35
Keats, John, *Lamia*, found in Shelley's pocket, 185 and n, 198
Kemble, Charles, 83n
Kemble, John Philip, 16n, 31
Kinnaird, Douglas, [*Vol. 2, 282–3*], 16, 36–7, 62; thinks *Cain* a 'puzzler', 61; and B.'s finances, 73, 92, 108, 186, 187–8, 193ff; publication of *Vision of Judgment*, 88, 89, 100; returns B.'s challenge to Southey, 102 and n, 109–10, 114–15, 117, 160 and n; to insure Lady Byron's life, 105–8 *passim*, 112, 113, 115, 124, 127, 188, 211, 214; and Masi affray, 151; B.'s budget, 206, 207, 209, 213–14, 215; B. describes Murray, 207

La Rochfoucauld, 117, 124
Lake Poets, 117
Lamb, Lady Caroline, [*Vol. 3, 283*], 16
Lansdowne, Sir Henry Petty-Fitzmaurice, third Marquess of, 14, 64
Lauderdale, James Maitland, eighth Earl of, 14
Le Despenser, Lord, 186 and n, 187
Leach, defends J. Johnston, 44 and n
Leghorn, 148, 149, 161n; villa Dupuy, 135n, 156, 157, 161–79; 161n; Tuscan authorities and the *Bolivar*, 178 and n, 192 and n; B.'s letter to the Governor, 178–9
Leigh (née Byron), Hon. Augusta, [*Vol. 1, 273*], 21, 25, 40, 52, 77,

83; invited to Pisa by B., 57; B. to provide for her children, 120
Leigh, George, s. of above, 120
Leone, Michele, translator of B., 157 and n
Leonidas, 48
Le Sage, Alain René, *Gil Blas*, 175
Lewis, Matthew Gregory, 22; hatred of B., 17–18; B. on, 18–19; 'Castle Spectre', 17
Liston, John, 71 and n
A Letter to Sir Walter Scott, Bart, an answer to *Remonstrance of Oxoniensis*, 142 and n
Lockhart, John Gibson and Sophie, 87, 154–5; *Memoirs. . . upon the Affairs of Scotland*, 156 and n
Londonderry, second Marquess of (formerly Viscount Castlereagh), *124n*; 197 and n, 209–10
Longman, publisher, 89, 91
Loughborough, Alexander Wedderburn, first Baron, 28
Lowe, Sir Hudson, Governor of St Helena, 26
Lucretius, *De Rerum Natura*, 126 and n
Ludlow, General Edmund, 41 and n
Lushington, Dr, attorney to Lady Byron, 145 and n, 176, 177, 187, 188, 194, 198 , 205, 211, 213
Lushington and Colborne, Lady Byron's trustees, 207 and n
Luttrell, Henry, 19, 156, 207; *Advice to Julia*, 136 and n
Lutzerode, Baron, translator of B., 165 and n
Lyttelton, William Henry Lyttelton, third Baron, *15n*; Sheridan on 15

Mackintosh, Sir James, 19, 20
Macready, William Charles, 83n
Malthus, Thomas Robert, 19
Maluccelli, Antonio, Teresa's servant, 139 and n, 160–1
Manchester, 'Reform' riot, 134 and n
Manton, Joe, gunsmith, 63, 75
Marcus Aurelius, *see* Aurelius
Masi, Sergeant-Major Stefani, 'jostling' affray with B. and party, 129 and n, 130–5, 138–40, 151–9 *passim*, 171–2; Taaffe's statement, 133n, 140; role of Papi, 139n, 172n; treatment of detainees, 139; effect

Papi, Vincenzo, B.'s coachman, 139n; and Masi affray, 172n

Parker, Augusta and Margaret, [*Vol. 1, 39n*], 79

Parr, Samuel, 34

Peacock, Thomas Love, Shelley's executor, 202

Peel, Sir Robert, 14, 22; at Harrow with B., 43

Persius, *Satires*, 76 and n

Perugino, Pietro, 50

Petrarch, 90

Pierrepoint, 'Dandy', 22n

Piron, Alexis, 'Epigrammatic Machine', 20 and n

Pisa, 50, 51–161, 179–219; Casa Lanfranchi, 74 and n, 75, 237

Pitt, William, 14, 27

Plato, 47, 117

Plutarch, life of Lysander, 47

Pope, Alexander, 11, 68; 'Epistle to Dr Arbuthnot', 74 and n, 197 and n; *Moral Essays*, 208

Priestley, Joseph, 100, 103, 116; Christian Materialism, 46

Proctor, Bryan Waller, *Mirandola*, B.'s alleged plagiarism, 83n, 83–4

Rae, Alexander, 36

Raphael, 11

Rivington, Francis and Charles, *A Remonstrance addressed to Mr John Murray*, 100 and n, 103 and n

Roberts, Capt. Daniel, RN, to build a boat (*Bolivar*) for B., 116, 137 and n, 236

Robins, George Henry, *16n*

Rochdale, 127, 195, 201; toll business, 106, 108, 111, 114, 163, 177; Coal Suits, 177; Burdett and its management, 188; appeal before the Lords, 188–9, 191, 211; proposed mortgage, 209, 211

Rochester, John Wilmot, Earl of, 'To Lord Brocklehurst', 20 and n

Rogers, Samuel, [*Vol. 2, 286–7*], 12, 16, 20, 27, 84; at Bologna, 50, 53, 55, 66; at Florence, 56, 66, 80; visits the Certosa with B., 66; in Pisa, 152; B.'s lines on, 213 and n

Roscoe, William, 16

Rousseau, Jean Jacques, contrasted with B., 11–12

Rowe, Nicholas, *Tamerlane*, 155 and n

Ruota, Count, on B., 42

Satanic School of Poetry, 98 and n

Savage, Richard, 11

Schlegel, August Wilhelm von, 26

Scott, Sir Walter, 35; accepts dedication of *Cain*, 54 and n; ignores reviews of himself, 55; reviews *Childe Harold* in the *Quarterly*, 85 and n, 86; admired by B., 86–7; *The Abbot*, 58; *The Antiquary*, 21 and n, 31 and n; *The Heart of Midlothian*, 87 and nn; *Kenilworth*, 97 and n; *Lay of the Last Minstrel*, 18 and n, 30; *The Monastery*, 58; *The Pirate*, 87; *Rob Roy*, 87 and n, 154 and n; *Waverley*, 45 and n, 101 and n, 154 and n, 164 and n

Selwyn, George, 97 and n

Seward, Anna, 34

Shakespeare, William, 11; *Coriolanus*, 81 and n, 213 and n; *Hamlet*, 71 and n, 80 and n; *Henry IV, Pt 1*, 33 and n, 66, 87 and n, 104 and n; *Julius Caesar*, 23 and n; *King Lear*, 196 and n; *Love's Labour's Lost*, 11 and n; *Macbeth*, 153 and n; *Much Ado about Nothing*, 213 and n; *Othello*, 119 and n, 165 and n, 199 and n; *Romeo and Juliet*, 41 and n; *The Tempest*, 209 and n; *Troilus and Cressida*, 14 and n; *Twelfth Night*, 12 and n

Shelley, Mary, 205 and n, 236

Shelley, Percy Bysshe, 30, 78n, 79n, 102n; B.'s 'fellow serpent', 81; and sale of B.'s *Memoirs*, 84–5; invites the Hunts to Italy, 95 and n, 110n; subscribes himself 'Atheist', 97n; B. on, 119, 189–90; denies religious influence over B., 119n; belief in immortality, 121; riding incident, 128n; shares a boat with Williams, 137n; and Tita, 147n, 178 and n; death of Allegra, 148n; and Masi affray, 160 and n; death at sea, 184 and n, 185 and n, 186, 187, 189; cremation on Viareggio beach, 192n, 197, 198; preservation of his heart, 197; financial affairs, 202, 218; his executors, 202 and n; B. quarrels with Mary, 202n; and his

246

will, 205; attacked by Hazlitt, 216n; and Taaffe, 236
Shelley, Sir Timothy, and his son's debts, 202–3, 205n
Sheppard, John, 75 *and n*
Sheridan, Richard Brinsley, speech on Hastings's Impeachment, 13; B. on, 14–16, 17, 20, 32, 48; liking for B., 16; *School for Scandal*, 15
Siddons, Mrs Sarah, 31, 34
Sinclair, Sir George, at Harrow with B., 43–4
Sismondi, Jean Charles, 74
Sligo, second Marquess of (formerly Lord Altamont), 67; origin of the *Giaour*, 80 and n
Smith, Horace, 119n
Smith, Edmund, Johnson's Life of, 69 and n
Smith, William, denounces Southey, 97
Smollett, Tobias, *Humphry Clinker*, 209; *Peregrine Pickle*, 188 and n
Socrates, 47
Sophocles, 11
Sotheby, William, 22, 29; *Ivan*, 35
Southey, Robert, 89, 191; B. on his 'Vision', 62, 96; abused in *The Two Foscari*, 86, 95, 104; letter to the *Courier*, and B.'s unpublished reply, 95 and n, 96–100, 100n; article in *Quarterly Review*, 96; and B. as leader of 'Satanic School', 98 and n; compares himself to the Hangman, 99; B. sends him an (undelivered) challenge, 102 and n, 109–10, 114–15, 160 and n; Coleridge's finances, 206–7, 208; *Vision of Judgment* and preface to, 62, 98; *Wat Tyler*, 97 and n
Spencer, Dowager Lady, Sheridan on, 15
Spencer, William Robert, 29; B. reviews his *Poems*, 42 and n
Staël-Holstein, Mme de, [*Vol. 3*, 272–3], 14, 18, 19, 22, 26; likens B. to Rousseau, 11; *De la Littérature*, 152 and n
Staël-Holstein (later de Broglie), Albertine, d. of above, 22
Statius, *Thebais*, iii, 661, 126 and n
Sterne, Laurence, letter to Ignatius Sancho, 49 and n
Sternhold, T. and Hopkins, J. H., 11, 59

Stith, Mrs Catherine Potter, asks B. for a 'souvenir', 161–3, 162n, 164
Stith, Major, 162
Strauss, Guiseppe, B.'s courier, hurt in Masi affray, 169 and n
Stuart, Sir Charles, Irish Committee, 183 and n; B.'s subscription, 198–9
Styles, Rev. John, preaches against *Cain*, 100n; describes B., 100n
Swift, Jonathan, 96; *The Grand Question Debated*, 191 and n; *Polite Conversation*, 85 and n

Taaffe, John, 62–3, *236*; riding accident, 80; to go to Lucca, 81, 236; wish to see himself in print, 90, 123, 236; and Masi affray, 129n, 130–1, 143, 157, 180, 236; B. on his statement, 133 and n, 140; friendship with Mme Regny, 238; translator of *Divine Comedy*, 90 and n; *Commentary on Dante*, 63, 90 and n, 122, 123, 126, 236
Tavistock, Marquess of, 16
Themistocles, 48
Thorwaldsen, Bertel, bust of B., 20–1, 55, 63, 69, 122 and n; B. on, 213
Thurlow, Edward Thurlow, first Baron, 28
Tiberius, Emperor, 11
Timon of Athens, 11
Todd, H. J., 'Oxoniensis', 151n
Tooke, John Horne, 16
Trelawny, Edward John, 143, 184, 186, 235, *236–7*; and B.'s boat, 137 and n, 203 and n, 204; arranges cremation of Shelley and Williams, 192n, 236; goes to Greece with B., 236–7; and Odysseus, 237; *Recollections of Byron and Shelley*, 237
Tulk, Mr, 25
Twiss, Horace, 22
Tyler, Capt., 156
Tyler, Wat, 97

Ugolini, Count, Pisan partisan, 74
Upton, William, 36 and n

Vega Carpio, Lope Félix de, 93
Virgil, *Æneid*, 103 and n
Voltaire, François Marie Arouet de, 20, 100, 116; *Candide*, 24 and n

Wallace, Capt., 19

Warburton, William, and Pope, 145n; *A Vindication of Mr Pope's Essay on Man*, 146 and n

Ward, Hon. John William (later first Earl of Dudley and Ward), [*Vol. 1, 214 and n*], 14, 19, 22

Watkins, John, and B.'s attack on Moore in *English Bards*, 190 and n; *Memoirs of . . . Lord Byron*, 190 and nn, 191

Webb, W., 202 and n

Webster, Sir James Wedderburn, [*Vol. 1, 171 and n*], 73

Wellington, Arthur Wellesley, first Duke of, 49; attacked in *Don Juan*, 182–3, 183n

Wentworth, Lord, 108, 145n

Wentworth, Mr, possible buyer of *Bolivar*, 186 and n

West, William Edward, to paint B.'s portrait, 162n, 164n, 198; proposed engraving, 211 and n, 214; portrait of Teresa, 211

Whitbread, Samuel, 14

White, Henry Kirke, [*Vol. 2, 76 and n*], 76

Wilberforce, William, 14, 41

Williams, Edward, 121, 237–8; and Shelley, 102n, 137n, 235, 237; drowned at sea, 184 and n, 185, 186, 187, 189, 237; cremation, 192n, 197; and Trelawny, 236; on B., 237

Williams, Jane, w. of above, 237

Wilson, Harriette, 21n

Wilson, John (Christopher North), alleged author of article on B. in *Blackwood's*, 58 and n

Wollstonecraft, Mary, Southey's professed attachment, 97

Wordsworth, William, B. reviews *Poems*, 1807, 42 and n

Young, Edward, 11

Zograffo, Demetrius, and Greek insurrection, 23